DICTIONARY
and
Help for Further Study
of
ALLEN'S KEYNOTES

by
DR SUBHAS SINGH, M.D. (Hom.)
Dept. of Organon of Medicine,
National Institute of Homoeopathy

DR PAMPA SAHA, M.D. (Hom.) (NIH)
DR BAISHAKHI GHOSH, M.D. (Hom.)
Lecturer, Mahensh Bhattacharya Homoeopathic Medical College,
(Govt. of West Bengal), Howrah
DR PULAKENDU BHATTACHARYA, M.D. (Hom.)
Lecturer, D.N. De Homoeopathic Medical College, (Govt. of West Bengal), Kolkata
DR SATYAJIT NASKAR, M.D. (Hom.)
Lecturer, D.N. De Homoeopathic Medical College, (Govt. of West Bengal), Kolkata

DR. ALOK MISRA, M.D. (Hom.)
Lecturer, Mahensh Bhattacharya Homoeopathic Medical College,
(Govt. of West Bengal), Howrah,

B. JAIN PUBLISHERS (P) LTD.
USA—Europe—India

Dictionary and Help for Further Study of Allen's Keynotes
First Edition: 2021
1st Impression: 2021

All rights reserved. No part of this book may be reproduced, stored in a retrieval system or transmitted, in any form or by any means, mechanical, photocopying, recording or otherwise, without any prior written permission of the publisher.

© with the Authors

Published by Kuldeep Jain for
B. JAIN PUBLISHERS (P) LTD.
D-157, Sector-63, NOIDA-201307, U.P. (INDIA)
Tel.: +91-120-4933333 • Email: info@bjain.com
Website: **www.bjainbooks.com**
Registered office: 1921/10, Chuna Mandi, Paharganj,
New Delhi-110 055 (India)

Printed in India

ISBN: 978-81-319-1381-9

PREFACE

Allen's Key Notes is the popular name of the book, *'Keynotes and Characteristics with comparisons of some of the Leading Remedies of the Materia Medica'* by Dr. H.C. Allen. It is indisputably the most read, most used and of course the most popular book not only in India but probably in the world. It has also become the book which is followed mostly for BHMS studies and for other curriculum bound studies.

However, those who are somewhat less fluent in English or whose mother tongue is not English, face difficulties in reading and understanding some of the words used in the book. Even for those who are much versed in English, some of the terminologies used in the book are difficult to comprehend. Many of the terminologies and nomenclature are quite out of use. We have tried to provide the word meaning to some of the selected words, terms and nomenclatures used in Allen's Key Notes.

Allen's Key Notes being the book which is most widely used by students, teachers, and practitioners, various attempts have been made to simplify it. Some of the writers have even attempted to rearrange the book without caring for the originality of the book. What we have done here is to segregate the symptoms (Keynotes) according to the various chapters and sub-chapters. We have tried to arrange the related symptoms of all the medicines of Allen's keynote at one place. Moreover, we have also tried to club the unrelated but similar-sounding symptoms at one place, which will make an easy comprehension and learning of Allen's keynote. The purpose of this effort is to make comparative study more interesting.

Those who have understood and grasped the basic structure, formation and underlying principle of Allen's Key Notes and especially those who have been fortunate enough to learn Allen's Key Notes from Masters like Dr S. K. Dubey, know that the utility and clinical applicability of the book depend mainly on comparisons. With this in mind and to share this, this book is being presented to the profession.

The relationship chapter is not merely compiling all that is given at end of each medicine in Allen's Key Notes but much has been added and put in one place which is scattered throughout the book. The arrangement of relationships in different headings will make it more palatable.

It is hoped that our efforts will be appreciated by the students, teachers and practitioners. We do not claim it to be perfect and free of all errors, but, your help by pointing out the errors, if any, will definitely help it to become more nearer to perfection, and which of course will be duly acknowledged.

PUBLISHER'S NOTE

Allen's Keynotes is one the widely read books of materia medica. Keeping into consideration, the difficulties faced by readers in reading and understanding the vocabulary used in Allen's Keynotes, Author have come up with this dictionary of Allen's Keynotes.

Author have done our best to provide the word meanings to all the difficult terminologies and nomenclature used in Allen's Keynotes.

In this book, the related symptoms of all medicines have been placed together. The Keynote symptoms have been placed under different chapters and sub-chapters.

The aim behind publishing this book is to make the study of Allen's Keynote much easier and efficient so that our readers can utilize Allen's Keynotes to its full potential. We hope this will make memorizing materia medica easier. We would like to thank our editor, DrSakshi Malhotra for her relentless efforts in completing the book. Suggestions are always welcomed.

Manish Jain
Director, B. Jain Publishers (P) Ltd.

CONTENT

Dr. H.C. Allen - Biography by *Dr. Mahendra Singh*

Prescription on Keynote or Keynote method of Precription by *Dr. Subhas Singh*

Preface	*iii*
Publisher's Note	*v*
Dr Henry Clarke Allen	*xi*
Prescription on Keynote Symptoms	*xv*
DICTIONARY TO ALLEN'S KEYNOTES	**1**
A	3
B	19
C	26
D	48
E	61
F	70
G	80
H	86
I	96
J	106
K	107
L	108
M	113
N	125
O	130
P	136

Q	158
R	159
S	167
T	191
U	203
V	207
W	214
X	219
Y	220
Z	221
HELPS FOR FURTHER STUDY OF ALLEN'S KEYNOTES	**223**
CHILD	225
MIND	228
VERTIGO	235
HEADACHE	237
EYE	247
EARS	250
FACE	252
MOUTH, SALIVA, TOOTHACHE, TONGUE	255
THROAT (E.N.T.) and DIPHTHERIA	261
• VOICE	266
GASTRO-INTESTINAL SYSTEM	268
• DESIRES and AVERSIONS	268
• VOMITING	270
• DIARRHEA	273
• CONSTIPATION	282
• HAEMORRHOIDS and ANUS	286
URINE	289

CONTENT

- GENITALIA 293
- FEMALE - GENITALIA 297
  - FEMALE CONDITIONS 297
  - MENSTRUATION 298
  - PROLAPSE 305
  - LEUCORRHOEA 306
  - AFTER-PAINS 308
  - BREAST 308
  - ABORTION 311
  - PREGNANCY and LABOR 312
  - LYING IN PERIOD/CHILD-BED 315
- RESPIRATORY SYSTEM 316
  - DYSPNOEA 316
  - COUGH 317
  - ASTHMA 322
  - WHOOPING-COUGH 323
  - CORYZA and SNEEZING 324
- HEART 326
- BACK 331
- EXTREMITY 333
- PAINS 338
- NERVOUS SYSTEM 344
- INJURY 350
- HAEMORRHAGES 354
- FEVER 357
- SKIN 360
- SENSATIONS 369
- TIME and TIME MODALITY 374
- MISCELLANEOUS 377

RELATIONSHIP OF REMEDIES 388
- ANTIDOTE 388
- BAD EFFECTS OF/ AILMENTS FROM 391
- WHEN FAILS 398
- ANALOGUE 401
- CHRONIC OF 402
- COMPLEMENTARY TO 402
- INIMICAL TO 404
- INSTRUCTIONS FOR PRESCRIPTION 406
- FOLLOWS WELL / AFTER 410
- FOLLOWED BY 416
- FOLLOWS AND IS FOLLOWED BY 418
- MISCELLANEOUS 419

Dr HENRY CLARKE ALLEN
(10.02.1836 - 22.01.1909)

BIRTH: Dr Henry Clarke Allen was born on February 10, 1836 in the village of Nilestown, Ontario, near London.

FAMILY and ANCESTRY: His parents were Hugh and Martha Billings Allen and inherited very famous and proud family name and tradition.

On his paternal side, he had a proud inheritance Vermonters family who had produced such famous warriors of revolution as Gen. Ira Allen and Ethan Allen.

On his maternal side, he belonged to the family of the Billings. The Billings were well known and respected name among the Colonial families of Massachusetts Bay. The present city of Salem is built on the farmlands which once belonged to the great-grand-father of Dr Allen who after selling this property (farmland), moved to Deerfield, in the Connecticut Valley and stayed there during the period when the Indians pillaged and ravaged that part of the country. Many left the area but Billings fought, guarded and protected their properties and stood their ground.

EARLY EDUCATION: Dr Allen received his primary education in the common and grammar schools at London. Later in the same school he worked as a teacher also for some time.

MEDICAL EDUCATION: He qualified from the College of Physicians and Surgeons of Canada. In 1861, He acquired his homoeopathic education from the Cleveland Homeopathic College at Cleveland, Ohio, which was then known as Western Homeopathic College.

LIFE IN ARMY: Shortly after graduation, he joined the Union Army, as a surgeon serving under General Grant.

LIFE AS A HOMOEOPATH: After the war, he was offered teaching job at his Alma Mater, Western Homeopathic College. He accepted the offer and started teaching and at the same time started practicing medicine for the first time at Cleveland.

He did continue at Western Homeopathic College, Cleveland for a long. He resigned and joined the Hahnemann Medical College of Chicago in the same chair, i.e. Professor of Anatomy.

Dr Allen did not stay in Chicago for long and his next shift was to Brantford, Ontario.

In 1868 he was offered the Chair of Surgery to succeed Dr Beebe, but was unable to accept.

In 1875 he again moved to Detroit, Michigan.

After being appointed Professor of Materia Medica at the University of Michigan in 1880, Dr Allen shifted his house for the last time to Ann Arbor.

MARRIAGE and CHILDREN: On 24th December 1867, he married Selina Louise Goold, In Brantford, Ontario. They had two children, Franklin Lyman Allen and Helen Marian Allen Aird.

HERING MEDICAL COLLEGE: He founded the Hering Medical College and Hospital in 1892 and worked there as Dean.

It was at this institute that he taught in the Department of Materia Medica, which gave him worldwide fame and respect as a teacher.

DEMISE: Dr H.C. Allen left this earthly world for his heavenly abode on **22nd January 1909.**

ATTACHMENTS:

Honorable senior member: The American Institute of Homeopathy,

Member: The International Hahnemannian Association,

Member: The Illinois Homeopathic Medical Association,

Member: The Englewood Homeopathic Medical Society,

M*ember:* The Regular Homeopathic Medical Society of Chicago

Honorary Vice-President: The Cooper Club of London, England;

Honorary Member: State Medical Society, Michigan

Honorary Member: State Medical Society, New York

Honorary Member: State Medical Society, Pennsylvania

Honorary Member: Ohio State Medical Society, and

Honorary Member: The Homeopathic Society of Calcutta, India.

LITERARY CONTRIBUTIONS:

JOURNAL: Dr Allen was the owner and editor of the *Medical Advance* for many years. He contributed many editorials and articles for Medical Advance and other magazines.

BOOKS:

1. *Keynotes of Leading Remedies,* lately placed on the *Council List of Books* for use in the Canadian Medical Colleges;
2. The Homeopathic Therapeutics of Intermittent Fever
3. The Homeopathic Therapeutics of Fevers
4. Therapeutics of Tuberculous Affections
5. *Materia medica of the nosodes with provings of the X-Ray*: This was his last work and completed only a short time before his death. The work was the result of years of study, experience,

and of proving and confirming the symptomatology of many of the nosodes.

REVISION and EDITING: Boenninghausen's *Slip Repertory*: Dr Allen edited the book and made many changes and annotations which made this work more clinically usable and easy to work with. His revision made it up to date and arranged for rapid and practical work.

PRESCRIPTION ON KEYNOTE SYMPTOMS
Or
KEYNOTE METHOD OF PRESCRIPTION

Homoeopathy faces many challenges and obstacles from outside world especially medical. But, the greatest challenges it faces is from its rank and files of followers. The different ways in which the principles of homoeopathy have been understood and interpreted and in the various modes in which it has been applied is a big problem facing homoeopathic system.

Keeping aside these, another of the serious challenges in homoeopathy is the sheer volume of information the student or practitioner has to contend with. To overcome this problem many ways and means have been suggested from time to time. The Keynote method of prescribing is one of such method which if properly understood makes the whole process of prescription much easier.

Though it is a method for which Dr H.N. Guernsey is being credited to be the founder, in reality, this has been practiced even before that. According to Dr Stuart Close, Dr Guernsey simply invented a new name for the old Hahnemannian idea. Guernsey himself has said that he believed Keynote System not to be a new doctrine but a true one in Homoeopathy.

The understanding and definition of Keynote have numerous variations, many of which conflict with each other. Again many are of view that the Keynote system is not homoeopathy.

The real Keynote system as taught and practiced by the late Dr H.N. Guernsey (but distorted t by many) does not conflict with the doctrine of the totality of the symptoms. It is in fact, strictly Hahnemannian.

Dr Guernsey defined Keynote (in music) as *'the fundamental note or tone on which the whole piece is accommodated'*. The word Keynote is mainly used in the music but it has other meanings also. One of the meanings which serve our purpose is that it is *'the fundamental or central idea'*.

However, there is no rationality going over all the fuss just over the term as Guernsey himself has said that the term "key-note" is not to be regarded as in itself definitive, nor did he, in first using it, wish or intend it to be taken as a piece of scientific nomenclature. To Guernsey it occurred as being in a very great degree expressive of a fact in medicine, and as such alone is it to be accepted. He categorically said that the term "key-note" is therefore *suggestive*, and merely provisional and to be continued in use only until its scientific successor is duly chosen and qualified by general acceptance.

Professor Guernsey while teaching Materia Medica to the students of Hahnemann Medical College of Philadelphia was very much aware of the problems that his students have to face in understanding and applying Materia Medica. To overcome this, he advocated that the characteristics be understood and memorised. When applying these medicines to the sick persons, it is these characteristics which are to be sought in the patient. And if these symptoms are found in the patient, rest of the symptoms will fall in line. He called these symptoms as Keynotes. During his professorship at the Hahnemann College, particularly during the session of 1871-73, he delivered lectures to the students in these lines and the collection of his lectures was ultimately published in the form of a book titles 'Keynotes of Materia Medica'. He aimed to present enough of the outline and the leading characteristics, which will turn the student's mind, when he will engage in practice, in the direction of the proper remedy, when prescribing for the sick. To him, Keynote is simply predominating symptoms or features, which directs one's attention to the totality of symptoms through which that individual case is expressed.

Dr Guernsey had coined the term 'keynote symptoms' in an article in 1868 titled 'The Key-note System' which was published in *The Hahnemannian Monthly, Vol. III, No. 12, pp. 561-569*. The article was a paper presented by Dr Guernsey before *The Philadelphia County Medical Society*. In my humble opinion before forming any opinion about the Key-note method of prescription, it will be only wise to once read this article and to know what the founder wanted to say and the way he wanted his system to be applied.

With all due regards and respect to great Dr J.T. Kent, his severe criticism of the system seems unwarranted. In his *Journal of Homoeopathics* which he was editing during the period (Vol. 2, 1899), he wrote "*The keynote system has done more mischief than anything else, although keynotes are not to be ignored, but until the relation of the generals and particulars is understood it is no matter how much you memorize about it.*" If the cases of Dr Kent given in his Lesser Writings or those published from time to time in different journals are to be anaysed, then we find that he criticized keynote prescribers on the one hand, and yet he used keynotes all the time. I am sure what Kent attacked was people using keynotes without looking for the general state of the patient. Kent's use of Keynotes is very much rational and he was giving more concrete support to the system when he was using keynotes, which represented the general state. Giving a reason for his criticism he said – '*The great trouble with keynote is that they are misused, the keynotes are often characteristic symptoms, but if the keynotes are taken as final and the generals don't confirm there will come failures.*'

Surprisingly we seem to forget the basic idea of Guernsey. If we read his article, then we find that he has used the two words

'Keynote' and 'Characteristics' as synonymously. Dr Close also agreed that misunderstanding and abuse of this method has caused it to fall somewhat into discredit. And that Guernsey's "keynotes" and Hahnemann's "characteristics" should be considered as synonymous terms, which they are. Guernsey never advocated prescriptions to be made on one symptom and calling it Keynote prescription. There cannot be better words than his own to know what he meant. He said – *'When a characteristic symptom or key-note presents itself in a given case, it means that the whole case is to be studied with reference to the remedy which correspondingly has that symptom or condition. Not that the totality of the case is to be disregarded, but that the characteristic presented is a key or key-note to the remedy that is almost certain to exhibit, in its pathogenesis, the tout-ensemble of the given case.'* Dr Charles G. Raue also pointed out that scarcely one of the "keynotes" or characteristic symptoms belongs exclusively to a single remedy, and cautioned us not to diagnose a remedy on one symptom only, be it ever so characteristic. "While in some cases, " he says, "it may point exactly to the remedy, it cannot do so in every case as it is not rational to suppose that the whole sphere of action of a remedy, which is often extensive and complex, should find its unerring expression and indication in one symptom. But such characteristics are of great aid in the selection of the remedy, as they define the circle of remedies out of which we must select." Dr Hering, in his quaint fashion, years before the "keynote system" was ever heard of, said: "Every stool must have at least three legs if it is to stand alone." He advised selecting at least three characteristic symptoms as the basis of prescribing.

Dr Stuart Close seems to have gone to the core of the proposed 'Keynote System' of Dr Guernsey. He realised that in Keynote we have the same idea underlying the phrase as of *Genius of the Remedy*. Genius, in this sense, is the dominant influence, or the essential principle of the remedy which gives it its individuality.

The real "keynote system, " is, in fact, strictly Hahnemannian. The truth is that Dr Guernsey simply invented a new name for the old Hahnemannian idea.

Later Dr H.C. Allen was as a big advocate of the system and gave it much popularity through his book *'Keynotes and Characteristics with Comparison of some of the leading remedies of the Materia Medica'* Dr Allen for the first time joined the two-term Keynotes and Characteristics. There appears to be a slight difference in his approach and application. Allen meant to use Keynotes more for comparison and differentiation of the remedies. In the Preface to the First Edition of his above-mentioned book, he says that so called Keynote are the pivotal point of comparison. Even Morgan called Keynotes as 'super-characteristics' and said they are 'almost always found in the cases cured by that drug'. Keynotes can be symptoms that fit only one remedy or a few selected remedies, and yet many of our best keynotes fit many remedies. It seems a keynote can, be strange, rare and peculiar, and it can be common, it can fit one remedy or many remedies, it can be a pathologic symptom that fits the disease or a physiological symptom that does not.

Both Guernsey and Allen made one thing clear that Keynotes are simply suggestive.

Loosely speaking, the following are the symptoms where one can expect to find Keynotes in a patient:

- Changes of personality and temperament
- Nature and peculiarities of disease
- Seat of the disease
- Concomitant
- Cause
- Modalities
- Time

Lastly, as a reminder and caution to all Keynote prescribers, I will like to quote an often repeated but maybe not properly understood warning that - **All the Keynotes are characteristics but all the characteristics are not keynotes.**

DICTIONARY TO ALLEN'S KEYNOTES

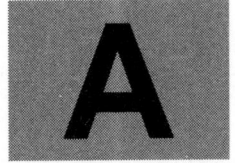

ABASHED (Phos.ac., Staph.): Embarrassed or ashamed or disconcerted especially because of shyness.

ABDOMINAL PLETHORA (Aloe.): Red florid complexion of the abdominal wall due to congestion of the blood the term is also loosely used to denote abdominal fat.

ABORTION (Act., Caul., Helon., Kali br., Kali c., Mill., Pyr., Sab., Thlaspi.): Expulsion or extraction from its mother of an embryo or fetus weighing 500 gm. or less when it is not capable of independent survival, this 500 gm. of fetal development is attained approximately at 22 weeks of gestation.

> **HABITUAL ABORTION (Caul.):** The spontaneous expulsion of a dead or non-viable fetus on three or more consecutive occasions at about the same period of development.
>
> **THREATENING ABORTION (Plb.):** There is risk or possibility of having abortion especially with prior family or personal history.
>
> **THREATENED ABORTION (Puls., Sec.):** It is a clinical entity where the process of abortion has started, but has not progressed to a state from which recovery is impossible.

ABOUND (Tereb.): To exist in large numbers or quantities.

ABRUPTLY LIMITED (Amyl.): Sudden or unexpectedly less in amount or degree.

ABSCESS (Hep., Mer., Pyr. Sil., Tar., Tub.): A painful, swollen area in the body that contains pus that results from invasion of pyogenic bacteria or other pathogens.

> **MAMMARY (Graph.):** Abscess in the female breast especially one involving the glandular tissue. It usually occurs during lactation or weaning.

ABSENCE OF MIND (Nuxm.): Forgets things or does not pay attention to what they are doing, often because they are thinking about something else.

ABSENT MINDED (Agnus., Kali br., Lac c.,): So deep, so far away from the thought that one is unaware of what one is doing, what is happening around , etc; preoccupied.

ABSORPTION (Anthr., Ars., Ham., Lyc., Sulph.): The process of being soaked up or taken in of a liquid, gas or other substance.

ABSTAINING (Cal.ars.): Staying away from doing something you could do, especially. that is pleasurable or unhealthy.

ABSTINENCE (Lys.): Act or practice of abstaining; especially refraining from an indulgence of food, alcoholic drinks, pleasures, for moral, religious or health reasons.

ABSURDITY (Anthr.): Unreasonableness; inappropriateness.

ABUNDANT (Iod.): Existing in large quantities; more than enough; a lot.

ABUSE (Agnus., Led.): To treat a person or animal badly or cruelly; to use or overuse something in a way that is harmful or wrong.

> **ABUSE OF ARSENICUMUM (Samb.):** Overuse or misuse of Arsenicum given as a medicine or non-medicinal intake.

ABUSE OF CHAMOMILE (Puls., Val.): Overuse or misuse of Chamomilla given as a medicine or chamomile tea.

ABUSE OF CINCHONA (Meny.): Overuse or misuse of Cinchona or quinine given for medicinal or non-medicinal purpose.

ABUSE OF MERCURY (Aur., Carbo v., Fluor. ac., Hep., Mez., Nit. ac., Pod., Puls., Sars., Staph.,): The practice in the 1800s of giving large doses of mercurial purgatives to cause loose bowels in order to treat patients suffering from syphilis and its bad effects. If repeated in large doses it can lead to a whole set of toxic symptoms, including headache, gingivitis, nausea, dizziness, heart pain, dermatitis, excess salivation, epistaxis, keratitis, neuritis, hematological abnormalities, albuminuria, purpura, and a metallic taste in the mouth.

ABUSE OF METALS (Sulph.): Overuse or misuse of medicines prepared from metals (heavy metals) or given for non-medicinal purposes.

ABUSE OF QUININE (Apoc., Meny.): Quinine has a long history of being used especially for malarial fever. When used non-homoeopathically, it was used in large doses producing serious side effects.

ABUSE OF QUININE BARK (Carbo v., Ipec, Puls.): Same as abuse of quinine.

ABUSE OF SILICEA (Flour.ac.): Overuse or misuse of Silicea given as medicine or from the intake of silica.

ABUSE OF TOBACCO (Tab.): Tobacco since long has been used for addiction, overuse, and misuse, even use of tobacco in any form produces serious, long-lasting and fatal effects.

ACONITE OF VENOUS CAPILLARY SYSTEM (Ham.,): Hamamelisvirg. is called *"Aconite of the venous capillary system"* to explain the action of Hamamelis on the venous capillary system. Its action on the venous capillary system can be compared to the action of Aconite on the arterial system.

ACCUMULATION (Carbo v., Sanic.): Something is collected together or increased gradually, especially over a period of time.

ACCUSTOMED STIMULANTS (Coca.): Frequently used, or habituated, or familiar with stimulants or excitants.

ACNE (Cal.p., Kali br., Psor.): An inflammatory follicular, papular, and pustular eruption caused by overactivity of sebaceous gland especially on the face, chest, and back and usually found in adolescence.

> **ACNE INDURATA (Kali br.):** Deep-seated acne with large papules and pustules with large hypertrophic scars and discoloured indurated surfaces.
>
> **ACNE PUSTULAR (Kali br.):** Acne with pustule formation and subsequent deep scar.
>
> **ACNE ROSACEA (Kali br., Psor.):** Acne involving the skin of nose, forehead and cheeks common in middle age and characterized by congestion, flushing, telangiectasia, deep seated papules and pustules.
>
> **ACNE SIMPLEX (Kali br., Psor.):** A synonym for acne vulgaris.
>
> **ACNE VULGARIS:** Chronic acne predominantly of the face, upper back, and chest, composed of comedones, cysts, papules, and pustules on an inflammatory base. The condition occurs in a majority of people during puberty and adolescence, due to androgenic stimulation of sebum secretion, with plugging of follicles by keratinization.

ACONITE OF CHRONIC DISEASE (Alum.): As Aconite is frequently used in acute diseases similarly Alumina frequently used in chronic diseases.

ACRID (Act., Arum., Carb.ac., Caul., Con., Euph., Graph., Iod., Kreos., Lac c., Mag.c., Mer., Mer.c, Mer.s., Nit.ac., Pyr., Staph, Sulph.): Having a strong, bitter, pungent, unpleasant smell or taste that causes a burning feeling.

ACUTENESS OF HEARING (Op.): Highly developed and sharp hearing producing ability to hear faintest of sound.

ACUTE IDIOCY (Hell.): Idiocy is the extreme mental deficiency due to incomplete or abnormal development of the brain, may be genetic, traumatic or due to severe disease. Acute idiocy is usually referred to severe mental deficiency which has been observed or has become marked recently (may be after some severe acute illness).

ADAPTED TO (Mag.m., Mer., Nit.ac., Nux., Nux.m., Petr., Phos., Plat., Pod., Samb., Spong.): Made more fit for a particular purpose.

ADHERING (Alum.): Sticking or be attached firmly to a surface.

ADHESIVE PLASTER (Calen.): Plaster made of a strong cloth coated on one side with an adhesive substance (plaster of Paris), used to immobilize the part, to relieve pressure upon sutures and to protect wounds, or to hold dressing in place.

ADIPOSE TISSUE (Graph.): Connective tissue of the body, containing large droplets of fat.

ADDISON'S DISEASE: A destructive disease marked by deficient secretion of the adrenal cortical hormone and characterised by extreme weakness, loss of weight, low blood pressure, gastrointestinal disturbances, and brownish pigmentation of the skin and mucous membrane.

AFFECTIONATE (Croc., Puls.): Showing caring feeling and love or fondness for someone; loving.

AFFLICTED (Spig.): To make someone badly affected or suffer from any pain or illness, physically or mentally.

AFFORDS (Lyc., Melil.): To provide.

AFRAID (Acon., Aur., Cina., Nux., Spig., Sulph.): Fearful, timid, or anxious.

AFTER PAINS (Act., Caul., Cup., Sab., Sec.): It is the infrequent, spasmodic pain felt in the lower abdomen after delivery due to contraction of uterus for a variable period of 2-4 days. Commonly seen in multipara.

AGGLUTINATE (Arg.n., Thuja.): To stick; to unite; to adhere; to glue together.

AGONY (Acon., Syph.): Extreme bodily or mental suffering; anguish.

AGONIZING (Coloc., Dios.): Extremely painful.

AGUE (Dros., Dul., Rhus.,): A fit or spell of shaking or shivering or chill; malarial fever, or any other severe recurrent symptoms of malarial origin, characterized by paroxysms of chill, fever and sweating that recur at regular interval.

> **AGUE-CAKE:** A form of enlargement of spleen, resulting from the action of malaria on the system.

> **DUMB AGUE (Gels.):** A sub-acute form of malaria without well-marked chill, and with only a slight periodicity.

ALAE NASI (Ant. t., Arum., Brom., Lyc., Med.): Wing of nose; the broad cartilaginous portion forming the outer (lateral) side of each nostril.

ALBUMINOUS (Med., Mer.c., Tereb.): Relating to or containing albumin; having the properties of albumin or albumen. (*Albumin:* A simple protein containing carbon, hydrogen, nitrogen, oxygen and sulphur, characterized by soluble in water and coagulable by heat. It is found in nearly every animal and in many plant tissue such as in blood as serum albumin, in milk as lacto-albumin and in egg white as ovalbumin.)

ALBUMINURIA (Apis., Tereb.): Presence of protein in urine, chiefly albumin but also globulin, usually indicative of diseases of kidney but sometimes a response to other diseases or physiological disturbances of benign nature.

ALCOHOLISM (Agar., Ars., Crot., Sulph., Syph.): A chronic progressive and potentially fatal disorder manifested by repeated drinking of alcohol to an extent that interferes the mental and physical health and also social, economic and occupational functioning; chronic alcohol abuse, dependence or addiction.

ALCOHOLIC BEVERAGE (Rat.): Alcoholic drinks as whisky, brandy, wine etc.

ALLEYED (Acon.): Diminish in strength; to put down.

ALL GONE (Anac., Puls., Sep., Sulph.): Sensation of emptiness.

ALOPECIA: Baldness; absence or loss of hairs from skin areas where it is normally present.

ALOPECIA AREATA (Bac.): A condition characterized by circumscribed, non-scarring, usually asymmetrical areas of baldness anywhere on the body especially on the scalp, eyebrows, and beard and usually reversible.

AMAUROSIS (Tab.): Partial or complete loss of vision or blindness occurring without apparent lesion of the eye, as from disease of optic nerve, spine, or brain.

AMBLYOPIA (Ruta.): Dimness of vision without detectable organic lesion of the eye associated especially with the toxic effects of certain drugs or chemical or with dietary deficiencies.

AMENORRHOEA (Acon., Calc., Euph., Phos., Sep.): Failure, suppression or absence of menstruation also known as *amenia*. Physiologically it is found before puberty, after menopause, during pregnancy and lactation.

AMIABLE (Ign.): Friendly, pleasant and good tempered, lovable, sweet and friendly disposition.

AMOROUS (Ver.): Showing, feeling or relating to love especially sexual desire.

AMPUTATION (All.c.): Cut off or removal of a limb, part of organ of the body; usually by surgery.

ANAEMIA (Puls.): A reduction in the number of circulating red blood cells per cu mm., the amount of haemoglobin per 100 ml., or the volume of packed red cells per 100 ml. of blood. Anaemia is not a disease, it is a symptoms of various diseases.

> **PERNICIOUS ANAEMIA (Pic.ac.):** A chronic macrocytic anemia marked by achlorhydria. It is an auto-immune disease.

ANAEMIC (Cal.p., Caul., Crot., Cyc., Kali c., Nat.c., Nat.m., Phos., Plb., Spig.): Pertaining to anaemia or suffering from anaemia.

ANAESTHETICS (Act.): Substances that produce anaesthesia i.e. partial or complete loss of sensation with or without loss of consciousness locally or generally as a result of disease, injury or administration of an anaesthetic agent.

ANAESTHETIC VAPOUR (Act.): Chloroform, Ethylene, Nitrous oxide or other gases that produce insensibility and were earlier used for anaesthesia.

ANASARCA (Apis., Ars., Dros., Dul., Tereb.): Generalized oedema of the whole body.

ANEURISM (Fluor.ac., Spig.): Localized abnormal dilatation of wall of a blood vessel (especially artery), or a blood containing tumour, connecting directly with the lumen of an artery. It is usually due to an acquired or congenital weakness of the wall of the artery or heart.

CAPILLARY ANEURISM (Fluor.ac., Spig.): Aneurism occurring in capillaries.

ANGINA PECTORIS (Spong.): Paroxysmal thoracic pain of short duration with a feeling of suffocation, oppression, severe constriction about the chest and impending death. It occurs due to inadequate blood supply to the cardiac musculature, and it precipitated by effort or excitement. The pain radiates from the precardium to the both shoulders and upper arm especially left, and also radiate to the elbow, wrist or even upto fourth and fifth fingers. Sometimes radiates to neck, upper jaw, throat, and back. It is usually found in coronary diseases.

ANGER (Lyc., Mur.ac., Nat.m., Nux., Plat., Staph.): A feeling of fierce annoyance because of something unfair or hurtful that has happened.

ANGRY (Ant.c., Bry., Caps., Caust., Cham., Coc., Coloc., Fer., Hep., Ign., Kali br., Mez., Val.): Person, feeling or showing annoyance, resentment, vexation, wrath, disapproval; irritable; cross; ill-tempered.

ANGUISH (Acon., Ars., Coff., Hell., Nit.ac.): Severe mental or physical pain or suffering.

ANNOYING (Tab.): Making someone feel slight angry and impatient; irritating.

ANIMAL HEAT (Alum., Am. c., Cal.p., Led.): Heat produced in the body of a living animal by functional, chemical and physical activity; the body's inherent heat or energy.

ANIMAL FLUID (Psor.): Natural fluid present in the body which is required for normal functioning and maintenance of health, e.g. blood, seminal fluid, etc.

ANIMAL MATTER (Ars.): Decayed meat.

ANOMALIES (Ruta.): Marked deviation from the normal standard, especially as a result of congenital or hereditary defects.

ANTEVERSION (Lil.): Inclining or tipping or tilting forward of an organ as a whole without bending. Used especially for the malposition of uterus.

ANTHRAX (Taren.): An acute infectious disease of warm-blooded animals (as cattle and sheep) caused by a spore forming bacteria (*Bacillusanthracis*) transmissible from animal to man through contact with contaminated wool, other animal products or by inhalation of air-borne spores, presents with symptoms of malignant pustules in skin and lesions of lungs, intestine, brain, etc.

ANTHRAX POISONING (Anthr., Ars., Taren.): Characterized by Wool sorters diseases (pulmonary form); *mycosis intestinalis* (gastroentric form); malignant pustules or malignant oedema (cutaneous form); occurs in man from infection with *Bacillusanthracis*. The disease is marked by haemorrhage and serous effusion in the organs.

ANTICIPATES (Med.): To imagine or expect that something will happen in the future, sometimes taking action in preparation for it.

ANTITOXIN (Vario.): An antibody produced by the body in response to a specific biologic toxin or deliberately introduced in the body by vaccination, which neutralizes those toxins released

by bacteria (usually exotoxins), animal (phytotoxins) or plant (zootoxins).

ANUS (Aesc., Aloe., Ant. c., Sec.): The opening at the end of the digestive system through which solid waste (stool) leaves the body.

ANXIETY (Acon., Aeth., Crot., Cup., Dig., Ham., Hyper., Ipec., Meny., Nat.c., Nit.ac., Nux., Plb., Samb., Sep., Spong.): A state of being anxious; uneasiness; a state of apprehension or fear, about some event or issue.

ANXIOUS (Acon., Ars., Asar., Aur., Camph., Hep., Iod., Kali br., Lach., Lil., Med., Nit.ac., Nux., Psor., Sil., Spong.): Experiencing worry or unease.

APPARENTLY (Puls.): Something that you have heard or read, seems to be true, although you are not sure whether true or not.

APPARENT RELISH (Cic.): Seemingly enjoy.

APATHETIC (Cinch., Diph., Phos., Phos.ac., Plb., Staph., Syph.): Indifferent; uncaring; feeling or showing little or no emotion or interest about anything.

APATHY (Agnus., Arum., Bor., Sul.ac.): Lack of interest or emotion.

APEX (Lil.): The pointed extremity of a conical or pyramidal structure, such as the heart or lung.

APHONIA (Arum., Caust., Cina., Sel.): Loss of voice; inability to produce vocal sounds which may be caused by hysteria, laryngitis, or some other disorder of the larynx or by brain damage.

APHTHAE (Bor., Sul.ac.): (Pl. form of *aphtha*) Small painful ulcer on the mucous membrane (as in the mouth or gastrointestinal tract or on the lips) of unknown etiology that are covered by grey exudates and surrounded by a red halo, and occurs as solitary or multiple lesions in recurrentaphthous stomatitis.

APOPLECTIC (Ver.v.): Relating to or suffering from or predisposed to apoplexy.

APOPLEXY (Arn., Aster., Crot., Hyos., Lach., Ver. v.): A classical but obsolete term for a cerebral stroke; a sudden loss of consciousness followed by paralysis, due to cerebral haemorrhage or blocking of an artery of the brain by an embolus or thrombus or rupture of an extracerebral artery causing subarachnoid haemorrhage; copious extravasation of blood within any organ.

SANGUINEOUS APOPLEXY (Cact): Apoplexy in sanguine persons whoare having excess amount of blood, plethoric.

APPETITE (Cic., Coc., Psor.): Natural strong desire, especially for food.

APPREHENSION (Cann.ind., Nat.c.): Anxiety or worry about the future; fear of something unpleasant or bad happening.

ARDENT (Nux.): Very enthusiastic; eager; passionate, showing strong feeling about something.

AREOLA (Mez.): The coloured ring around the nipple, or around the vesicle or pustule; that portion of iris which borders the pupil of the eye.

ARROGANT (Plat.): Unpleasantly proud and behaving as if you are better or more important than other people.

AROUSE (Nux., Pyr.): To make responsiveness to sensory stimulation or excitability; the act of state of waking from or as if from sleep.

ARTHRITIS (Benz. ac., Led.): Inflammation of one or more joints of the body due to infectious, metabolic, or constitutional causes.

ARTHRITIS VAGA (Benz.ac., Bry.): Wandering gout. Now it commonly means inflammation of the joints.

ARTICULATION (Aesc., Calen., Cham., Pyr.): A joint; a place of union between bones in the skeleton of a vertebrate; distinct utterance, enunciation of words and sentences.

ARTICULATION DIFFICULT (Pyr.): Difficulty in speech.

ASCARIDES (Cina., Spig., Tereb.): Pl. form of Ascaris. (*Ascaris:* A genus of large intestinal nematode parasites of the sfamily ascarididae).

ASCERTAINABLE (Equis.): To find out for certain; to discover the truth or correct information; to assure to make certain; to insure.

ASCITES (Apis., Fluor.ac., Tereb.): Effusion and accumulation of serous fluid in the abdominal cavity, also known as abdominal or peritoneal dropsy, hydroperitonia, and hydropsabdominis.

ASHY HUE (Pyr., Sec.): Grey or black like the colour of burnt tobacco, wood, coal, etc.

ASIATIC CHOLERA (Camph., Ipec., Cup.): An acute infectious epidemic and endemic disease of man especially in Asia involving the small intestine, characterized by severe effortless diarrhea with rice water stools, vomiting and muscle cramps, marked by toxaemia, dehydration and collapse, caused by a bacteria Vibrio cholera, and spread by contaminated food and water.

ASPHYXIA (Ant.t.): A condition due to lack of oxygen in inspired air resulting in impending or actual cessation of apparent life, due to interruption of effective gaseous exchange in the lungs.

ASPHYXIA NEONATORUM (Ant.t.): Respiratory failure in new-born.

ASSIMILATION (Ars., Calc., Petros.): The processes where the byproduct of digestion are converted to the chemical substances of the body tissues; the constructive phase of metabolism i.e., anabolism.

DEFECTIVE/IMPERFECT ASSIMILATION (Petros., Sil.): The assimilation is not occurring properly due to any disease of gastro-intestinal tract or any general cause. Hence there is no problem in the intake of food, but the utilization is faulty.

ASTHENIC (Led., Mur.ac.): Lack or loss of strength and energy; weakness; debility.

ASTHENOPIA (Ruta.): Weakness or tiring of the eyes accompanied by pain, headache and dimness of vision.

ASTHMA (Can.s., Carbo v., Hep., Kali c., Med., Sang., Tab., Tub.): A respiratory condition marked by attacks of spasm in the bronchi of the lungs due to narrowing of airways and extra mucous production, that causes difficulty in breathing. It is usually connected to allergic reaction or other forms of hypersensitivity and also of hereditary origin.

ASTHMATIC BREATHING (Ars.): Difficult breathing as in asthma.

ASTHMATIC COUGH (Ipec.): Cough occurring during an attack of asthma.

HUMID ASTHMA (Nat.s.): Asthma resulting from long time residing in damp houses, air or climate.

ASTHMA SPASMODIC (Lob.): Uncontrollable, repetitive, paroxysmal cough during attack of asthma.

ASUNDER (Asar.): Apart; to separate into two or more pieces.

ATHEROMA: Fatty degeneration or thickening of the inner surface of an arterial wall, occurring in atherosclerosis.

ATROPHY (Plb., Staph., Tab.): Wasting away or diminishing in size and strength of an organ or tissue or muscles resulting from death and resorption of cells, diminished cellular proliferation, pressure, ischemia, malnutrition, decreased activity or hormonal changes.

ATONY (Caul., Helon., Fer., Lil., Mill., Plb.): Lack of normal tone or strength.

ATONY OF FUNDUS (Mill., Tereb.): Lack of muscle tone or strength of fundus part of bladder or uterus.

ATONY OF UTERUS (Sab.): Lack of contraction of muscles of uterus.

ATROCIOUS (Spig., Taren.): Very bad; extremely cruel; shocking.

AUDITARY CANAL (Pic.ac.): It is a tube that connects the pinna, or fleshy outer visible part of the ear, and tympanic membrane, or eardrum. Together, the pinna and the auditory canal make up the external ear and measure about 1 inch long. The ear canal has two primary functions: helping the auditory process by funnelling sound towards the eardrum and protecting the eardrum from injury.

AURA (Cup.): A subjective, but recognizable sensation that precedes and signals the onset of convulsion or an epileptic attack. It may be psychic or sensory with olfactory, visual, auditory or taste hallucination.

AURA EPILEPTICA (Cup.): A subjective sensation before an attack of epilepsy. It may precede the attack by several hours or only by a few seconds. It may be of a psychic nature or sensory with olfactory, visual, auditory, or taste hallucinations.

AUTUMN (Ant. t.): The 3rd season of the year from August or September to October or November (in northern hemisphere). This is the period when leaves change colour and fall and harvests ripen. That particular season of the year which is characterized by hot days and cold nights.

AVARICIOUS (Lyc.): Greedy of gain; excessive desirous for money, possessions, property, etc.

AVERSION (Bap., Calad., Kali c., Nat.c, Nat.m., Sel., Stram.): A strong feeling of disliking.

AWKWARD (Apis., Bov., Nat. m.): Causing or feeling embarrassment; clumsy; ungraceful; not comfortable.

AWLS (Led.): A small pointed instrument for boring small holes, especially in leather.

BACKACHE-LUMBO-SACRAL (Aesc., Fer., Kali.c., Lac c., Nux.m., Nux., Phyt., Psor., Ruta.): Pain in the lower back. Pain in the lumbosacral region.

BACK GIVES OUT (Aesc.): Weakness and loss of strength of back causing inability to stand; has to sit, lie or support the back.

BAD BEERS (Nux.m.): Beers that are decayed or are of low-standard in quality.

BAD EFFECTS OF MERCURY (Hep., Pod.): Adverse effects of abuse of mercury.

BAD EFFECTS OF SYPHILIS (Aur.): Bad effects of suppressed, maltreated or untreated syphilis.

BALANITIS: Inflammation of glans penis or glans clitoris.

BALDNESS (Phos.): The partial or total loss of hair from parts of the body where it normally grows, especially the head; alopecia.

BALLOONING (Coca): An adventurous game in which large hot air filled balloons are used for lifting and ascending.

BALM OF GILEAD (Con.): Gilead is a region of Palestine, known for its balm. Balm means gold-coloured oleoresin exudates from the tree, *Balsamodendrongileadense*, once esteemed as an antiseptic and useful in healing wounds. In ancient times, Balm of Gilead was thought to be a panacea (a cure-all for any ill, problem, etc.) for all types of wounds and diseases. Similarly Conium maculatum is esteemed as panacea for all types of sufferings of old maids and old bachelors.

BARBER'S ITCH: Tinea barbae; a pustular folliculitis of the hairy areas of the face and neck and nape of neck. Pustules form around hair follicles after which they may break and form hard brown crust. This crusts slough off in a few days, leaving purple pimples which gradually disappears.

BARREL (Nit.ac.): A round bulging vessel or cask, of greater length than breadth, made of staves, bound with hoops, and having flat ends or heads of equal diameter.

BASHFUL (Cina., Coca.): Shy; easily embarrassed; timid; wanting confidence.

BEARING DOWN (Aloe., Lil., Mag.m., Murex., Nat.c., Plat.): To push or press downwards with steady pressure.

BEDSORE (Nux.m.): Decubitus ulcer; a chronic ulcer that appears in the pressure areas in debilitated patients lying in bed for a long time. It is due to a circulatory defect in the area under pressure.

BELCHING (Act, Ars., Cinch, Lyc., Mag.c.): Voiding of wind noisily from the stomach by the mouth; eructation.

BELLIES OF MUSCLES (Act.): The enlarged, prominent, thick, central fleshy body of a muscle between the usual slender points of its attachments.

BEND DOUBLE (Mag.p.): To lean forward and down, usually because of pain or laughter.

BESEECHING (Stram.): To ask someone earnestly; to beg; to solicit.

BESOTTED (Bap., Diph.): Confused; stupid; foolish or silly.

BESOTTED DRUNKEN EXPRESSION (Bap.): Stupid or foolish expression of the face as in drunk or intoxicated state.

BEVERAGES (Ran.b.): Any liquid for drinking other than water as tea, milk, fruit juice, alcohol etc.

BIG BELLIED (Sulph.): Large bulging of stomach.

BILIOUS (Mag. m.): Pertaining to or relating to bile, or disorder arising from excessive bile; Peevish, ill-natured, ill-humoured, bitter, resentful, discontented.

>**BILIOUS ATTACK (Aesc., Bry., Pod., Tar.):** A nondescript state assumed to result from hepatic dysfunction. It is characterised by coated tongue, loss of appetite, constipation, headache, dizziness and vomiting of bile.

>**BILIOUS MEN (Ign.):** Persons of bilious temperament or constitution.

>**BILIOUS TROUBLES (Aesc.):** Troubles due to bile disorder or hepatic dysfunction.

BITTERS (Nux.): A strong bitter alcoholic liquid that is made from plants and added to other alcoholic drinks to give flavour.

BLAND (All.c., Puls.): Non-irritating; insipid; mild or gentle.

BLAND CORYZA (Euph.): Non-irritating, non-corroding coryza.

BLINDNESS (Kali bi., Lac d., Nat.m., Psor., Pyr.): Inability to see, caused by disease of the lens, retina, optic nerve, structures of eye or lesion of the visual cortex or pathway of the brain.

>**DAY BLINDNESS (Ran.b.):** An inability to see in daylight.

BLISTER (Anthr., Calc., Canth., Nat.s., Thuja.): A small swelling on or just beneath the surface of the skin, containing watery fluid and occasionally blood or pus, usually caused by friction or a burn.

BLOATED (Lyc., Op., Spig.): Much larger than normal usually because of fluid, gas, food or excessive fat in a way that is unpleasant and uncomfortable.

BLOND HAIR (Calc.): Light, golden-light or pale yellowish-brown hair.

BLOND (Brom, Calc., Chel., Nit.ac., Phos., Sel., Tub.): A person of fair complexion, with yellowish brown or golden hairs and light or blue or grey eyes.

BLOOD BLISTER (Sec.): Subcutaneous swelling containing blood, resulting from a minor pinch or crushing injury.

BLOOD POISOINING (Crot.): Outdated term for septicemia where whole body is affected by toxins produced by microorganisms in the circulating blood; pyemia.

BLOODSHOT (Ver.v.): The white part of the eyes showing red or pink due to local congestion of the smaller blood vessels found as in lack of sleep, tiredness, drinking much alcohol, etc.

BLOTCHES (Sul.ac.): A spot or mark or area of discolouration on the skin especially when large or irregular.

BLUSHING (Fer.): Become redder or darker in the face, usually from ashamed or embarrassment or from heat or may be caused by any systemic disease like carcinoid syndrome, pheochromocytoma.

BLUR OR FILM (Phys.): An ill-defined spot or smear in the field of vision causing a confused and dim impression.

BLURRED (Kali bi; Rum., Ruta.): A dim, confused ill-defined appearance, indistinctness of vision in which the object seems dim, vague and the outlines are indistinct.

BLUSH (Amyl., Fer.): Sudden brief erythema (redness) of the face and neck, resulting from vascular dilatation due to heat, shame or other emotions.

BOIL (Arn., Lach., Mer.s., Sec., Sulph., Tereb.): Furuncle; a painful nodule formed in the skin by circumscribed inflammation of the dermis and subcutaneous tissue after staphylococci enter the skin through hair follicles.

BLOOD BOILS (Crot., Sil.): Boils containing mainly blood.

BOOK WORMS (Coca., Coc.): A person unusually devoted to reading and studying books.

BORBORYGMUS (Cinch.): A gurgling, splashing noise heard over large intestine caused by the passage of gas through the liquid content of the intestine.

BORING (Cina., Hell.): Digging.

BOYISH GO (Aur.): The vigour or energy of the young boys; like a boy in appearance or behaviour.

BRADYCARDIA: Slowness of the heart beat as evidenced by slowing of the pulse rate to less than 60 beats per minute.

BRAIN FAG (Pic.ac.): A tired condition of the nerves or brain after overwork of an intellectual character; mental fatigue.

BRAN LIKE (Tub.): Like the outer covering of grains.

BREEDS VERMIN (Mez.): To produce noxious small animals or parasitic insects, as lice.

BRIGHT'S DISEASES (Dig., Kali bi., Kali br., Lac d., Mer.c., Mer.cy., Plb.): (Syn.*Glomerulonephritis*) A non-suppurative inflammatory or degenerative renal disease characterised by proteinuria, haematuria and occasionally hypertension, oedema and nitrogen retention.

BRINE (Sanic., Med.): Very salty water, used especially for preserving food.

BRITTLE (Calc.p., Graph., Thuja): An object or substance that is hard but easily broken, or apt to break or snap; fragile.

BRONCHITIS (Dul., Puls., Sang.): Inflammation of the mucous membrane of the bronchial airways caused by irritation or infection by pathogens..

BROODS (Ign., Naja.): To think continuously or moodily on a gloomy subject; to be in a state of gloomy, serious thought.

BRUISE (Arn., Caust., Eup., Ham., Med., Mer.s., Led., Ran.b., Ruta., Petr., Phyt., Pyr., Spong., Sul.ac., Sulph.): A superficial injury produced by a blow or collision transmitted through unbroken skin to underlying tissue causing rupture of small blood vessels and escape of blood into the tissue with resulting discolouration.

BRUNETTE (Nit.ac., Tub.): A girl or women of dark pigmentation or pertaining to a dark type, having brown or olive skin and brown or black hair and eyes; applied especially to the darker division of the race.

BUBBLING SENSATION (Berb.): Sensation of water bubbles.

BUBO (Mer.s.): An enlarged and inflamed lymph node often suppurating particularly in the axilla or groin, due to infections such as plague, syphilis, gonorrhoea, lymphogranuloma venereum, andtuberculosis.

BULIMIA: Voracious appetite, in which a person repeatedly eats too much and forces himself or herself to vomit.

BUNGHOLE (Thuja.): A hole in a barrel or cask, used to fill or empty it.

BUNION (Hyper., Rhod.): Inflammation and thickening of the bursa of the joint of the great toe usually associated with marked enlargement of the joint and lateral displacement of the toe.

BURIED (Psor.): Hiding something by covering it.

BURN (Caust., Hell., Ruta., Psor.): Tissue injury resulting from excessive exposure to thermal, chemical, electrical, or radioactive agent. The effect may be local or both local and systemic. Four degrees are recognized- 1. Erythema without vesiculation, 2. Vesiculation with erythema 3. Destruction of epidermis and 4. Destruction of skin and subcutaneous tissue.

BUSINESS EMBARASSMENTS (Hyos., Kali br.): Shy, awkward or guilty feelings in various situations of business, like financial loss, inability to repay loan, etc.

CACHECTIC PEOPLE (Bar., Bell., Carbo v., Hydr, Nat. m., Nit. ac., Sec.): People having the symptoms of cachexia, especially thin, emaciated body.

CACHEXIA (Carbo. v., Eup., Iod., Staph., Thyr.): A condition characterized by physical weakness, wasting of muscles, malnutrition, abnormally low body weight and general ill-health, usually associated with a chronic disease such as cancer or tuberculosis.

CADAVEROUS (Carbo. v., Kreos.): Of or relating to a corpse or cadaver i.e. the dead human body.

CAGE (Cact.): An enclosure having some open work (as of wires or bars), specially for confining birds or animals.

CALAMITY (Lil.): It is an event that causes a great deal of damage, destruction, or personal distress e.g. earthquake.

CALCULI (Med., Sars.): Stone;a hard solid mass consisting of mineral salt, formed around organic material, and found mainly within hollow body structure such as kidney, urinary bladder, gall bladder, or bile ducts.

CALISTHENICS (Brom.): Physical exercises intended to improve the strength, suppleness, balance and health of the body.

CALLOUS (Cal.p., Symph.): A substance that is exuded around the ends of a broken bone and that by conversion into true bone, bridges the gap and restore the continuity of bone.

CALVARIUM (Cann. ind.): The dome like upper portion of the skull, comprising the superior portion of the frontal, parietal and occipital bones

CANCER (Anthr., Carb. ac., Con., Graph., Hydr, Kreos., Med., Mur. ac., Phos., Psor.): General term frequently used to indicate various types of malignant neoplasm, most of which invades surrounding tissues, may metastasis to several sites, and are likely to recur after attempted removal and to cause death of the patient unless adequately treated, such ascarcinoma or sarcoma, but, in ordinary usage, speciallythe former; have also been used to denote a severe and fatal illness.

CANCER UTERI (Thlaspi.): Cancer of the uterus.

CANCEROUS TENDENCY (Con.): Tendency or prone to develop cancer.

CANCRUM ORIS: Gangrenous stomatitis; gangrenous process of the mouth, it begins as a small gingival ulcer results in gangrenous necrosis of surrounding facial tissues.

CANINE HUNGER (Cina., Fer., Lyc.): A morbidly voracious appetite; excessive and insatiable appetite; a condition when person can eat again even after just having eaten.

CANKER SORES (Ant. c.): Recurrent ulcerative disease of mouth specially lips; obsolete term for aphthous stomatitis.

CANTHUS (Bor.): The angle at either end of the fissure between the eyelids, medial (nasal canthus) and lateral (temporal canthus).

CARBUNCLE (Anthr., Canth., Carboan., Carb.ac., Carbov., Crot., Diph., Dul., Kali bi., Lach., Pyr., Sil., Taren.): A circumscribed inflammation of the skin and deeper tissues, characterized by the presence of several drainage ducts. This painful necrotic lesion most commonly occurs on the back of the neck, shoulders, hips, and thighs and terminates in a slough and suppuration and is accompanied by marked constitutional symptoms, e.g. fever, leucocytosis, prostration.

CARCINOMA (Med.): Any of the various types of malignant neoplasm derived from epithelial tissue and may infiltrate locally or produce metastases. It may affect almost any organ or part of the body and spread by direct extension, through lymphatics or through the blood stream.

CARDIAC ASTHENIA (Pyr.): Weakness of heart.

CARDIALGIA (Bis.): Literal meaning is pain in the heart. But the term is used to denote pain in the pit of the stomach or region of the heart usually occurring in paroxysm. Sometimes also used to mean heartburn due to acidity or indigestion.

CARDITIS (Naja.): Inflammation of the heart muscle; myocarditis.

CARIES (Coca., Fluor. ac., Mez., Phos. ac., Ther.): Gradual decay, destruction or necrosis of the teeth or bone and if the decay progresses, the surrounding tissue becomes inflamed and an abscess forms.

CARIOUS (Mez.): Affected with or of the nature of caries. *Caries* means the progressive decomposition and decay of a tooth or bone, accompanied by softening and discolouration.

CARPHOLOGIA: An aimless plucking at the bed clothes, as if one were picking off threads or tufts of cotton observed in condition of exhaustion, delirium, fever or stupor.

CARSICKNESS (Coc.): Sickness caused by riding on a railway or in an automobile with resultant nausea, weakness, malaise, dizziness and vomiting.

CASTING THEM OFF (Plat.): Get rid of; no longer wanted.

CASTS (Nit. ac., Tereb.): An elongated or cylindroid mold formed in a tubular structure that may be observed in histological sections or in materials such as urine or sputum.

CASTS FIBROELASTIC (Kali bi.): Casts composed of collagen and elastic fibres.

CATALEPSY (Graph., Sabad.): A condition where body become stiff and temporarily becomes unconscious, seen in some patients after parietal lobe strokes and found in some sycotic patients.

CATAMENIA (Glon.): Menstruation.

CATARRH (Lyc., Nat. c., Nux., Thuja): Inflammation of a mucous membrane especially of throat and nose with discharge of mucous.

CATARRHAL (Aesc., Diph., Euph., Kali bi., Mer.dul.): Relating to or affected with catarrh.

CATARRHAL INFLAMMATION (All.c., Mer.dul.): Inflammation of mucous membrane, characterized by congestion and copious discharged of mucous and epithelial debris.

CATARRHAL DULL HEADACHE (All.c.): Dull pain in head associated with catarrhal discharge usually occurring after or with attack of cold.

CATARRHAL ISCHURIA (Dul.): Retention or suppression of urine due to catarrh (inflammation of mucous membrane of the bladder wall).

CATARRHAL LARYNGITIS (All.c.): Acute congestive inflammation of larynx with excessive secretion of mucous.

CATHETERIZATION (Mag. p.): Use or passage of a catheter that is a hollow tube designed to be passed into the body for evacuating fluids or injecting them into body cavities.

CAULIFLOWER (Staph.): A large, round vegetable that has a hard white center surrounded by green leaves and is eaten cooked or raw.

CAUTERIZATION (Nat.m.): Destruction of tissue with a caustic, an electric current, a hot iron or by freezing, usually done in os uteri and cervix for treating leucorrhoea.

CAUTIOUSNESS (Graph.): Carefulness in order to avoid possible danger or risks.

CAVITY (Trill.): A hollow space, such as a body organ or the hole in a tooth produced by caries.

CAYENNE PEEPER (Caps.): A very hot and pungent red powder which is made by drying and grinding the whole fruits or seeds of dried pepper and is used to flavour food.

CEREBRAL TYPHOID OR TYPHUS (Phos.ac.): Typhoid or typhus associated with cerebral symptoms.

CEREBRO-SPINAL DISEASE (Ver.v): Diseases of central nervous system.

CESSATION (Thuja.): The ending of a condition or the stopping of an activity; pause.

CHAFING (Sul.ac): To make or become damaged or sore by rubbing between opposing surface.

CHAGRIN (Bry., Cham., Caul., Murex., Petros., Plat., Staph.): Is a feeling of disappointment, upset, or annoyance caused by the humbling or wounding of pride, by failure, troubles, vexation etc.; acute vexation or mortification.

CHALAZAE (Staph., Thuja.): (Syn.*Meibomiancyst*) A chronic inflammatory granuloma in the tarsus of the eyelid due to inflammation of a meibomian gland.

CHANCRES (Lac c., Mer.s., Syph.): A hard ulcer, the first sign of syphilis, appearing 2-3 weeks after infection begins as a papule of dull red colour and the centre of which usually becomes eroded or breaks down into an ulcer.

CHANCROIDS (Mer.s.): A sexually transmitted infection, caused by the *Haemophilusducreyi*. Its hallmark is the appearance of one or more painful ulcers on the genitals (where chancre is the painless ulcer). The incubation period is typically 2 to 5 days, although longer incubation has been reported.

CHAPPED HANDS (Petr.): Dry, scaly, fissured skin of hands, usually caused by cold, eczema etc.

CHARPIE (Mez.): Straight threads obtained by separating old linen cloth; used for surgical dressings.

CHATTERS (Hyos.): To talk quickly or continuously usually about things that are not important or for no serious purpose.

CHECKED (Acon): Sudden arrest or stoppage of course.

CHEERFUL (Alum.): Happy and showing this in their behaviour; in a good mood.

CHILLBLAINS (Abrot., Agar., Petr., Zinc.): An erythema and swelling of toes, fingers, nose, ears, heels and sometimes in cheeks that are caused by cold injury (frostbite) producing vascular constriction accompanied by itching, burning, blistering and sometimes cracking and ulceration of skin.

CHILLINESS (Mag.c., Nux., Ver.): The sensation of cold, or the sensation of being cold with or without shivering.

CHLOROSIS (Calc., Cyc., Fer., Phyt., Puls., Thlaspi.,): A form of chronic hypochromic microcytic (iron deficiency) anemia, characterized by a great reduction in haemoglobin out of proportion to the decreased number of red blood cells; marked by a greenish colour of the skin, weakness and menstrual disturbances;

observed chiefly in females from puberty to the third decade and usually associated with diets deficient in iron and protein.

CHOCKING (Can.s., Hep., Med., Naja., Spig., Tereb.): To prevent or interrupt respiration by obstruction or compression of the larynx or trachea or the condition resulting from such interruption or fumes, emotion etc.; to suffocate.

CHOLERA (Am.c., Crot., Cup., Kreos., Ver.): An acute epidemic infectious disease of small intestine caused by the bacterium Vibrio cholera, due to ingestion of contaminated food and water, resulting in profuse watery diarrhea, vomiting, extreme loss of food and electrolytes, dehydration, muscle cramps and collapse.

> **ASIATIC CHOLERA (Cup.):** Cholera that is chiefly occurs in Asia (especially India and Pakistan).
>
> **CHOLERA MORBUS (Ant. t., Bis., Camph., Cup., Pod., Sec., Ver.):** An acute severe gastroenteritis characterized by severe colic, vomiting, and diarrhea and watery stool usually occurring in summer or hot weather.
>
> **CHOLERA INFANTUM (Ipec., Kali br., Pod.):** Infantile cholera;an acute, noncontagious intestinal disturbances of infants and young children, common in congested areas of high humidity and temperature, characterized by vomiting, profuse watery diarrhea, fever, prostration and collapse.
>
> *Nearly all references consider cholera infantum and cholera morbus to have the same symptoms, with the only difference being in name: cholera infantum is used when referring to infant and young children.*

CHOLERIC (Coff., Lach., Phos.ac., Taren.): Irritable; quick-tempered without apparent causes.

CHLOROTIC (Phos.): Relating to chlorosis.

CHOREA (Act., Agar., Caul., Cic., Coc., Croc., Nit.ac., Phos., Stram., Zinc.): Involuntary, irregular, spasmodic, uncontrollable, purposeless, rapid, jerky, dyskinetic movements of body and face and marked incoordination of limbs.

CHRONIC BLUE CONDITION (Lac c.): Always depressed and gloomy.

CHRONIC OTITIS (Thuja.): Chronic inflammation of ear.

CHUBBY (Kali bi.): Slight fat in a way that people usually find adorable; fatty.

CICATRICES (Caust., Flour.ac., Graph., Sul.ac.): (Pl. of *Cicatrix*) Scar marks left after healing of wound; scar; fibrous tissue replacing the normal tissue during the process of healing.

CIDER (Nit.ac.): An alcoholic drink made from apple juice.

CIDER VINEGAR (Act., Carb.ac.): vinegar made from fermented cider.

CILIARY NEURALGIA (Act.): Pain of severe throbbing character in the course of distribution of a nerve supplying the ciliary structures of eye i.e. ciliary body, ciliary process, ciliary muscles etc.

CIRCULATION (Carboan., Sep.): The system of blood vessels that supplies oxygenated blood pumped by the heart to all parts of body, and that transport deoxygenated blood to the lungs.

CIRCUMSCRIBED (Ign., Sang., Stram.): Bounded or limited; confined to a limited space; to draw a line around; to surround.

CIRRHOSIS (Apoc.): A disease of liver characterized by loss of the normal microscopic lobular architecture, degeneration, fatty infiltration, interstitial inflammation, atrophy with fibrosis and nodular regeneration, interfering function of the liver.

CLAIRVOYANCE: The supposed ability to perceive things that are out of the natural ranges of human senses or ability to see into the future (or ability to communicate with dead people).

CLAMMY (Ars., Ver.v.): Unpleasantly damp or sticky or cold; humid.

CLASPED (Cact.): A firm grip or act of gripping; to hold something tightly with arms or hands.

CLAYEY (Alum., Plat.): Containing clay or like clay (*Clay* is a kind of earth that is soft and dark green when wet and hard when it is dry).

CLAVUS (Nat.m.): A sharp pain in the head sharply defined and typically describe as feeling like a nail being driven into the head. The correct term is "Clavushystericus".

It also means a corn or small conically callosity caused by pressure over a bony prominence, usually on a toe.

CLENCHED (Aeth., Cup.): To close tightly; to grasp; to grip firmly.

CLERGYMAN (Arum., Dros.): Religious preacher; a male priest or minister in the Christian Church.

CLERGYMAN'S SORE THROAT (Arum., Dros.): (Syn. *Anginagranulosa, granularpharyngitis*) Sore throat of religious preacher.

CLIMACTERIC (Cact ., Caust., Cinch., Con., Croc., Dig., Glon., Graph., Lach., Med., Murex., Plb., Psor., Sab., Sang., Sep., Sulph., Sul.ac., Thalaspi., Ther., Trill.,): The syndrome of endocrine, somatic and psychic changes occurring at the termination of the reproductive period in the females (menopause); it is the normal diminution of sexual activity in the male (male climacteric).

CLIMAXIS (Lach., Psor.): Physiological stoppage of menses occurring usually around 40-45 years of age; climacteric; menopause.

CLINKER (Kali bi.): A hard, dried mass of mucous in the nasal cavity; hard mass.

CLOSET (Aloe., Alum.): Though the word means an apartment or small room for retirement or privacy but earlier the term was used to mean 'toilet'.

CLOTTED (Mag.m., Med., Sab.): A mass which is thickened or coalesced in soft thick jelly like or semisolid consistency.

CLOVES (Alum.): The pungent fragrant aromatic reddish brown dried flower bud, used as a spice.

CLUB (Tab.): A heavy tapering stick, knobby or massy at one end, used to strike with.

CLUMSY (Caps.): Lacking intellectual skill or grace; unskillful with the hands or awkward and ungainly in movement.

CLUTCHING (Ipec.): Seizing or grasping or holding firmly in a tight, powerful grip.

COALESCING (Hep.): To unite or join together into one body or product; become integrated into a whole.

COARSE (Psor., Sel.): Not fine or delicate; composed of somewhat large or rough parts or particles.

COBWEB (Brom., Graph.): A web of fine sticky thread spun by a spider to catch its prey.

COCCYDYNIA: Neuralgic or rheumatic pain of coccygeal region.

COLIC (Abrot., All.c., Aloe., Alum., Am. c., Cal.p., Chel., Cinch., Collin., Coloc., Dios., Graph., Kali br., Kali s., Lyc.,

Mag.c., Mag.p., Mer., Mill, Nux., Plb., Rheum., Sab., Stan., Staph., Thlaspi.): (Pertaining to the colon) A paroxysm of acute abdominal pain localized in a hollow organ or tube and caused by spasm, obstruction or twisting. Different types of colic are biliary colic, appendicular colic, renal colic, gall stone colic etc.

> **DOUBLING-UP COLIC (Mag.p.):** Bending forward due to colic.
>
> **FLATULENT COLIC (Ipec.):** Colic due to flatulency.
>
> **RENAL COLIC (Med., Sars., Tab.):** Pain in the region of one of the flanks (renal area) that radiates inferiorly, towards the lower abdomen, groin, scrotum, labia or thigh, may be associated with impaction or passage of calculus.

COLLAPSE (Carb.ac., Crot., Diph., Med., Sec., Tab., Ver.): A state of extreme prostration and physical depression resulting from circulatory failure, great loss of body fluids, or heart disease and occurring terminally in diseases such as cholera, typhoid, pneumonia etc.

COLLIQUATIVE (Phos.ac.): Characterized by excessive discharge of fluid, or by liquefaction of tissue.

COLLIQUATIVE SWEATS (Phos.ac.): Excessive sweat and weakening.

COMA (Nux.m., Op.): A state of profound unconsciousness from which one cannot be roused. It differs from drowsiness or stupor in which the patients are slow to respond, but comatose patients are completely unresponsive.

COMEDONS: A blackhead; a collection of sebaceous (oily) material and dead cells retained in the hair follicle and excretory duct of the sebaceous gland, the surface covered with a dark dot. It is the primary lesion of acne vulgaris.

COMMENCEMENT (Sec., Syph.): Beginning.

COMMISSURES (Hep.): A site of union of corresponding parts; a general term used to designate such a junction of corresponding anatomical structures, frequently, but not always across the mid-plane of the body, as the lips, eyelids or labia.

COMMOTION (Spig.): A disturbance (physical or mental); noisy confusion or excitement; violent motion or agitation.

COMPEL (Coloc.): To force someone to do something; to make something necessary.

COMPLEXION SALLOW (Caul., Lyc.): Pale, yellow and unhealthy appearance.

COMPETENT (Vario.): Having the skills or knowledge to do something well enough to meet a basic standard.

COMPOSITORS (Caust.): A person who arranges types and pictures of a book, magazine, newspaper before printing (of printing press especially where lead types were used).

CONCIOUSNESS (Cic., Cup., Graph., Hell., Helon.): The physical and mental state of being awake and fully aware of one's environment, thoughts and feelings.

CONCUSSION (Arn., Cic., Hyper., Spig., Sul.ac.): A violent shaking or jarring of the brain, caused by injury to the head as a result of a severe blow or fall and usually resulting in disturbance of cerebral function and sometimes marked by permanent damage.

CONDYLOMATA (Nit.ac., Thuja., Sab.): (Pl. of *Condyloma*) Wart like excrescence on the outer skin or the adjoining mucous membrane.

CONFINEMENT (Lyc., Pyr., Ruta., Sil.): Restraint within a specific area; used especially to designate the period of childbirth when the mother is confined to bed; lying-in.

CONFLUENT (Vario.): Denoting certain skin lesions which become merged, forming a patch which is not discreet or distinct one from the other; joining together.

CONFUSION (Act., Aeth., Calc., Carboan., Dul., Gels., Lil.): State of being confused mentally; lack of certainty, orderly thought, or power to distinguished, choose, or act decisively.

CONGESTION (Acon., Aesc., Aloe., Cact., Collin., Glon., Lob., Mel., Sulph., Tereb., Ver.v.): Abnormal accumulation of blood in the blood vessels of an organ or part whether naturally or artificially induced.

> **CEREBRAL CONGESTION (Glon., Hyos.):** Abnormal accumulation of blood in cerebral vessels.
>
> **CONGESTION OF PORTAL CIRCULATION (Aloe.):** Over fullness or abnormal accumulation of blood in portal circulation.
>
> **VENOUS CONGESTION (Ham.):** Congestion in large and small veins.

CONGESTIVE CHILL (Camph.): Historical term for a form of pernicious malaria in which the paroxysm is accompanied by congestion of the gastro enteric tract and profuse diarrhea preceded by a chill, vomiting and prostration.

CONJUNCTIVITIS TRAUMATIC (Ham.): Inflammation of conjunctiva due to any trauma to the eye.

CONSCIENCE (Cyc.): The feeling that we know and should do what is right and should avoid doing what is wrong, and that makes us feel guilty when we have done something wrong.

CONSEQUENCES (Staph.): A result of an action or situation, especially the bad result.

CONSOLATION (Hell., Lil., Nat.m.): Comfort or sympathy is given to someone who is sad or disappointed.

CONSTIPATION (Abrot., Aesc., Alum., Anac., Ant.c.): A condition in which bowel movements are irregular, infrequent, abnormally delayed and insufficient or incomplete (dry, hard faeces).

HABITUAL CONSTIPATION (Graph.): Regularly suffers from constipation.

OBSTINATE CONSTIPATION (Aloe., Am.m., Can.s., Coc., Lac d., Psor., Pyr., Syph.): A constipation whichis not easilycured or relieved.

CONSTITUTION (Aster., Aur., Colch.): The physical make-up of the body, including the mode of performance of its function, the activity of its metabolic processes, the manner and degree of its reaction to stimuli and its power of resistance to the attack of pathogenic organisms. Though in Homoeopathic literature the term is used to denote the physical and mental make-up of the person.

HYDROGENOID (Ant.t., Nat.s., Thuja.): A homoeopathic term denoting a constitution that will not tolerate much moisture; One of the three constitutions put forth by Edward von Grauvogl (1811-1877). It is characterized by an excess of water in the tissues and blood and heightened sensitivity of the patient to cold and dampness; it corresponds to the sycoticmiasm of Hahnemann (1755-1843). The two other Grauvogl constitutions are CARBO-NITROGENOID (psoric) and OXYGENOID (syphilitic).

LYMPHATIC (Aster., Bap., Bell., Hep.): It is marked by pallor, slow and shallow respiration, and sluggish circulation, hyperplasia of the lymphatic glands and tendency to inflammation of the skin and lymphatic.

STRUMOUS (Apis., Bar., Crot., Diph.): Scrofulous.

CONSTITUTIONAL EFFECTS OF ONANISM (Arg.m.): Constitutional effects occur due incomplete coitus or coitus interruptus.

CONSTITUTIONAL REMEDY (Calc., Nat.c., Tub.): A remedy which has been selected on the basis of constitutional symptoms of the patient and is expected to act on the person's constitution as a whole.

CONSTRICTION (Cact., Can.s., Caps., Dros., Ipec., Lach., Lob., Med., Melil., Plat., Stram.): A feeling or sensation of tightness, narrowness, or compression; a normally or pathologically constricted or narrowed portion of a luminal structure.

CONSTRICTED FAUCES (Aesc.): Feeling of constriction in the space between the cavity of the mouth and the pharynx, bounded by the soft palate and the base of the tongue,

CONSUMPTIVE (Fer., Med.): (Adj. of *Consumption*)A progressive wasting away of the body especially that attendant upon pulmonary phthisis, is called pulmonary consumption or tuberculosis; obsolete term of tuberculosis.

CONTEMPTUOUS (Plat.): Haughty, scornful; who consider others unworthy, arising out of feeling of superiority and dislike; one who looks down upon other.

CONTORTION (Stram.): The state of the face or body being twisted out of its natural shape.

CONTRACTION (Can.s., Caust., Coc., Croc., Hell., Nat.m., Plb., Sec.): The action or process of becoming smaller, shorter or pressed together; a tightening of the muscles caused by a shortening in length of the muscle fibre.

CONTRACTIVE STIFFNESS (Med.): Tightening and shortening of muscles with inability to fold easily or rigid in action.

CONTRADICTION (Aster., Aur., Con., Fer., Helon., Ign., Lyc., Puls.): Disagreement; opposition of facts, forces, tendencies, qualities or events.

CONTRARY (Nat.m.): A fact or opinion, event or situation that is the opposite of one already stated; opposite.

CONTUSION (Arn., Con., Euph., Ham., Led., Sul.ac.): Any mechanical injury (usually caused by a blow) resulting in haemorrhage beneath unbroken skin; a bruise.

CONVALESCENCE (Calc., Tar.): A period between the end of a disease and the patient's restoration to complete health; during which the patient is recovering his strength and health.

CONVERGE (Syph.): To move toward the same point and come closer together or meet.

CONVULSION (Acon., Act., Caust., Cham., Cinch., Cic., Coc., Cup., Glon., Hell., Hyos., Lys., Nux.): A sudden, violent and irregular movement of the body due to involuntary spasmodic contraction of muscles.

> **APOPLECTIC CONVULSION (Crot.):** Convulsion accompanied with apoplexy i.ea sudden loss of consciousness followed by paralysis.

> **PUERPERAL CONVULSION (Cic., Cup.):** (Syn. *Puerperal eclampsia*) Convulsion during puerperal period.

CONVULSIVE GAGGING (Bis.): Spasmodic type of unpleasant feeling in mouth and stomach as if going to vomit or cause to retch or heave.

CONVULSIVE TREMBLING (Sab.): Trembling occurring during convulsive attacks.

COPIOUS (Act, Am.c., Carb.ac., Kreos., Led., Lob., Mez., Nat.s., Sabad., Sars., Sec., Spig., Trill.): In large amount; abundant; plentiful.

COPPERY HUE (Mer.): Of coppery colour (reddish brown).

CORNS (Ant.c., Hyper., Ran.b., Thuja.): A horny painful induration and thickening of the epidermis of the skin usually on or between toes, produced by friction or pressure and form into a central conical mass extending into the dermis.

CORPSE LIKE (Plb.): Resembling a dead human body.

CORPULENT (Aur., Carbo v., Calc., Lob., op.): Fat; flabby; bulky; obese.

CORPUSCLES (Am.c., Sec.): Any small rounded body or mass; a blood cell.

CORRODES (All.c., Cham., Iod., Mer.c.): To destroy slowly especially by chemical action; to weaken or destroy by a gradual process of impairment.

CORROSIVE (Kreos., Mer.): Having the power to corrode; a substance that destroy or wears away the texture of the tissues of the body.

CORYZA (Aesc., Eup., Euph., Lac.c., Nux., Phos., Sabad., Samb., Sel.): An acute inflammatory contagious disease involving the upper respiratory tract; acute rhinitis.

>**SPRING CORYZA (All.c.):** Coryza especially occurring at the time of season of spring.

COSTIVENESS (Nux.): Tendency to suffer fromconstipation; especially by reason of dryness of faeces rather than as a consequence of muscular atony.

COUGH

COUGH (Acon., Alum., Ambr., Caust., Cina): Expel air from lungs with violent effort and characteristic noise produced by abrupt opening of glottis, in order to remove obstruction or relieve irritation in air passages.

BARKING (Dros., Hep., Spong.): Loud, short cough like the bark of a dog.

CONCUSSIVE (Stan.): A violent coughshaking or jerking the whole body.

DEEP (Med., Stan.): A low pitched sound as if coming from a long distance or deep inside.

EXPLOSIVE (Caps.): Characterised by sudden and violent coughing.

FATIGUING (Mer., Rum.): Prolong excessive, repetitive, painful cough producing fatigue or tiredness.

HACKING (Tereb.): Dry painful repetitive cough with a harsh, unpleasant sound

HOLLOW (Med., Samb., Stan.): Sound as if producing from an empty space or cavity, within a solid substance.

MINUTE GUN (Dros.): Rapid coughs in short paroxysms.

PAROXYSOMAL (Kali c., Stan.): A sudden, periodic attack or recurrence of cough.

RACKING (Bry., Mer.): To cause great physical pain; agonizing cough.

SHATTERING (Stan.): Very loud or the sound as if something is broken down into small pieces suddenly.

SIBILANT (Spong.): Hissing or whistling in character, found in certain abnormal lung condition.

SUFFOCATIVE (Samb.): Feeling of suffocation during coughing as if seen in different obstructive and restrictive lung diseases.

SPASMODOMIC (Caps., Chel., Con., Cup., Dros., Hyos., Ign., Ipec.): Cough which occurs suddenly for short period of times and at irregular intervals; relating to or consisting of a spasm or spasms.

STOMACH COUGH: A reflex cough excited at times by irritation of the gastric mucous membrane.

SYMPATHETIC (Naja.): Cough associated with heart disease.

TEASING (Rumex): Annoying, irritating cough.

TICKLING (Am.c., Ham.): A slight irritating, uncomfortable feeling in throat producing cough.

TITILATING (Dros.): Sensation produced by tickling and causing cough.

WHEEZING (Spong.): The sound made by air passing through the fauces, glottis, or narrowed tracheobronchial airways in difficult breathing.

WHISTLING (Spong.): Cough like a clear shrill musical sound produced by the forcing of air or steam against a thin edge or into a cavity (may be through a small hole between nearly closed ups).

WHOOPING (Ambr. Ant.c., Cup., Dros., Ipec., Kali br., Samb., Sang., Stram): .): Pertussis; an acute infectious disease marked by recurring attacks of spasmodic coughing continued until the breath is exhausted, then ending with a deep, noisy inspiration.

COUNTENANCE (Acon., Sec.): A person's face or facial expression; appearance.

COURAGE (Glon.): The ability to control fear and to be willing to deal with something that is dangerous, difficult, or unpleasant; bravery.

CRACKED (Hell., Hep., Nat.m., Nit.ac., Petr., Pyr., Sars.): Damaged something by causing thin lines or spaces to appear on its surface; broken down slightly.

CRAMPS (Cup., Sulph., Med., Pod., Ver., Thlaspi.): A sudden pain caused by sudden contraction of a muscle.

CRAVING (Alum., Calad., Cal.ars., Mag.c., Mag.m., Med., Nat.m., Staph., Syph.): A strong desire for something; desire to satisfy a vague inner need; longing.

CRAWLING (Dros.): Move or progress slowly or with great difficulty; movement or feeling like that of movement of a worm.

CRAZY (Acon., Act., Lil.): Insane; mentally unbalanced.

CRIB (Bor., Gels.): Cradle; a child's bed with side railings.

CRIPPLED (Graph., Sil.): To make lame; to lame; to disable, impair the efficiency of; one lacking the natural use of a limb or the body.

CRI ENCEPHALIQUE (Hell.): Sudden shrill cry by an infant. Usually indicative of a cerebral disease, e.g. meningitis, encephalitis.

CROAKING (Acon., Lyc.): To utter a deep hoarse sound, as a frog or raven or similar sound.

CROPS (Sulph., Tub.): A group of things that have appear together at the same time.

CROSS (Abrot., Aesc., Cina., Cham., Lac c., Lyc., Med., Nat.m., Sanic.): annoyed.

CROUP (Acet. Ac., Acon., Ars., Arum., Hep., Kali bi., Iod., Ipec., Samb., Spong., Staph.): A condition resulting from inflammation and consequent narrowing of the larynx and trachea usually in infants and children and characterized by resonant, barking cough, suffocative and difficult breathing, hoarseness and persistent stridor. (*Stridor* means a harsh whistling sound of obstructed breathing)

MEMBRANOUS CROUP (Brom., Iod., Merc.c.): Inflammation of the larynx with exudation forming a false membrane characterized by loss of voice, difficult and stridulous breathing, weak, rapid pulse, livid skin and moderate fever.

METALLIC CROUP (Kali bi.): Cough with characteristic of croup but with metallic, ringing sound as if produced by striking on a metal.

CROWING (Ambr., Op.): A loud, noisy, harsh sound.

CROWING INSPIRATION (Ambr.): Inspiratory sound resembling loud cry of cock.

CRUDE (Amyl., Arg.n., Camph., Diph., Mag.c., Vario.): The natural state of any substance, before it has been treated with chemicals.

CRUEL (Abrot.): Disposed to inflict pain; indifferent to pain of others; pleased by hearting others; devoid of kindness, pity, merciful.

CRUMBLE (Graph., Mag.m., Nat.m., Sanic., Staph., Thuja.): Broken out into small pieces; disintegrate.

CRUMBLING AT VERGE OF ANUS (Am.m., Mag.m., Nat.m.): Broken out into small pieces at the opening of anus.

CRUSTA LACTEA: (Syn.*Milkcrust*) Thick dried exudates on the scalp of nursing infants.

CRUSHED (Carb.ac., Phos.ac., Rhod.): To press something very hard so that it is broken or its shape is destroyed.

CRUST (Ant.c., Mez., Carb.ac., Cic., Dul., Graph., Hyper., Lyc., Mez., Sars.): Dry, brittle outer layer or covering which forms especially above the soft substance; cutaneous crusts are often formed by dried serum or pus on the surface of a ruptured blister or pustules.

CULPABILITY (Phos.ac.): feeling of guilt; liability to blame; responsible or deserving of blame or disapproval.

CULPABILITY OF THE ACT (Phos.ac.): Feeling responsible or guilt for having done something.

CUPPED (Syph.): Hollowed out like a cup; shaped like a cup (convex from outside, concave from inside).

CURDLED MILK (Aeth.cyn., Val.): Milk that is changed into curd or become sour.

CURE (Lac d.): Restoration of sick to health.

CURSE (Anac., Lac.c., Lil.): An appeal to God or some other divine power to harm someone; something that causes harm or evil.

CYANOSIS (Carboan., Dig.): Bluish or purple discolouration of the skin and mucous membrane due to presence of increased amount of reduced haemoglobin (> 5 gm/dl) or of haemoglobin derivatives in the capillary blood vessels.

CYSTITIS (Tereb.): Inflammation of urinary bladder.

CYSTS (Med.): An abnormal sac or pouch, with a definite wall, that contains fluid, gas, semisolid, or solid material may result from developmental anomalies, obstruction of ducts or parasitic infection.

D

DAMP BASEMENTS (Ant. t.): Moisture laden, humid bottom of lowest storey of a building beneath the principal one especially one below ground level.

DAMP HOUSES OR CELLARS (Nat. s.): Moist, humid houses or underground rooms often used for storage things.

DAMP PLACES (Nux. m.): Wet, moisture laden places which are unpleasant.

DANDELION (Taren.): A common yellow flowered composite (*Taraxacum Officinales*) with jagged-toothed leaves.

DANDRUFF (Phos.): White flakes or scales that exfoliates from the outer layer (epidermis) of the skin, especially in the hair of the scalp. This condition may be more pronounced in diseased state.

DAPHNE MEZEREUM (Mez.): A genus of *thymelaeaceous* shrubs of Europe and Asia, having tetramerous, often fragrant apetalous flowers, with a coloured calyx. Mezereum is used in medicine as stimulants, vesicatories, and purgatives.

DARK HALO (Mer.): A disc or dark luminous or coloured circle of light (such as the coloured circle seen around the light in glaucoma).

DASHED TO PIECES (Coff.): To hit or smash or crash violently so as to break into pieces.

DAZZLING (Lys., Nat. m.): To daze or overpower with strong light; unable to see properly for a short time or confuse the sight by an excess of light.

DEAFNESS (Kreos., Mer. dul.): Congenital or acquired lack, loss or impairment of the sense of hearing without designation of the degree or cause of the loss.

DEATH LIKE PALLOR (Tab.): Paleness of the skin of a person in any diseased condition, which resembles the pallor found in death.

DEATHLY PALLOR (Ver.): Death like pallor.

DEATH-RATTLE (Ant. t.): A respiratory gurgling or rattling in the throat of a dying person caused by the loss of cough reflex and accumulation of mucous.

DEBAUCH (Agar., Carbo v., Nux., Nux m., Sel.): To indulge in excessive sensual pleasure; to cause or persuade someone to take part in immoral, especially sexual, activities or excessive drinking.

*DEBILITY (*Calc.p., Carb.ac., Carbo v., Caul., Cinch., Coc, Con. etc.**):** Weakness; feebleness; quality or state of being weak, feeble or infirm especially physical weakness.

DEBILITATING (Fer., Nat. c, Phos. ac., Spig., Stan.): To make someone weak or weaker; weakening; enervating.

DECAY (Kreos., Mer., Staph., Syph., Thuja.): To make or become rotten, ruined, weaker in health or power, etc.; to undergo decomposition.

DECEPTION (Nux.): An act of deceiving or the state of being deceived; to cause someone to have a false impression or belief.

DECK (Tab.): A platform extending from one side of a ship to the other, and forming a floor or covering in outside.

DECOMPOSED (Colch., Phos. ac., Pyr.): To be destroyed gradually by natural chemical processes, usually as a result of the activity of fungi and bacteria.

DECREPIT (Sec.): Weak or worn out by the infirmities of old age; in the last stage of decay.

DECUBITUS (Bap., Flour. ac., Lach., Petr., Pyr.): Bed-sore; the position of lying down in bed.

DEFECTIVE NUTRITION (Helon., Lac d.): Wanting or lacking of the process by which the living things receive the food and other nourishing material necessary for them to grow and be healthy.

DEFECTIVE VITALITY (Am.c., Zinc.): Wanting or lacking in the normal functioning and zeal of life processes i.e. the vital functions. (*Vitality* means the state or quality of being alive).

DEFICIENT CAPIILLARY CIRCULATION (Carbo v.): Lack of course of blood through the capillaries for maintaining the normal functioning of the body.

DEFICIENT HEAT (Bar., Bell.): Wanting or lacking in natural heat of the body.

DEEP SIGHING (Dig.): To release a long deep audible breath, expressive of sadness, longing, tiredness or relief, that may be voluntary or involuntary.

DEFORMED (Graph., Thuja.): To change the shape of something without breaking it, so that it looks ugly, unpleasant, unnatural or spoiled.

DEFORMITY (Med.): A deviation from the normal shape or size, resulting in disfigurement; may be congenital or acquired.

DEGENERATION (Tereb.): Physically, morally or intellectually worse than before; a retrogressive pathologic change in cells of tissues, in consequence of which their function often impaired or destroyed, sometimes reversible.

> **CANCEROUS DEGENERATION (Iod.)**: An irreversible pathologic changes in cells of tissues, in consequence of which their function often impaired or destroyed in cancer.

DEGLUTITION (Caps.): The act or process of swallowing.

DELETERIOUS SUBSTANCE (Anthr.): Harmful, destructive, damaging substance.

DELICATE (Caust., Ign., Psor., Sep.): Of weak or poor health; easily made sick.

DELICATE CHILDREN (Benz. ac.): Feeble, weak children who becomes ill easily.

DELIRIUM (Agar., Arn., Ars., Bap., Bry., Hyos., Nat. s., Op., Petr., Plat., Plb., Sabad., Stram., Syph.,): A mental disturbance of relatively short duration usually reflecting a toxic state, marked by illusion, hallucination, delusion, excitement, restlessness, impaired memory, and incoherence often caused by fever or other illness, drugs, etc.

> **MANIACAL DELIRIUM (Hyos.)**: Delirium relating to or characterized by mania; delirium that is extreme, violent, wild or furious.

> **MUTTERING DELIRIUM (Lach., Phos. ac.)**: Delirium common in low fevers in which the subject is unconscious, but constantly mutters incoherently.

DELIRIOUS TREMENS (Cann. ind., Hyos., Op., Ran. b.): A severe sometimes fatal, form of delirium due to alcoholic withdrawal following a period of sustained intoxication.

DELUSION (Plat.): A persistent false psychotic belief regarding the self or persons or objects outside the self that is maintained despite indisputable evidence to the contrary.

DELUSION MELANCHOLIC (Kali br.): Delusion occurs in a sad, gloomy, depressed person.

DENTITION (Mag. p., Mag. m., Melil., Nux. v., Phyt., Pod., Zinc.): Development and cutting of teeth; the number, arrangement and type of teeth of an individual.

DEPRESSING EMOTION (Pic.ac.): A feeling that causes sadness.

DEPRESSION (Calad., Calc ars., Con., Gels., Helon., Hyper., Kali br., Kreos., Lil., Nat. s., Sul. ac., Phos. ac., Pod., Psor.): A mental state or disorder, either organic or circumstantial, characterized by prolonged and disproportionate feelings of sadness, pessimism, helplessness, apathy, low self-esteem and despair; a lowering of vitality or functional activity.

DEPRESSION OF SPIRIT (Nux.): Lowering of normal energy and functional activity of the person.

DEPRESSION OF VITALITY (Med., Murex.): Lowering of physical or mental energy and strength.

DEPRIVED (Tereb.): To take something away from.

DERANGED (Caul., Croc., Hydr, Puls.): Disordered; disarranged; unbalanced; disturbance in the regular order or arrangement.

DERANGED MENSES (Cyc.): Any disturbances in the regular menstruation function.

DERANGEMENT (Pod.): Lack of order or organization, especially as compared with the previous condition, whether in mind or body.

DESIRE TO BE MAGNETIZED (Calc., Phos.): Want to be rubbed, massaged or stroked.

DESIST (Sulph.): To stop doing something.

DESPAIR (Cham., Coff., Fer., Hell., Phos. ac., Psor.): To lose or lack hope; to give up all expectation.

DESPITE (Sanic.): In spite of; introduce a fact which makes the other parts of the sentence surprising.

DESPONDENT (Abrot., Aesc., Apis., Cinch., Croc., Dios., Graph., Lac c., Lac d., Lach., Mez., Psor., Stan., Staph., Tab., Tub.): Feeling of extreme discouragement, dejection, depression or complete loss of hope.

DESQUAMATION (Arum.): The shedding of the cuticle of skin or the outer layer of any surface in scales or shreds.

DETACHED (Mer. b. iod.): A voluntary or involuntary separation from normal association or environment; separation of a structure from its support; indifferent.

DIABETES (Act, Fluor. ac., Helon., Lac d.): Any disorder characterized by excessive urine excretion. When used alone, the term refers to Diabetes mellitus. (*Diabetesmellitus*: It is a clinical syndrome characterized by hyperglycaemia due to absolute or relative deficiency of insulin.)

DILATED (Hell.): To become or to make something larger, wider or more open.

DIARRHEA (Abrot., Act.): Abnormally frequent evacuation of semisolid or fluid faecal matter from the bowel.

> **CHRONIC INFANTILE DIARRHEA (Crot.t.):** Chronic diarrhea in infants.

DIATHESIS (Psor.): The constitutional or inborn state disposing to a disease; a state or condition of the body or the combination of attributes in an individual causing susceptibility to a disease.

> **GOUTY DIATHESIS (Benz. ac., Bry.):** A constitutional or hereditary influence or predisposition to develop gout.

HAEMORRHAGIC DIATHESIS (Am. c., Cinch., Croc., Fer., Ham., Ipec., Kreos., Lach., Phos., Sec.): Predisposed to haemorrhage easily, active or passive.

LITHIC DIATHESIS (Sars.): Pertaining to calculi or stone; a supposed tendency to the formation of lithic acid in excess, with resulting calculus formation or gouty symptoms.

PHELGMATIC DIATHESIS (Caps.): Predisposed to or having a slow, sluggish, apathetic, unexcitable condition of mind; or pertaining to phlegm, a stringy, thick mucous secreted from the respiratory tract..

PSORIC DIATHESIS (Sil.): Predisposed or proneness to being affected by the chronic miasm.

RHEUMATIC DIATHESIS (Benz. ac., Bry., Led., Phyt., Rhus., Spig.): Tendency to suffering from rheumatism.

SCROFULOUS DIATHESIS (Sulph.): Predisposed to suffering from scrofula.

SYCOTIC DIATHESIS (Aster., Med., Nat. s., Phos. ac., Sars., Thuja.): Patients of this diathesis are suspicious, cross and irritable, deceitful, jealous, cruel and vindictive. They suffer from diseases associated with proliferation and infiltration of tissues; warty growths and gouty concretions; valvular diseases of the heart. Complaints ameliorated by abnormal discharges (e.g. Leucorrhoea, coryza etc.) They are prone to be attacked by Asthma, Rheumatism, diseases of genito-urinary organs. (S)

TUBERCULAR DIATHESIS (Chel., Rum., Spong., Tub.): Predisposed or proneness to being affected by the tubercular (psoro-syphilitic) state.

DIGNIFIED (Staph.): Calm, serious and deserving respect.

DIM SIGHTED (Tab.): Having greatly reduced vision.

DIOSCORIDES (All.c., Agar.): *Padacious Dioscorides.* A Greek scholar and herbalist who lived during the first century. He wrote on medical botany as an applied science and was the first to write a Materia Medica. His works were regarded as the ultimate authority on Materia Medica for 1600 years. He wrote De Materia Medica.

DIPHTHERIA (Act., Brom., Caust., Diph., Kali. bi., Lach., Lac c., Lyc., Mer., Mer. b. iod., Mur. ac., Mer. p. iod., Phyt., Pyr., Sabad., Tereb., Vario.): An acute infectious disease caused by *Corynebacterium diphtheriae* and it toxin marked by formation of a false membrane upon nose, throat, larynx, pharynx and sometimes in tracheobronchial tree and it produces fever, pain, respiratory obstruction and suffocation. It may also cause degeneration in peripheral nerves, heart muscles and other tissues. Had a high fatality rate esp. in children; now rare due to an effective vaccine.

GANGRENOUS DIPHTHERIA (Mer. cy.): Diphtheria relating to or affected with gangrene.

LARYNGEAL DIPHTHERIA (Diph.): Diphtheria affecting the larynx, usually with asphyxiation due to obstruction of the airway by the membrane that forms, with fatal outcome.

MALIGNANT DIPHTHERIA (Crot.): Diphtheria taking a serious course and advancing towards fatality.

DIPHTHERITIC CROUP (Brom.): Croup associated with infection Corynebacterium diphtheriae (causative organism of diphtheria).

DIPLOPIA (Gels., Syph.): A disorder of vision in which two images of a single object are seen due to unequal actions of the eye muscles may be seen in alcoholism or in any other illness.

DISAPPOINTED AFFECTION (Phos. ac.): Disappointed feeling or love.

DISAPPOINTED LOVE (Cal. p, Ign., Lach.): One is frustrated or upset due to having unfulfillment or failure of hopes or expectations in love.

DISGUST (Canth., Pod.): A feeling of very strong dislike or disapproval.

DISLOCATION (Can. s., Eup., Nat. c., Ruta.): Displacement of an organ or any part specifically disturbance or disarrangement of the normal relation of the bones entering into the formation of a joint.

DISPOSED TO (Mur. ac., Nux., Phos.ac.): Inclined to; prone to; tendency to.

DISPOSITION (Alum., Am. c., Ars., Bell., Calc., Cinch., Coc., Colch., Dios., Kali bi., Lach., Lil., Mag. c., Mer. p. iod., Nat. m., Nit. ac., Nux., Petr., Sep., Stram., Tub., Val.): A tendency or proneness, either physical or mental towards certain diseases.

> **EASY DISPOSITION (Sep.):** Relaxed, pleasant temperament
>
> **IRRITABLE DISPOSITION (Nux.):** Tendency to easily angered, annoyed, excited, or to react immoderately to a stimulus.
>
> **MILD DISPOSITION (Alum.):** A person is gentle, calm, quite in behavior or attitude.
>
> **NERVOUS DISPOSITION (Nux.):** Disposition of easily excited, agitated, or apprehensive.
>
> **YIELDING DISPOSITION (Ign., Phos. ac., Puls., Sil.):** Submissive temperament i.e., who does not oppose, who comply easily.

DISPUTES (Lyc.): A disagreement or argument about something important.

DISPUTATIVE (Fer.): Disposed or prone to dispute, disagree, argue or quarrel.

DISQUIET (Acon.): Lack of quiet; a feeling of anxiety, uneasiness, or restlessness.

DISTENSION (Tereb., Sars.): The state of being swollen, inflated or stretched out in all directions.

DISTINCT CONCIOUSNESS (Pyr.): Clear, obvious, noticeably different or separate physical and mental state of being aware of one's environment, thoughts and feelings.

DISTORTION (Cic.): An undesirable change in shape, appearance, etc.

DISTORTS (Stram.): To twist or change in shape, appearance, sound or facts, ideas etc.

DISTRESSING (Cham., Cup., Lach., Med., Nux.m, . Phos. ac., Thuja.): Feeling upset; mental or emotional pain.

DOMINEERING (Con.): Trying to control other people without considering their opinions or feelings; over bearing, arrogant.

DOOMED (Diph.): People who desires destined death.

DRAUGHTS (Acon., Caust.): A current of air especially at confined space, as room, ventilator, furnace, or chimney.

DRAWING (Mez.): Act of pulling, attracting, extracting etc.

DRAWN CONDITION (Aeth.): Pulled out of shape of the face, distorted or strained condition of face, (looking very tired or worried) from fear, anxiety, or pain.

DREADS (Calad., Caps., Lyc., Rhod., Sanic.): Great fear or apprehension; frightful.

DREAM (Nat.m.): A series of unconscious thoughts and mental images or emotion that are experienced during sleep.

DRENCHING (Act.): To wet all over with falling liquid; to soak or cover thoroughly with liquid.

DRENCHING NIGHT SWEAT (Act.): Profuse sweating during sleep i.e. sometimes a symptom of febrile disease of tubercular origin.

DRENCHING PERSPIRATION (Crot.): Excessive perspiration making wet all over the body.

DRIBBLE (Sars., Sel.): To fall or flow in drops or in a thin stream.

DRIVING OUT (Rum.): To urge or force someone or something to move out.

DROOPING (Caust., Syph.): Hanging or leaning downwards with no strength or firmness especially because of being weak or tired.

DROPSICAL (Phyt.): Swollen with an excessive accumulation of fluid.

DROPSY (Act., Apis., Apoc., Cinch., Colch., Collin., Dig., Dulc., Fer., Hell., Kali c., Lac. d., Sulph.): (Old term of oedema) It is an abnormal accumulation of watery fluid in any part of the body i.e. cells, inter cellular spaces, tissues, serous cavities.

DROWSINESS (Helon., Nux. m., Sulph.): Disposition to sleep; sleepiness; a very sleepy state.

DRUNKARDS (Cal. ars., Carb. ac., Coc., Fluor. ac., Lach., Sulph.): One who habitually drinks strong liquors immoderately; toper.

DULL (Med.): Slow or blunted in perception or sensibility; stupid.

DUNG (Chel., Mag. m.): Solid waste (stool) from animals especially from large ones such as cow, sheep, horse etc.

DWARFED (Med., Syph.): The condition of being abnormally small that may be hereditary or a result of endocrine dysfunction, nutritional deficiency, renal insufficiency, diseases of the skeleton or other causes.

DWELLINGS (Nat. s., Tereb.): Residence; habitation; a place where someone lives.

DWINDLE (Iod.): To grow less; to waste away; to grow feeble; to become degenerate.

DYSCRASIA (Sul. ac.): A term formerly used to indicate an abnormal state of the four humours, now used generally to indicate a morbid condition specially in which an imbalance of component elements occur. Those elements of weakness transmitted from parents to child which of itself produces certain definite results, and which renders the individual more susceptible to the ordinary diseases and also changes the normal course of those diseases.

> **CACHECTIC DYSCRASIA (Hydr):** Susceptible to physical weakness, wasting of muscles, malnutrition, abnormally low body weight and general ill-health, usually associated with a chronic disease such as cancer or tuberculosis.
>
> **MALIGNANT DYSCRASIA (Hydr):** Tendency to be affected by malignant diseases.

DYSENTRY (Abrot., Carb. ac., Coloc., Kali bi., Mer., Mer. cor.): A diseased condition marked by frequent passage of watery stool containing blood and mucous with abdominal pain and tenesmus.

> **AUTUMNAL DYSENTRY (Colch., Ipec.):** Dysentry occurring in autum.

HAEMORRHOIDAL DYSENTRY (Collin.): Dysentry associated with haemorrhoids.

DYSMENORRHOEA (Act., Collin., Croc., Tub., Ver.): Difficult and painful menstruation.

MEMBRANOUS DYSMENORRHOEA (Brom.): Dysmenorrhoea accompanied by an exfoliation of the menstrual decidua.

RHEUMATIC DYSMENORRHOEA (Act.): Painful menstruation where the pain is very similar to that of rheumatism.

DYSPEPSIA (Arg. n., Ars., Cal. p., Med., Nat. s., Nux. m., Samb., Sep., Spig., Tab.): A condition of disturbed digestion characterised by nausea, heartburn, epigastric pain, gas and sense of fullness due to local causes or to disease elsewhere in the body.

INTERMITTENT DYSPEPSIA (Ipec.): Dyspepsia occurring intermittently means stopping and starting often over a period of time, not regularly.

DYSPNOEA (Act., Can s., Coca., Ipec., Kali bi., Lil., Mer. sul., Psor.): Difficult or labored breathing usually associated diseases of heart and lungs.

EAR COUGH: A reflex cough excited by irritation in the ear that stimulates Arnold's nerve (ramus auricularisnervivagi).

EARTHY (Berb., Spig.): Earth like colour of the skin of face; muddy complexion.

EAST WIND (Rhod.): East wind then wind that originates in the east and blows west and sends down cold rains upon the earth.

EBULLITION: Effervescence; a boiling or bubbling up, such as when blood rushes to the face or hot flushes; subjective feeling of flushes of heat.

ECCHYMOSIS (Led., Sec., Sul.ac., Tereb.): A small haemorrhagic spot; larger than a petechiae, in the skin or mucous membrane forming a non-elevated, rounded or irregular, blue or purplish patch caused by extravasation of blood.

ECLAMPSIA (Melil., Mill.): A severe hypertensive disorder of pregnancy characterized by hypertension, oedema, proteinuria, convulsions and coma, occurring between the 20th week of pregnancy and at the end of the first week of postpartum.

ECSTACY (Lach.): A feeling or state of extreme happiness or pleasure.

ECSTATIC (Ant.c., Lach.): Very happy, excited and enthusiastic; feeling or showing great enthusiasm.

ECSTATIC LOVE (Ant.c.): Exalted state of feeling about love.

ECZEMA (Cic., Crot., Graph., Nat.m., Psor., Staph., Tub.): an inflammatory condition of the skin, of acute or chronic nature, typically erythematous, with a composite picture of papules, vesicles, crusts and scales, and often accompanied by itching, burning and various paraesthesias.

ECZEMA CAPITIS: Eczema affecting the scalp.

ECZEMA SOLARIS (Mur.ac.): An archaic term used to denote eczema of the sole.

EFFLUVIA (Crot.): A harmful exhalation, especially one of bad odour or injurious influence; harmful, foul, disagreeable odours, fumes or exhalations from decaying matter.

EFFUSION (Colch., Hell., Kali br., Tub., Zinc.): The escape of fluid from the blood vessels or lymphatics into the tissues or a cavity.

ELASTIC PLUGS (Lyc.): Anelastic, stretchable mass of dried mucous present in the nose, almost filling the nasal cavity or closing an orifice.

ELONGATED (Hyper., Mer., Mez., Rat.): Longer and thinner than usual, as if stretched.

EMACIATION (Abrot., Acet. ac., Cal.p., Graph., Helon., Iod., Kreos., Lach., Led., Lyc., Mag.p., Mez., Nat.c., Nat.m., Op., Phos.ac., Phyt., Plb., Sanic., Samb., Sel., Sulph., Syph., Tab., Tub.): Becoming abnormally thin from extreme loss of flesh; wasted condition of the body; leanness.

EMBOLISM: A mass of undissolved material, usually a part or all of a thrombus carried in the blood stream and frequently obstructing a vessel.

EMBRACE (Calad., Lyc., Murex., Nat.c., Nat.m.): To hug; to put one's arm around in greeting or affection.

EMIGRANTS (Plat.): Who goes from one's own country to another to settle there.

EMISSION (Calad., Canth., Dios.): A discharge, specifically an involuntary discharge of semen.

    NOCTURNAL EMISSION (Canth., Dig., Mer.): The involuntary discharge of semen during sleep, usually occur in conjunction with an erotic dream.

    PREMATURE EMISSION (Lyc.): An imprecise term that usually indicates ejaculation occurring very shortly after the onset of sexual excitement or ejaculation occurring before copulation or before the partner's orgasm.

EMOTION (Cal.ars., Caust., Cinch., Coff., Colch., Collin., Fer., Gels., Ign., Kali br., Lach., Lyc., Mag.p., Nux., Phos.ac., Psor., Samb.): A strong feeling such as love, happiness, fear, anger, hatred.

EMPHYSEMA (Am.c.): A chronic pulmonary disease characterized by beyond the normal increase in the size of air spaces distal to the terminal bronchiole with destructive changes in their walls.

ENDOCARDIUM: The inner endothelial lining of the heart.

ENDURE (Cham., Lyc.): To remain firm under; to tolerate; to suffer; to experience and bear something painful or unpleasant, esp. for a long time, or to continue for a long time.

ENEMA (Lac d., Syph.): Injection of solutions into the rectum and colon in order to stimulate bowel movements and to cause defecation, mostly used in constipated persons.

ENERVATED (Hclon.): Deficient in nervous strength; weakness.

ENFEEBLE (Helon.): To make feeble; to weaken.

ENGORGEMENT (Melil.): Vascular congestion; distension with fluid or other material.

ENGRAFTED (Nit.ac.): To implant to insert; to join on; to fix deeply.

ENGRAVING (Ruta.): The act or art of cutting a picture or design, or letters into the surface of a hard substance such as metal, wood, or stone; to impress deeply.

ENORMOUSLY (Glon., Nux.m.): Very or very much.

ENNUI: Boredom; listlessness and dissatisfaction resulting from lack of interest; loathing of life.

ENTREATING (Stram.): To ask earnestly; to ask seriously; to beg for.

ENURESIS (Equis., Mag.p., Psor., Sec., Sep.): Involuntary passage of urine, usually occurring at night or during sleep; bed-wetting.

>   **NOCTURNAL ENURESIS (Mag.p., Med.):** Urinary incontinence during night. It is unaccompanied by urgency or frequency.
>
>   **ENURESIS DIURNA ET NOCTURNA (Equi.):** Involuntary passage of urine, day and night.

ENVY (Staph.): Uneasiness at the sight of another excellence or good fortune, accompanied with some degree of hatred and a desire to possess equal advantage; jealousy.

EPIDEMIC (Cina., Dros., Eup., Mez., Nux.m.): Appearance of an infectious disease or condition that attacks many people at same time in the same geographical area; excessively communicable, contagious, widely diffused and rapidly spreading.

EPILEPSIES (Cal.ars., Caul., Cic., Cup., Hyos., Kali br., Lach., Mill., Plb.): Paroxysmal transient disturbances of brain function due to repetitive abnormal electrical discharges that may be manifested as episodic impairment or loss of consciousness, abnormal motor phenomena, psychic or nervous symptoms such as tonic-clonic convulsion of all extremities, urinary and faecal incontinence and amnesia.

CONGENITAL EPILEPSY (Kali br.): Epilepsy resulting from congenital brain diseases such as lipid storage disease, tuberous sclerosis, cortical dyscrasia, anoxic brain injury, etc.

EPILEPTIFORM CONVULSION (Plb.): Tonic, clonicconvulsion stimulating epilepsy with violent character and irregular movement of the body due to involuntary spasmodic contraction of muscles.

EPISTAXIS (Act., Carbo v., Diph., Dros., Kreos., Melil., Mill., Mez., Trill.): Nose bleeding; haemorrhage from the nose.

EPULIS: A fibrous tumour of the gum.

ERADICATE (Psor.): To pull up by the roots; to root out; complete elimination.

ERRATIC (Lac c.): Roving or wandering; eccentric; deviating from an accepted course of thought or conduct; irregular (as in course or direction); wandering.

ERECTION (Calad., Carbo v., Lyc., Sel.): The state of swelling, hardness and stiffness observed in the penis and to a lesser extent in the clitoris, generally due to sexual excitement. It is caused by engorgement with blood of the corpora cavernosa and the corpus spongiosum of the penis in men and the corpus cavernosaclitoridis in women.

ERETHITIC CHLOROSIS (Fer.): Anemia with flushing and redness of skin.

EROTOMANIA: Morbidly exaggerated sexual behavior.

ERUCTATION (Bry., Calad., Calc., Cham., Fer., Iod., Mag.c., Mag.m., Nux., Psor., Sul.ac.): The act of belching, or of casting up wind from the stomach through the mouth, usually with a characteristic sound.

ERUPTION (Dul., Graph., Kreos., Mez., Psor., Sang.): A breaking out, especially the appearance of lesions on the skin; redness, spotting or other visible phenomena on the skin or mucous membrane, mainly appearing as a local manifestation of a general disease, such as measles, typhoid fever, etc.; the passage of a tooth through the alveolar process and perforation of the gums.

> **HERPETIC ERUPTION (Aeth., Sars.):** The term, like most others which refer to cutaneous diseases, has not been accurately defined. The term pertains to eruptions resembling the Herpes i.e. an eruption of deep-seated vesicles on an erythematous base.
>
> **REPERCUSSED ERUPTION (Cup.):** The driving in of an eruption or the scattering of a swelling; an eruption having an unwanted effect after not being allowed to come out fully but has been driven in.
>
> **VESICULAR ERUPTION (Crot.t.):** Eruptions containing vesicles filled with liquid.

ERYSIPELAS (Calen., Carbo v., Lach., Ruta.): An acute contagious febrile disease associated with a local, intense, reddish inflammation of the skin and subcutaneous tissue usually due to infection with group-A streptococcus virus, accompanied with constitutional symptoms like fever, chills, sweats or vomiting etc., sometimes may be present with vesicular and bullous lesions.

> **ERYSIPELAS PHLEGMONOUS (Graph.):** Erysipelas, marked by invasion of the subcutaneous tissues, with the formation of deep-seated abscesses

VESICULAR ERYSIPELAS (Canth.): Erysipelas forming vesicles.

ERYTHEMA (Canth.): Redness of the skin that is non-specific sign of skin irritation, injury or inflammation caused by dilatation of superficial blood vessels in the skin.

ERYTHISM (Nit.ac., Sep., Sil.): Redness of the skin, produced by congestion of capillaries, which may result from a variety of causes

EUSTACHIAN TUBE (Mer.dul.): A canal, partly bony, partly cartilaginous, measuring 38.0 to 50.8 mm in length, connecting the pharynx with the tympanic cavity. It allows air to pass into the middle ear, so that the air pressure is kept even on both sides of the eardrum.

EUTHANASIA (Amyl.): An easy or painless death; Mercy Killing; the deliberate ending of life of a person suffering from an incurable and painful disease.

EVACUATION (Anar., Arn., Crot.t., Lac d., Plb., Sanic.): The act of emptying or clearing the bowels; defecation.

EVERSION OF LIDS: A turning outward of eyelids.

EXAGGERATION (Can.ind.): A statement or description that makes something seem larger, better, worse or more important than it really is.

EXANTHEMA (Apis., Bry., Hell., Op., Tereb.): Any eruption or arash that appears on the skin as opposed to one that appears in the mucous membranes. Term is often used to describe infectious rashes (as in measles or scarlet fever), but also applies to other rashes.

EXANTHEMATA (Hell., Tereb., Thuja., Zinc.): Plural of exanthema.

EXCITABLE (Caust., Coff., Gels., Lach., Lac c., Phos.): Capable of being excited or roused into action.

EXCITED (Mag.p., Med., Nux.): Feeling or showing happiness and enthusiasm; aroused emotionally; nervous or upset and unable to relax.

EXCITEMENT (Acon., Coc., Collin., Con., Fer., Glon., Gels., Ran. b., Puls.): The state of being excited.

EXCITIBILITY (Acon., Murex., Pic.ac., Val.): The quality of being readily excitable; irritability.

EXCORIATION (Graph., Sanic., Sulph.): Any superficial loss of substances such as abrasion of the epidermis of skin by trauma, burns or other causes

EXCRESCENCES (Merc.s.): Any abnormal growth from the surface of a part.

EXCRETION (Apoc., Plb., Psor.): The elimination of waste products from the body.

EXECUTION (Hyp., Ign.): The act of, or skill in, doing or performing; effective action or operation.

EXERT (Nat.c., Stan.): To use the power or the ability to make something happen; to make a great physical or mental effort or work hard to do something.

EXERTION (Bry., Cup., Fer., Gels., Hep., Iod., Lob., Lys., Mag.p., Mer., Mill., Nat.c., Nat.m., Pic.ac., Psor., Sep., Ver.): Act of exerting; an effort specially a laborious or perceptible effort as exertion of strength or power.

EXHAUSTED (Caps., Carbo v., Caul., Caust., Cina., Coca., Crot., Cup., Diph., Ign., Lach., Lac d., Phos.ac., Sel., Sec., Staph., Sul.ac., Thlaspi., Ver.): Deprived of energy or strength, mentally or physically; worn out; very tired.

EXHAUSTION (Dig., Med., Nat.c., Phyt., Sil., Stan., Syph., Tereb., Zinc.): Loss of energy with consequent inability to respond to stimuli; lassitude.

EXHILARETED (Med.): To make hilarious or merry; to raise the spirits of; to enliven; to cheer.

EXOPHORIA: Deviation of visual axis away from that of other eye when fusion is prevented.

EXOSTOSIS (Fluor.ac., Mez., Ruta.): A benign bony growth that arises from the surface of a bone, often involving the ossification of muscular attachments.

EXPECTORATE/EXPECTORATION (Caust., Euph., Kali bi., Lyc., Psor., Rum., Stan., Trill.): The act or process of spitting out saliva or coughing up materials from the air passage way leading to the lungs.

EXPELLED (Nit.ac., Sab., Sanic., Sil., Thuja.): Driven out or forced out or ejected.

EXPULSIVE (Sec.): Having the power of expelling.

EXTORT (Hyp., Lac d.): To obtain by force or threat.

EXTRACTION (Kreos., Trill.): The act or process of removing or drawing out or obtaining something; removal of tooth.

EXTRAVASATION (Ham., Led.): The escape of fluid from its physiological contained space, e.g. Bile, blood, CSF into the surrounding tissue.

EXUBERANT (Nit.ac., Thuja, Sabina): Copious or excessive in production; showing excessive proliferation.

EXUBERANT GRANULATION (Nit.ac., Sab., Thuja.): Excessive proliferation of granulation tissue in healing wounds.

EXUDATION (Caust., Cic., Hell., Merc.b.iod., Staph.): Pathological oozing of fluids, usually the result of inflammation.

FACILITATED (Sulph.): To make possible or easier or less difficult.

FAINT (Acon., Caust., Cham., Colc., Crot., Dig., Hep., Lil., Lob., Lac c., Mer., Nux.m., Puls., Sec., Sep., Trill., Ver.): A sudden loss of consciousness.

FAINT HEARTED (Sil.): Wanting in courage; depressed by fear; easily discouraged or frightened; cowardly.

FAINTNESS (Asar., Bry., Phos.ac., Phyt., Pic.ac., Plum., Sep., Spon., Tab.): A sensation of impending loss of consciousness.

FALLS OUT IN CLOUDS (Phos.): Falls out in bunches, in good quantity.

FALSE STEP (Spig.): Stumbler.

FANCY (Sulph.): Having a particular liking or desire for.

FARINACEOUS FOOD: Food rich in starch; food made from flour or other grains.

FATAL (Acon., Sabad.): Causing death; destructive; deadly.

FATIGUE (Cyc., Lac d., Med., Nux m., Plat., Rum., Sel., Sil.): Tiredness.

FATTEN (Tub.): To make fat; to make fleshy or plump with fat.

FATTY DEGENERATION (Aur., Bell., Kali c., Lac d.): A change involving the deposition of fat in the cytoplasm of cells; Cell degeneration associated with the formation of fat.

FATTY HEART (Kali bi.): A heart which have been the subject of fatty degeneration or infiltration.

FAUCES (Aesc., Caps., Crot., Dros., Kali bi., Kali br., Lyc., Mer.b.iod., Mer.cy., Sabad., Sanic.): The constricted opening leading from the oral cavity to oropharynx, bounded by soft palate, the base of the tongue, and the palatine arches.

FAULT FINDING (Hell.): Finding, or disposed to find fault.

FEAR (Acon., Cact, Caust., Gels., Glon., Hyos., Lac c., Lac d., Lil., Lys., Lyc., Plat., Phos.ac., Psor., Sep.): A painful emotion caused by impending danger or evil; apprehension of danger or pain.

FEEBLE (Carbo.an., Cyc., Dios., Lach., Sec.): Very weak; lacking in necessary strength or endurance; lacking force; debilitated.

FEELING: It is an emotion, such as anger or emotion; a sensation which may involve touch, temperature, etc. or physical pain or pleasure.

ALL GONE FEELING (Sulph.): Felling of emptiness.

EMPTY FEELING (Sulph.): Sensation of having nothing inside the any part of the body

FAINT FEELING (Sulph.): Sensation as if going to lose the consciousness.

FELON (Anthr., Dios., Tar., Taren.): Panaratia; a painful inflammation of a finger or toe, especially near or around the nail.

FERMENTATION (Cinch., Lyc.): A process in which an agent causes an organic substance to break down into simpler substances; especially, the anaerobic breakdown of sugar into alcohol; gas formation.

FEVER: Pyrexia; a disease state of the system, marked by increased body temperature, acceleration of the pulse and a general derangement of the function including usually thirst and loss of appetite.

AFRICAN FEVER (Tereb.): Black water fever. Haemoglobinuria or malignant malaria in which more than half of the circulating R.B.C. are haemolysed, characterised by the passage of dark red or black urine.

BILIOUS FEVER (Eup., Tar.): Fever accompanied by the vomiting of bile; A term loosely applied to intestinal fevers and malarial fever with digestive disturbances (bitter vomiting, copious clayey stools).

ENTERIC FEVER (Sel.): Typhoid fever.

HAY FEVER (All.c., Nat.m., Psor., Tub.): A catarrhal affection of mucous membranes of the eyes, nose, and respiratory tracts, accompanied by itching and profuse watery secretion, followed occasionally by bronchitis, fever and asthma. It occurs annually, usually in the spring and late summer, and is caused chiefly by inhaling pollen of various flowers which are subjected to the disorder are especially sensitive.

HECTIC FEVER (Abrot., Acet.ac.): A type of fever occurring usually at an advanced stage of exhausting disease, as in pulmonary tuberculosis, septicaemia etc. and marked by a daily recurring rise of temperature, profuse perspiration, and flushed countenance.

INTERMITTENT FEVER (Caps., Cinch., Eup., Ipec., Lac d., Lach., Nat.m., Petros.): Fever that recurs in cycles of paroxysms and remissions, such as in malaria.

CONGESTIVE INTERMITTENT FEVER (Ver.): In fever with prominent heat stage, marked by redness and heat of head, face and another parts due to congestion of blood vessels.

PERNICIOUS INTERMITTENT FEVER (Ver.): A term usually to denote malignant malaria, caused by the *Plasmodiumfalciparum* species and spread by Anopheles mosquito and it is the most dangerous form of malaria with the highest rates of complications and mortality.

MALARIAL FEVER (Crot., Tereb.): Fever caused by animal parasite (genus-*Plasmodium*) in the RBCs and occurs in paroxysm, each marked by a chill, followed by high fever and sweating, and is usually either intermittent or remittent.

SCARLET FEVER (Dros., Phyt.): Same as scarlatina i.e. an acute exanthematous disease, caused by bacterial infection and marked by fever and other constitutional disturbances and a generalized eruptions of closely aggregated points or small macules of a bright red colour followed by desquamation.

EPIDEMIC SCARLET FEVER (Mer.bin.i.): Scarlet fever which has spread in large number of people in a geographical area in a very short time taking the characteristic of an epidemic.

TYPHOID FEVER (Agar., Apoc., Bap., Carbov., Caust., Crot., Gels., Hell., Hyos., Kreos., Lach., Mur.ac., Nit. ac., Pyr., Sel., Tar., Tereb.): An acute infectious caused by *Salmonella typhi*, characterised by a continued fever rising in a step like curve in the first week, great physical and mental exhaustion, an eruption of rose-coloured spot on the chest and abdomen, diarrhea, and sometimes intestinal haemorrhage or perforation, and the definite lesions located in Payer's patches (intestine), mesenteric glands and spleen. It is usually spread by contamination of food, milk or water.

FEVER BLISTER (Nat.m.): (Syn. *Cold sore*) Small painful, hard or crusty ulcer which often breaks open and oozes and usually appearing on the lips or mucous membrane of the mouth and caused by herpes simplex virus type I.

FIBRINOUS (Kali bi., Rhod.): Having or partaking of the properties of fibrin.

FIBROID (Cyst.): Benign tumour that consists mainly of fibrous tissue occurring in the uterine myometrium; fibroma; myoma; leiomyoma.

FIDGETY (Apis., Graph., Kali br., Med., Phos., Sil., Zinc.): A restless condition, shown by incessant changes of position or nervous movements; restless; uneasy.

FIERCE RAGE (Hyos.): Aggressive and violent uncontrollable anger.

FIERY SPARKS (Cyc.): Brilliant fire like particles produced by striking flint or hard metals and stone together.

FIG WART (Sab., Staph., Thuja.): *Condylomaacuminatum*; growth of filiform projections usually occurring on genitalia and anal region often in groups of large size; a primary manifestation of Sycosis.

FILTHY (Psor., Sulph.): Foul: unclean; dirty.

FINGERS' GO TO SLEEP (Dig.): A temporary state of numbness and anaesthetic condition of the fingers where they do no react to external stimuli and there is no voluntary movement.

FIRST AND SECOND CHILDHOOD (Bar., Op.): Childhood and old age.

FISSURED (Graph., Nit. ac., Petr., Phyt., Rat., Sil., Sulph., Syph., Thuja.): Ulcer or crack like sore.

FIST (Acon., Symph.): The closed or clenched hand, esp. as used in boxing.

FISTULA DENTALIS (Fluor.ac.): An abnormal passage or communication with the apical periodontal area of a tooth, which permits appearence on the mucous membrane of the skin of an inflammatory or suppurative discharge; called also *alveolar fistulae*.

FISTULA LACHRYMALIS (Fluor.ac., Sil.): An abnormal passage communicating with the lachrymal sac or duct.

FISTULA (Cal.p., Phos., Phyt., Sil.): A pathologic sinus or abnormal passage leading from a normal cavity or a hollow organ to the surface, or from one abscess cavity or organ to another.

FISTULA-IN ANO (Sil.): Fistula opening at or near the anus or into the rectum above the internal sphincter.

FLABBY (Abrot., Acet.ac., Calc., Cal. p., Camph., Chel., Hep., Iod., Mer., Pyr., Sanic., Sars., Sec.): Hanging loose by its own weight; flaccid; feeble; lacking muscle tone or firmness.

FLAKES (Kali bi., Sars., Ver.): A thin loose filmy mass or a thin chip like or scale like layer of anything; a small flat mass.

FLATULENCY (Cal. p., Cinch., Collin., Dios., Kali bi., Lyc., Mag.p): Abdominal gas or flatus; the presence of an excessive amount of gas in the stomach and intestines.

FLATUS (Lac c., Phos.ac., Pyr., Sabad., Sanic.): Gas in the stomach or intestine; expelled gas from the anus.

FLAXEN (Brom.): Of light golden or pale yellow colour.

FLAXEN HAIR (Brom.): Light golden or pale yellow coloured hair.

FLESH (Cic., Iod.): The soft tissues of the animal body, especially the muscles.

FLESHY (Calc.ars, Calc., Dul., Iod., Kali bi., Kali br., Lach., Lob., Samb.): Marked by abundant or excessive flesh; plump; fat; obese.

FLICKERING (Cyc., Psor.): The visual sensation produced by intermittent flashes of light occurring at a certain rate; to burn or shine with an unsteady light.

FLORID (Glon., Lob.): Having a lively reddish colour; flushed with red.

FLUENT (Euph., Mer.): Flowing or capable of flowing specially with ease or freedom.

FLUID POLLUTION (Sars.): The discharge of semen, either voluntary or involuntary, other than during coitus.

FLUSHED (Cinch., Dig., Fer., Glon., Mag.p., Melil., Sul.ac.): Become red in the face, esp. as a result of strong emotions, heat, or alcohol.

FLUTTERING (Nat.m., Lil.): A rapid and irregular vibration or pulsation; a rapid and unwanted vibration.

FOETID (Caps., Carb.ac., Kreos., Med., Mer., Mer.s., Mur. ac., Nux.m., Pyr., Phyt., Pod., Sep., Tereb., Tub., Zinc.): Very strong, unpleasant, offensive smell.

FOETUS (Plb.): The product of conception from the end of the eighth week to the moment of birth.

FOLLICULAR PHARYNGITIS (Aesc.): Chronic inflammation of the pharynx in which lymphoid follicles are enlarged, studding the mucous membrane as minute nodules or granules.

FONTANELLES (Calc., Cal.p., Sil.): An unossified space or a soft spot, such as one of the membrane covered spaces remaining in the incompletely ossified cranial bones of a foetus or infant.

FORBIDS (Psor.): To oppose, hinder, or prevent as if by an effectual command.

FOREBODINGS (Phos., Psor.): A perception beforehand; apprehension of coming evil or misfortune.

FORGETFUL (Can.i., Kali bi., Lac c.): Act to forget; unable to recall; having a poor memory.

FOSSA (Petr.): A general term for a hollow or depressed area; a furrow or shallow depression.

FOSSA NAVICULARIS (Petros.): The terminal dilated portion of the urethra in the glans penis; the depression between the posterior commissure of the labia majora and fourchette.

FOUL (Petr.): Extremely unpleasant, offensive to the senses; very ill-smelling.

FRACTURE (Ruta.): It is a condition where the continuity of the bone is broken.

FRAGMENTARY (Vario.): Existing only in small parts and not complete; made of small or unconnected pieces.

FRAENUM (Merc.s.): A fold of mucous membrane that connects two parts, one more or less movable, and checks the movement of this part.

FRAME (Spig.): The form or structure of a person or animal's body.

FRECKLES (Lach., Mur.ac.): A brownish pigmented spot on the skin due to discrete accumulation of melanin (as a result of the stimulant effect of sunlight acting on clusters of melanocytes which have higher than normal tyrosinase activity). Called also ephelis, *lentigo*.

FREE SWEAT (Eup.): Excessive sweating.

FRENZY (Mag.p.): Violent maniacal excitement or mental agitation; a brief madness or delirium; violent action.

FRETFUL (Ars., Ant.c., Cham., Mur.ac., Psor., Tub.): Prone to easily angered or irritated; peevish.

FRETS (Acon., Psor.): A agitation of mind; worry unnecessarily or excessively.

FRIGHT (Caust., Cup., Gels., Glon., Hyos., Hyper., Kali br., Lach., Lyc., Nat.m., Op., Plat., Psor., Samb., Spong., Ver.): The feeling of fear, esp. if felt suddenly, or an experience of fear which happens suddenly usually of short duration.

FRIGHTENED (Tub., Zinc.): Affected with fright; made afraid.

FROG SPAWN (Hell., Melil.): The eggs (in mass) of frogs; a large collection or production of tadpoles.

FRONTAL EMINENCE (Arg.n.): A rounded prominence on forehead either side of the median line and a little below the center of the frontal bone.

FROSTBITE (Agar.): Damage to tissues as the result of exposure to excessive cold, occurs in exposed areas such as ears, cheeks, nose, fingers, toes.

FROTH (Mag.m.): A mass of small bubbles produced by fermentation, especially, on the surface of a liquid.

FROTHY (Mag.c., Med., Sanic.): Consisting of froth, foam or light bubbles.

FROWSY (Bor.): Untidy.

FULL BLOODED (Ver.v.): Exhibiting great physical or mental health, ruddy (looking red and healthy).

FULL MOON (Alum.): The moon with its whole disc illuminated as when opposite to the sun.

FUNGUS EXCRESCENCES (Mer.s.): Any fungated abnormal growth from the surface of a part.

FURIOUS (Stram.): Extremely angry; full of violent in effect; mad; insane.

FURROW (Lyc.): A narrow channel or groove or trench.

FURUNCLE (Abrot., Mer.s.): A boil; a painful nodule formed in skin by circumscribed inflammation of the corium and subcutaneous tissue, enclosing a central slough or "core" .This localized pyogenic infection most favoured by constitutional or digestive derangement and local irritation.

G

GAGGING (Bry., Cina., Dros., Euph., Ipec., Kali bi., Kali c., Lyc., Lys., Pod.): Make an unsuccessful effort to vomit; strain to vomit.

GAIT (Aster.): The posture, manner or style of walking.

> **STAGGERING GAIT (Kali br.):** Moving or walking awkwardly or unsteadily as if the balance were lost.

GALL STONE (Chel., Cinch.): A concretion or stone in the gall bladder or a bile duct, composed chiefly of cholesterol crystals; cholelithiasis.

GANGRENE (Calen., Crot., Sec., Sul.ac., Taren.): Death of tissue, usually in considerable mass, usually resulting from deficient or absent blood supply and followed by bacterial invasion and putrefaction.

GANGRENOUS (Sil.): Pertaining to gangrene.

GAPING (Phyt.): An opening or hiatus; a break in continuity.

GASPING (Samb., Spong.): To take a short quick breath through the mouth, esp. because of surprise, pain, or shock or due to breathlessness.

GASPING AT FLOCKS (Hyos.): To take a short quick breathtogether in large numbers through the mouth.

GASTRALGIA (Bis., Petr.): Pain or discomfort in the stomach from any cause.

GASTRIC ATTACKS (Tar.): Any acute, sudden and violent illness of stomach.

GAY (Nux m., Plat.): Merry; joyous; happy; cheerful.

GELATENAOUS (Arg.n.): Thick and sticky, like a jelly.

GENU: Knee;any structure of angular shape resembling a flexed knee.

GENUINE COLLAPSE (Crot.): Sudden and extreme prostration or exhaustion.

GENUS EPIDEMICUS (Merc.cy.): A medicine that is used in epidemic diseases as a curative as well as preservative.

GIDDY (Acon.): Dizzy; having lost the power of preserving balance of the body and thus wavering and inclined to fall.

GIVES OUT (Aesc.): To become exhausted;to cease from exertion, as because of the expenditure of all one's strength; to refuse to act, operate or perform its function to break down.

GIVES WAY (Med., Nat.c.): To stop functioning or operating; to break down.

GLABELLA: The hairless space between the eyebrows.

GLAIRY (Ipec.): Anything slimy or sticky resembling the white of an egg.

GLASSY (Op.): Fixed, blank and uncomprehending.

GLAUCOMA: A disease of the eye characterized by high fluid pressures within the eyeball, damaged retina, hardening of the eyeball and partial or complete loss of vision.

GLAZED (Lac c., Tereb.): Glossy (as by polishing).

GLEET (Agnus., Petros., Sel., Sep.): A mucus discharge, from the urethra in chronic gonorrhoea.

GLITTERING (Cyc.): A bright, sparkling (light); brilliant; bright and colourful.

GLOBE OF THE EYE (Symph.): Eyeball.

GLOBUS HYSTERICUS (Lac d.): The subjective sensation of a lump in the throat, a condition frequently seen in hysteria.

GLOOMY (Aesc., Aur., Cinch., Nat.s., Phos.): Depressed in spirits; melancholy; hopeless; unhappiness.

GLOSSY (Op., Tereb.): Smooth and shiny; reflecting lustre polished.

GLUED (Mez., Psor.): Adhered; pressed firmly together.

GNASHING (Zin.): Striking or grinding the teeth, as in anger, pain or worm infection.

GNAWING (Acon., Nat.s., Nit.ac.): To biting or eating away with a scraping or mumbling movement little by little; causing constant pain.

GOES RIGHT THROUGH HER (Calc.): Penetrating through her body.

GOITRE (Fluor.ac., Iod., Stan.): A chronic enlargement of thyroid gland may cause by thyroiditis, benign thyroid nodules, malignancy, iodine deficiency or any condition that causes hypo function or hyper function of gland.

GONORRHOEA (Med., Merc.s., Nat.s., Petros., Psor., Phyt., Rhod., Sars.): A specific, contagious, catarrhal inflammation of the genital mucous membranes of either sex due to *Neisseria gonorrhoea* transmitted venereally in most cases, but also by contact with infected exudates in neonatal children at birth. It is marked in males by urethritis with pain and purulent discharge, but is commonly asymptomatic in females, although it may extend to produce suppurative salpingitis, oophoritis, tubo-ovarian abscess, and peritonitis. Bacteremia occurs in both sexes, resulting in cutaneous lesions, arthritis, and rarely meningitis or endocarditis.

CHECKED GONORRHOEA (Sars.): Suppressed gonorrhoea.

INFLAMMATORY STAGE GONORRHOEA (Can.s.): In this stage of gonorrhoea the symptoms of inflammation of the urethra, prostrate, cervix, fallopian tubes, rectum and/or pharynx are usually present.

MAL-TREATED GONORRHOEA (Med., Thuja.): Gonorrhoea which was not treated properly (Homoeopathically), resulting in suppression, palliation or over medication.

SUPPRESED GONORRHOEA (Med., Nat.s., Spong.): Gonorrhoea which is not run out in its full course. Its normal course is checked by strong non-homoeopathic medicines.

GONORRHOEAL POISON (Nat.s.): Bad effects of gonorrhoea.

GOUT (Abrot., Colc., Kal., Led., Med., Rhod.): A disease due to disorders of purine and pyrimidine metabolism in which there is an excess of uric acid in the blood that is deposited as sodium biurate called tophi in and around the joint causing recurrent paroxysmal attacks of acute inflammatory arthritis initially involve the first metatarsophalangeal joints of great toe followed by other joints, bones, ligaments, cartilages and usually affecting a single peripheral joint and followed by complete remission.

GOUTY CONCRETIONS/STONES (Benz.ac., Bry., Led): Stony hard deposits (of sodium urate) in the joints affected by gout especially great toe, or the external ear (*pinna*).

GRANULATION (Calen., Thuja.): The formation of minute, rounded, fleshy connective tissue projections on the surface of a wound, ulcer, or inflamed tissue surface in the process of healing.

GRANULAR CONJUNCTIVITIS (Arg.n.): Granular lids; trachoma that is achronic contagious form of viral conjunctivitis, noted by hypertrophy of conjunctiva and formation of minute yellowish or greyish translucent granules with subsequent cicatrical changes, caused by Chlamydia trachomatis.

GRANULAR LIDS (Nat.s.): Granular conjunctivitis; granulation on the lids due to conjunctivitis.

GRASPED (Dios., Gels., Iod., Lil.): To seize and hold.

GRATIFIED (Con., Petros.): Pleased; satisfied.

GRAUVOGL (Ant.t., Thuja.): Eduard Von Grauvogl (1811-1877), was a German orthodox physician who converted to Homoeopathy as the first Homoeopathic physician in Finland. He described three types of constitution and was an advocate of high potency remedies.

GRAVE (Nux m.): A serious, critical or dangerous character.

GRAVEL (Collin., Sars.): A term applied to fairly coarse concretions or crystalline dust of mineral salts, as from the kidney or bladder, of smaller size than the so-called stones. Generally made up of phosphates, calcium, oxalate and uric acid.

GREASY (Caust., Puls., Psor.): Like grease or oil; smooth; slippery; covered with or full of grease.

GREASED (Nat.m.): Smoothed or made slippery by any thick lubricant.

GREEDY (Hell., Lyc., Sep.): A person of an eager and selfish desire or longing for something, desirous.

GRIEF (Cal. p., Caust., Coccu., Colc., Coloc., Ign., Kali br., Lach., Nat.m., Pic.ac., Plat., Phoa.ac., Samb., Staph.): Mental suffering, especially such as follows from affliction, bereavement, remorse or the like; sadness; suffering; distress.

GRIEVES (Staph.): To feel or show grief; to injure or harmor hurt; to afflict.

GRIMACES (Agar.): A distortion of the face, whether involuntary or from annoyance, disgust or contempt.

GRINDING (Cic., Cina., Kali br., Pod.): Rubbing together with force, harshly, producing a grating noise.

GRIPPE: Influenza like symptoms.

GRIPING (Ipec.): To seize or lay hold on tightly and tenaciously; to grasp firmly.

GROINS (Act.): The junctional region between the abdomen and thigh; the inguinal region.

GRUMBLING (Lyc.): To make a low heavy sound as of thunder; to snarl in deep tones as a feeding lion.

GRUMOUS (Graph., Ham., Plat.): Clotted or lumpy.

GURGLING (Thuja): To make a sound like that of gurgling liquid; to run or flow in a broken, irregular, noisy current.

GUSHES (Chel., Graph., Lac c., Nat.s., Petr., Pod., Ver.): To flow out suddenly with violence and in volume.

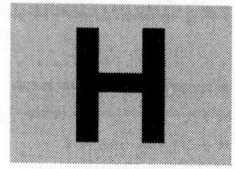

HABITUALLY COLD (Ver.): Lacking vital heat.

HAEMATIC (Crot.): A drug used in treating anemia.

HAEMATURIA (Kreos., Tereb.): Presence of blood in the urine.

HAEMOPTYSIS (Cact., Coca., Ham., Hyos., Kreos., Mill., Phos., Trill.): Expectoration of blood arising from the oral cavity, larynx, trachea, bronchi or lungs.

HAEMORRHAGE (Acet.ac., Bry., Cact): The escape of blood from the ruptured blood vessels; bleeding.

> **ACTIVE HAEMORRHAGE (Ipec., Trill.):** Haemorrhage occurring from arteries.
>
> **PASSIVE HAEMORRHAGE (Ham., Helon., Kreos., Ipec., Tereb., Thlaspi., Trill., Sec.):** Bleeding occurring from veins.
>
> **INTRAOCULAR HAEMORRHAGE (Ham.):** Haemorrhage within the eyeball.
>
> **POST-PARTUM HAEMORRHAGE (Mill., Nit.ac.):** Blood loss more than 500 ml from or into the genital tract following birth of the baby up to the end of puerperium.
>
> **VENOUS HAEMORRHAGE (Ham.):** Haemorrhage of a vein characterised by steady profuse bleeding of rather dark blood.

HAEMORRHOIDS (Acet.ac., Caust., Coc., Mur.ac., Nux., Sep., Sul.ac.): Piles; a mass of dilated tortuous vein in the ano-rectum involving venous plexus of that area, resulting in painful swelling with or without bleeding.

HALLUCINATIONS (Act., Bell., Stram., Tub.): A false perception having no relation to reality and not accounted for by any exterior stimuli, may be visual, and auditory or olfactory. Judgment may be impaired and the patient will not be able to distinguish between the real and the imagined.

HAMSTRINGS (Am.m., Med., Nat.m.): Any of three muscles at the back of the thigh that function to flex and rotate the leg and extend the thigh.

HANGNAILS (Nat.m.): Partly detached piece of skin at root or lateral edge of fingers or toenails.

HANGS (Abrot., Merc.b.i., Mur.ac.): To suspend; to drop; to bend or let something bend downwards.

HARD THUMP (Aur.): Hit hard with the hand, fist, or some heavy instrument.

HASTE (Acon., Bry., Coffe., Hep.s., Nat.m.): Speed; hurry.

HASTILY (Coccu.): Quickly; speedily; impatiently.

HASTENS (Phyt., Ruta.): To make something go or happen faster; to make haste; to hurry; to be quick.

HATEFUL (Lac c., Nit.ac.): Filled with or causing strong dislike; an emotion of intense aversion, usually springing from anger, fear, or a sense of injury.

HAUGHTY (Plat.): Behaving in an unfriendly way towards other people because you think that you are better than them.

HAWKING (Ant.c., Euph., Hydr, Nat.c.): Clear mucus or food from one's throat loudly; an audible effort to force up phlegm from the throat.

HEADACHE (Acet.ac., Bry., Cact., Nat.c., Nux.m., Pic.ac., Plat.): Pain in the head.

AMERICAN SICK HEADACHE (Lac d., Sang.): Periodic hemicranias (migraine).

ANAEMIC HEADACHE (Nat.m.): Headache occurring in anaemic persons.

CONGESTIVE HEADACHE (Cact., Lach.): Headache occurring due to abnormal accumulation of blood in the blood vessels of supplying the head.

DULL HEADACHE (Carb.ac.): Mild discomfort in head, that is often difficult to describe.

FRONTAL HEADACHE (Carb.ac.): Headache in the frontal region of head.

MENSTRUAL HEADACHE (Croc.): Headache occurring during the time of menstruation.

SICK HEADACHE (Coccu., Sanic., Sil., Sulph., Ver.v., Indigo.): Migraine that is a symptom complex of periodic headache, usually temporal and unilateral, often with irritability, nausea, vomiting, constipation or diarrhea and photophobia.

HEADSTRONG (Nit.ac., Sanic., Sil.): Habitually disposed to disobedience and opposition; obstinate; stubbornly bent on having one's own way.

HEAL (Sec., Sulph.): To cure or restore to a sound or healthy condition from disease, ailment or wound.

HEART BURN (Aur., Lyc., Mag.c., Sul.ac.): Pyrosis, i.e., the raising of small quantities of acid, i.e. sourliquid from the stomach, associated with burning feeling in stomach which may extend up to oesophagus.

HECTIC (Acet.ac., Eup.): Characterized by excitement, bustle (to be full of or busy with) or feverish activity, restless; relating to hectic fever.

HECTIC FEVER (Acet.ac.): A daily fluctuating but persistently recurrent fever accompanied with profound sweating, chills, flushed cheeks and hot skin, often associated with certain wasting diseases of long duration specially tuberculosis or septicaemia.

HELMINTHIASIS (Spig.): Having intestinal parasites or worms.

HEM AND HAWK (Arg.m.): Making an effort to bring out mucous and clear the throat noisily.

HEMICRANIA (Amyl., Arg.n.): Pain or aching in one side of the head; one-sided headache.

HEMIOPIA (Aur.): A defect of sight in which the person sees only one half of an object; hemianopia.

HEMIPLEGIA: Paralysis of one side of the body.

HERNIA (Nux.): The protrusion of an organ, its part, or tissue through an abnormal opening of the wall of the cavity that normally contains it.

>**FEMORAL HERNIA (Plb.):** The escape of a part of intestine through the femoral canal.
>
>**INGUINAL HERNIA (Plb.):** Hernia of the intestine at the inguinal region. A direct inguinal hernia passes directly through the abdominal wall between the deep epigastric artery and the edge of the rectus muscle. An indirect inguinal hernia passes through the inguinal canal.
>
>**STRANGULATEDHERNIA (Nux., Plb.):** Hernia that is both reducible and incarcerated and in which the blood circulation is also arrested causing gangrene occurring unless speedy relief is afforded.

UMBILICAL HERNIA (Coccu., Nux., Plb.): One in which bowel or omentum protrudes through the abdominal wall under the skin at the umbilicus.

HERPES (Hep., Nat.m., Petro., Tab.): A spreading skin eruption of deep-seated vesicles on erythematous bases, caused by herpes virus.

HERPES CIRCINATUS (Sep., Tell.): (Syn. *Herpes bullosis, dermatitis herpetiformis*) any inflammatory skin disease characterized by presence of severe, extensive itching eruptions of vesicles and papules which occur in groups, spontaneous healing, rarely occurs except in children. Relapses are common.

HERPES SIMPLEX: An infection by the herpes simplex virus *(Herpesvirushominis)* marked by the eruption of one or more groups of vesicles on the border of the lips, at the external nares, or on the glans, prepuce, or vulva. Such infection commonly reappears during other febrile illnesses or even physiologic states such as menstruation.

HERPES ZOSTER: An acute painful inflammatory disease of the skin, consisting of grouped vesicles corresponding in distribution to the course of the cutaneous nerves. Also called Zona or Shingles.

HERRING (Agnus., Sanic.): A type of fish (*Clupeaharengus*) that is abundant in the temperate and colder parts of the North Atlantic and that in the adult state is preserved by smoking or salting and in the young state is extensively canned and sold as sardines.

HICCOUGH (Ran.b., Tab.): (Syn.*Singultus)* an involuntary spasmodic contraction of the diaphragm causing a beginning inspiration which is suddenly checked by closure of the glottis causing the characteristic sound.

HIDEOUS 91

HIDEOUS (Bell.): Exciting horror and fear, frightful, terrifying, dreadful; shocking.

HIGH GAME (Crot.): Living with uncontrolled and undisciplined habits.

HIGH NOTES (Arg.n.): High tune; musical sound of very high pitch.

HILARITY (Croc.): Gaiety; pleasurable excitement; boisterous fun; cheerfulness.

HIPPOCRATIC FACE (Camph., Carbo v., Cinch., Sec., Ver.): Dark brown, livid or lead-coloured skin; hollow, sunken appearance of eyes, collapse of temples, sharpness of nose, lobes of ears contracting and turning outward, the skin of the forehead tense and dry, lips pendent, relaxed and cold.

HISSING (Acet.ac.): An act or instance of emitting a hiss (i.e to make a prolonged sibilant sound like the sound made by various animals-snakes, goose etc. and gas escaping from narrow hole.

HISSING RESPIRATION (Acet.ac.): Respiration with hissing sound.

HIVES: An allergic disorder marked by raised edematous patches of skin or mucous membrane and usually intense itching and caused by contact with a specific precipitating factor (as a food, drug, or inhalant) either externally or internally — called also urticaria.

HOARSE (Acon.): Having a rough, harsh grating voice as when affected with cold.

HOARSENESS (Calc., Carbo v., Caust., Dros., Hep., Nuxm., Rum., Stan.): An unnaturally deep, husky and croaking of the voice.

HOLLOW (Berb., Coccu., Lyc., Med., Phos., Samb., Stan., Thuja.): Having an empty space or cavity, natural or artificial, within a solid substance.

HOMESICKNESS (Caps., Phos.ac.): Sadness and depression from a longing or love for home or loved ones when away from home.

HOOP (Tub.): A rigid circular band of metal or wood or other material used for holding or fastening or hanging or pulling.

HOPELESS (Caust., Lac c.): Abscence of hope; despairing; having no expectation.

HORN (Spong.): A hard, pointed part, usually one of a pair, on the head of cows, goats, and other animals.

HORRIBLE (Asar., Psor., Pyr., Sabad., Sep.): Dreadful; terrible; shocking.

HORRIPILATION, GOOSE FLESH: A temporary condition in which small raised swellings appear on the skin because of cold, fear, or excitement; cutis anserine; goose bumps; goose skin.

HOT FLUSHES (Lach., Sulph.): In women symptom of declining ovarian function, falling estradiol levels, and impending menopause, marked by the sensation of sudden, brief flares of heat followed by sweating.

HOUR-GLASS CONTRACTION (Sec.): Constriction of the middle portion of a hollow organ such as stomach or gravid uterus to resemble a sand hourglass which runs out in one hour.

HOVERING (Asar.): To remain suspended in or near one place in the air.

HUE (Mer.): The particular shade or tint of a colour.

HUMID (Nat.s.): Moist; damp.

HUMID ASTHMA (Nat.s.): Asthma occurring in damp weather with profuse mucus and expectoration.

HUMID SCURF (Psor.): Moist scales of epidermis that continually comes out of skin.

HUMMING (Kreos.): To make a low, dull, continuous sound as of a bee.

HUMOR (Nux.m.): The ability to laugh at things that are amusing.

RAVENOUS HUNGER (Abrot., Iod., Med., Sec., Staph., Zinc): Violently hungry; voracious; craving for satisfaction or gratification.

HUNTERIAN CHANCRE (Mer.s., Mer.p.iod.): Indurated, syphilitic chancre that is a hard, syphilitic primary ulcer, the first sign of Syphilis, appearing 2-3 weeks after infection.

HURRIED (Mer.): Quickly; hastily.

HUSKY (Stan., Sel.): A dry, hoarse almost whispering voice.

HYDRANT (Phos.): A large, upright street pipe from which water may be obtained from a water main for fighting fire, cleaning street, etc.

HYDROCEPHALOID (Cinch., Hell., Kali br.): Resembling hydrocephalus; a state resembling chronic hydrocephalus, but attended with depression of the fontaneles.

HYDROCEPHALOUS (Hell.): An abnormal accumulation of fluid in the cerebral ventricles, causing enlargement of skull and compression of the brain.

POST-SCARLATINAL HYDROCEPHALOUS (Hell.): Hydrocephalous developed as asequelae of scarlatina.

TUBERCULAR HYDROCEPHALOUS (Hell.): Abnormal accumulation of fluid in the cranial cavity due to tubercular affection as in tubercular meningitis.

HYDROPHOBIA (Lys., Stram.): Fear of water; inability to swallow water owing to a contraction in the throat. Rabies in man.

HYDROTHORAX (Mer.sul.): A non-inflammatory collection of watery fluid in the pleural cavity; pleural effusion with transudate.

HYPERAEMIA: Congestion; the presence of an increased amount of blood in a part.

HYPERAESTHESIA (Taren.): Excessive sensitivity to stimuli; increased sensitivity to sensory stimuli such as pain or touch; oxyesthesia.

HYPERTROPHY (Hep., Iod., Naja.): The enlargement or overgrowth of an organ or part due to an increase in size of its constituent cells (not increase in numbers of cells).

HYPOCHONDRIUM (Chel., Pod.): Part of the abdomen beneath the lower ribs on each side of the epigastrium.

HYPOCHONDRIACAL (Mez.): Suffering from hypochondria (i.e. extreme anxiety and depression of mind often centred on imaginary physical ailments)The word comes from the Greek '*hypochondrion*', because the imaginary disease is often referred to the stomach region. The hypochondriac's symptoms are usually referred to as being 'all in the mind', and in our society not worthy of much attention. However, this can be looked at in another way, namely, that the person is announcing his life suffering in the language of bodily symptoms. In its own words, so to speak, the body is expressing concerns about its life circumstances.

HYPOCHONDRIACS (Alum., Hep., Mez., Nux., Nux m.): A morbid concern about the health and exaggerated attention to any unusual bodily or mental sensations, very often leading to an unfounded belief that one is suffering from some disease.

HYPOGASTRIUM (Tereb.): Region below the umbilicus or navel, between the right and left inguinal region.

HYSTERIA (Act., Caul., Croc., Hyos., Mag. m., Nux m., Plat.): A nervous disorder accompanied by extreme emotional excitability and lack of control, especially in fits which alternate between laughing and crying. This disorder was formerly believed to be confined to just young women but is now known to affect either sex, and thus is no longer called 'hysteria', but 'histrionic personality disorder'.

HYSTERICAL (Mag.m., Pic.ac., Sep.): Prone to hysteria.

IATROGENIC: Relating to an abnormal state or condition produced by a doctor by his medicines or poor treatment (either procedures or drugs).

ICHOROUS (Carb ac., Coccu., Kreos., Mez., Phyt., Psor.): Relating to or resembling ichor that is a burning, thin, acrid, pus-like discharge from an ulcer, wound or sore.

ICICLE (Mer.s.): A long hanging, tapering piece of ice formed by the freezing of dropping water.

ICTERUS (Ant.t.): Jaundice; yellowness of the skin.

IDIOCY (Hell.): Extreme deficiency in intelligence, commonly due to incomplete or abnormal development of the brain and the deficiency is usually congenital or due to arrest of development following disease or injury in early childhood. According to Binet-Simon intellect tests, an idiot is one who does not advance beyond the age of 3 years. The term 'idiot' is archaic and no longer used in the field of psychology.

IDIOPATHIC (Ham.): Denoting or pertaining to a disease or illness whose cause is unknown or uncertain or as yet undetermined.

IGNORENCE (Lac c.): Having no knowledge or awareness of something; state of being uneducated or uninformed.

ILL-DEVELOPED (Kreos.): Defectively or poorly developed.

ILL-HUMOUR (Caps., Cina., Cyc., Staph., Sel.): Bad tempered, bad mood.

ILL-NATURED (Abrot.): Bad-tempered; a disagreeable mood marked by irritability.

ILLUSION (Sabad.): A false perception; the mistaking of something for what it is not.

ILL-WILLED (Nit.ac.): Unkind feeling; enmity.

IMAGINARY TROUBLE (Naja.): Sufferings or troubles not really present, but in mind or imaginary.

IMBECILITY (Nat.c.): Weak mindedness; foolishness; stupidity.

IMMENSE (Can.ind.): Huge; unmeasured; immeasurable; infinite.

IMMODESTY (Hyos.): The perverse act of exposing and attracting attention to your own genitals.

IMPACTED (Sel.): Firmly fixed; driven together or close.

IMPACTION (Plb., Pyr., Ruta.): Act of becoming or state of being impacted; a lodgement of something in a strait or passage.

IMPAIRED LOCOMOTION (Phys.): Damaged power of any movement or walking.

IMPAIRMENT (Puls.): State of being impaired or deterioration or damage or diminution of strength, quality or value.

IMPATIENT (Cham., Coloc., Ign., Med., Rheum.): Not willing to wait for something to happen and becoming annoyed at delays; easily irritable.

IMPEDED (Caust., Hep.): Obstructed; hindered; stopped in progress.

IMPENDING (Abrot., Lil., Meny., Zinc.): Usually something unpleasantthatis going to happen soon; to threaten from near at hand or as in the immediate future.

IMPERATIVE (Psor., Tub.): Extremely important or urgent or must be done; obligatory.

IMPERFECT OXIDATION (Carbo v.): Improper or inability to utilization of oxygen by the blood.

IMPETIGO: Contagious skin disease caused by *Streptococcus* or *Staphylococcus* and characterised by yellow to red pustules which ripen, rupture or become crusted, especially around the nose, mouth, and cheeks or on the extremities. The disease is common in children and adults and may develop after trauma or irritation to the skin.

IMPOTENT: Incapable of sexual intercourse, usually refers to male; lacking physical strength or vigour; weak.

IMPOTENCY (Calad., Ign., Lyc., Nat.m.., Thuja., Tab., Sel.): Inability to achieve penile erection or to achieve ejaculation or both.

IMPRESSION (Nux., Op., Phos., Staph.): An effect produced upon the mind by some external object acting through the organ of sense as light, noise etc.; a mark seemingly made by pressure of one structure or organ upon another; an idea, feeling or opinion about someone or something.

IMPRINT (Hydr., Mer.): To mark a surface by pressing something into it, or to fix something firmly in the memory.

IMPUDENT (Graph.): Rude and not respectful; marked by casual disrespect; improperly forward or bold.

INABILITY (Nat.c., Nat.s.): A lack of ability to do something; want of sufficient power, strength, recourses or capacity.

INACTIVE RECTUM (Sel., Sil., Ver.): Having no power for effort or urge in rectum for defecation; no feeling of urge for stool.

INACTIVE BOWEL (Tab.): Loss of function of bowel or intestine specially the peristaltic movement.

INANITION: A debilitated physical condition (exhaustion) resulting from lack of sufficient food material essential to the body, such as in starvation or malabsorption syndrome.

INAPTNESS (Sul.ac.): Unfitness, awkwardness; inability.

INCARCERATED FLATUS (Coca.): Flatus that is not passing out or cannot escape.

INCESSANT (Kali bi., Kali br., Kreos., Lac d., Med., Mer.cor., Rum., Stram., Tab., Zinc.): Uninterrupted; continuous.

INCIPIENT (Bar., Med., Mill., Trill., Zinc.): Beginning to be or to appear; becoming apparent; just beginning.

INCLINATION (Con., Kali c., Lac c., Nux., Phos.): A preference or tendency, or a feeling that makes a person want to do something.

INCOHERENT (Hyos., Stram.): Without proper sequence;not clear; confused (Speech).

INCONSTANT (Ign.): Variable, irregular; in anatomy denoting a structure, such as an artery, nerve etc., that may or may not be present.

INCONTINENCE (Apis., Arn., Hyos., Kreos., Sanic.): Inability to retain, to control the excretory functions (usually refers to the bladder, e.g., 'an incontinent bladder').

INCOORDINATION (Kali br., Mag.c.): Want of co-ordination; inability to produce harmonious, rhythmic, muscular action due to loss of voluntary control.

INCREDIBLY (Ign.): Extremely or unusually good.

INCURABLE (Cact.): Not capable of being cured; not admitting of remedy or correction.

INDECISIVE (Ign., Puls.): Inconclusive; hesitant; uncertain.

INDIFFERENT (Cinch., Con., Mez., Nit.ac., Nux.m., Phos.ac., Phyt., Sep., Syph.): Lacking in interest or feeling; not responding to normal stimuli; apathetic.

INDIGESTION (Carb.v., Collin., Mag.m., Staph., Tab.): Righteous anger at injustice etc., feeling caused by an unjustified slight etc.Angerespecially at something unjust.

INDIGESTABLE (Puls.): Not easily digestible; not easily convertible into products fitted for absorption.

INDIGNATION (Coloc., Staph.): Feeling caused by an unjustified slight etc.; anger especially at something unfair or unreasonable.

INDOLENT (Caps., Con., Helon., Lach., Sep.): Inactive, sluggish; (painless or nearly so, as in 'indolent ulcer').

INDULGENCE (Con., Samb.): Gratification; to satisfy desires, whims etc.

INDURATED (Bell., Carboan., Con., Iod., Kali br., Phyt., Plb., Rhod.): Hardened; rendered hard; The hardening of a tissue or part.

INDURATION (Tar., Sars., Spong.): The act or process of becoming extremely hard; a hardened mass.

INEBRIATES (Crot., Eup.): To make drunk, to intoxicate; achronic drinker.

INEFFECTUAL (Caust., Fer., Lac d., Plb.): Not producing the proper or usual effect; useless; without the ability to achieve much.

INERTIA (Collin., Med., Plat., Pyr.): Denoting inactivity or lack of force; lack of mental or physical vigor; sluggishness of thought or action.

INEVITABLE (Hep., Phyt.): Not to be evaded or avoided; certain to happen; exactly right, giving the feeling that thing could not have been other than it is, unavoidable.

INFANT (Mag.m., Nux., Samb., Symph.): A child in the first year of the life.

INFECTION (Pyr.): A disease caused by microorganisms, especially those that released toxin or invade body tissue.

> **SEPTIC (Vario.):** Pertaining to sepsis that is systemic inflammatory response to infection to which there is fever or hypothermia, tachycardia, tachypnea and evidence of inadequate blood flow to the internal organ.
>
> **TUBERCULAR (Vario.):** Affected with tuberculosis.

INFECTIOUS (Vario.): Capable of being transmitted by infection, with or without actual contact; denoting a disease due to the action of a microorganism.

INFLAMMATION (Acon., Mer., Mez., Naja., Sab., Sil., Tereb., Ver.v.): A protective tissue response to injury or destruction of tissues, which serves to destroy, dilute or wall off both the injurious agent and the injured tissues. The classicalsigns of acute inflammation are pain (dolor), heat (calor), redness (rubor), swelling (tumor) and loss of function (functiolaesa).

INFLAMMATORY (Canth., Hyos., Ran.b., Rhod.): Accompanied by or tending to cause inflammation.

INFLAMMATORY EXUDATE (Sulph.): An inflammatory process in which the fluid leaving the capillaries is rich in plasma proteins.

INFLAMMED (Calen., Caps., Cham., Con., Kreos., Lac c., Nat.m., Psor., Ran.b.): Affected with inflammation; red, sore and hot due to infection or injury.

INFLUENZA (Eup., Ipec.): An acute contagious respiratory infection marked by fever, muscle ache, headache, prostration, cough and sore throat. The causative organism is influenza A or B virus.

INGESTA (Fer., Kali c., Phos.): Solid or liquid nutrient taken into the body through mouth.

INGROWING TOENAILS (Sil.): Nails of toe are growing inwards so that a portion normally free becomes covered.

INGUINAL GLAND (Merc.p.iod.): Lymph gland present in the region of groin or inguinal region.

INHUMAN (Abrot.): Not human; brutal; cruel; without human feeling; lacking the qualities of mercy, pity, kindness, or tenderness.

INIMICAL (Nit.ac.): Unfriendly; hostile; unfavourable opposed; like an enemy; antagonistic; hostile.

INJURIOUS (Acon.): Inflicting or tending to inflict injury; hurtful; harmful; mischievous.

INSANE (Lac c., Thuja., Syph.): Mentally deranged and therefore legally incompetent; of unsound mind.

INSANITY (Lil., Melil., Tub.): In legal medicine, the inability to managed one's own affairs or take responsibility for one's actions as a result of cognitive deficit, absence of self-control or psychosis; severe mental illness.

INSATIABLE (Eup., Med.): Incapable of being satisfied or appeased; not satiable.

INSENSIBLE (Hell., Hyos., Nux.m., Op., Stram.): Unconscious; without feeling or consciousness; not perceptible.

INSOLENT: Insulting in manner, speech, or behaviour; arrogant, impudent, impertinent.

INSTINCT (Con.): An inherited tendency to react to an environmental stimulus in a predictable but limited fashion.

INSUFFICIENT (Sep.): Wanting in strength, power, ability, capacity or skill; incompetent; inadequate to need, use or purpose.

INSULAR (Nat.m): Restricted, not connected with others.

INTELLECTUAL (Lyc.): Possessing intellect; pertaining to the mind; having the power of understanding.

INTENSE (Acon., Caust., Crot.t., Hyos., Lac c., Lac d., Led., Med., Melil., Mer., Mer.cy., Psor., Puls., Sab., Ver.): Extreme physical and emotional feelings; very strong; in a strain or extreme degree.

INTENTLY (Ruta.): Paying attention; do something eagerly.

INTERSECTING RINGS (Sep.): The rings meeting and crossing at a point, at two lines.

INTENSITY (Sul.ac.): A state of increased energy or force; marked tension.

INTERMITS (Mur.ac.): To cease for a time or at intervals; to be intermittent as a fever.

INTERMITTENT (Caul., Coff., Con., Dig., Fer., Hell., Kreos., Puls.): Coming and going at interval; recurring; periodic.

INTERSTITIAL INFLAMMATION OF BONE (Phos.ac.): One in which the inflammatory reaction occurs chiefly in the supportive fibrous connective tissue or stroma of bone.

INTERTRIGO (Caust.): Superficial dermatitis occurring in the folds of the skin, as the creases of the neck, folds of the groin and armpit, and beneath pendulous breasts. It is characterized by erythema, maceration, burning itching, and sometimes erosions, fissures, and exudations. It is caused by moisture, warmth, friction, sweat retention, and infectious agents; obesity is a predisposing factor.

INTOXICATED (Nux.m., Petr.): Under the influence of intoxicating liquor or drug; inebriated; being poisoned.

INTOXICATION (Coc., Gels., Lil., Nux.m., Petr.): The state of being poisoned. The condition produced by over indulgence in alcoholic beverages.

INTEGRITY (Hyper.): Unimpaired or unmarred state; state or quality of being complete, undivided or unbroken; entirety.

INTUSSUSCEPTION (Plb.): The infolding of one part of the intestine into the lumen of an immediately adjoining part.

INVERTED (Nit.ac.): To turned in or inwards; arranged in reverse order by inversion; turned upside down, outside in or inside out.

INVERTED SAUCER (Calc.): Concave in shape or turned inwards.

INVETERATE (Nit.ac.): Chronic; firmly by established long continuance; deep rooted; stubborn.

INVOLUNTARY (Carbo an., Carbo v., Caust., Chel., Cina., Dig., Hell., Hyos., Mur.ac., Op., Phos.ac., Psor., Pyr., Ruta., Rum., Sel.): Not under the control of the will, as an organ or its action; unwilling; reluctant; occurring as a result of a reflex.

INVOLUNTARY SIGHING (Ign.): A deep inspiration followed by a slow audible expiration as the involuntary expression of weariness, dejection, grief, regret, sadness, longing or relief.

IRASCIBLE (Nux.): Marked by outburst of temper or irritability; easily angered.

IRIDECTOMY (Led.): Surgical removal of part of the iris.

IRRELEVANT (Hyos.): Not applicable or pertinent; extraneous; unrelated; inconsequent, unessential.

IRRESISTABLE (Sel., Petros., Phos.ac., Phyt.): That cannot be successfully resisted; superior to opposition.

IRRESOLUTE (Ign., Mez.): Not firm in purpose; hesitant; undetermined; fickle mind.

IRRITABLE (Abrot.): Likely to become impatient, angry, or disturbed; easily excitable; easily annoyed; excessively or unduly sensitive to irritant or stimuli.

IRRITABILITY (Melil., Nat.s., Nit.ac., Nux., Symp.): Quality or state of being irritable.

IRRITATION (Kali br., Lil., Mag.p., Ran.b.): A reaction to a noxious or unpleasant stimulus; excitement of impatience, anger or passion; a condition of morbid excitability or over sensitiveness of an organ or part of the body.

IRRITATING (Med., Naja., Sars.): Provoking causing displeasure, annoyance, anger, impatience etc.

ISCHAEMIA: A local anemia caused by mechanical obstruction of the blood supply. If prolonged, death of tissue can occur.

ISCHURIA (Ars., Dul.): Suppression or retention of the urine.

ISOMORPHIC (Phos.): An organism or crystal superficially which is like another morphologically. (In genetics, denoting genotypes of polypoid organisms, which produce similar gametes even though containing genes in different combinations on homologous Chromosomes).

ITCHING (Crot., Iod., Kreos., Merc., Mez., Petr., Sab., Sars., Sel.): Pruritus; an uncomfortable sensation of irritation of the skin or mucous membranes which causing scratching or rubbing of the effected part.

JAGGED (Caust.): Having a sharply uneven surface or outline.

JAUNDICE (Chel., Eup., Plb., Tar.): A yellowishstaining of the integument, sclerae and deeper tissues and the excretionswith bile pigments; icterus.

> **JAUNDICE HAEMATIC (Crot.):** Haemolytic jaundice which is resulting from excessive amounts of haemoglobin released by any process (toxic, congenital or immune) causing haemolysis of erythrocytes.
>
> **JAUNDICE MALIGNANT (Crot.):** Jaundice that has a tendency to become fatal.

JEALOUSY (Hoys., Lach.): Unhappy and slightly angry because you wish you had someone else's qualities, advantages, or success.

JERKING (Ign., Tar., Ver.v., Zinc.): To move or make something move with a sudden, short, quick, sharp movement.

JERKS (Acon., Ver.v., Zinc.): Chorea or any form of tic; a sudden pull; a sharp muscular contraction following a tap on the muscle or its tendon; deep reflex.

JOLTING (Ham.): Shaking with jerks from seat, as on rough road journey.

JOVIAL (Caps.): Merry; very cheerful, friendly and good-humoured.

JOY (Caust.): Feeling of great happiness and pleasure.

KEEN (Lyc.): Very sharp.

KELOID GROWTH: A fibrous, excessive growth of the tissue usually at the site of scar caused by cut or burn. It is elevated, firm having whitish ridges or nodules with ill defined borders.

KERATITIS (Crot.): Inflammation of the cornea.

KERATOIRITIS (Crot.): Inflammation of both cornea and Iris.

KLEPTOMANIA: A diseased condition in which the patient has uncontrollable impulse to steal something which may be of no use for the patient.

KNUCKLES (Med.): A prominence produced by the head of any of the metacarpal bones.

LABIAL COMMISURE (Graph.): The upper end of vulva, where both sides of labia majora join.

LABYRINTHINE VERTIGO (MENIERE'S DISEASE) (Ther.): Distension of membranous labyrinth of middle ear from excess fluid pressure causes ischemia and failure of function of nerve of hearing and balance, thus there is fluctuating deafness, tinnitus and vertigo.

LABOR (Calen., Caul., Cham., Hoys., Kali c., Lil., Med., Mill., Sec., Thlaspi.): Series of events that takes place in the genital organ in an effort to expel the viable products of conception out of the womb through the vagina into the outer world is called labor.

> **PREMATURE LABOR (Sab.):** It is defined as one where the labor starts before the 37th completed week (< 259 days), counting from the first day of the last menstrual period.

LABOR PAIN (Nux.): Pain during labor, it may be false or true labor pain.

LABOURED (Glon.): To try very hard to do something difficult; to exerts one's powers of body or mind, especially with painful or strenuous effort.

LACHRYMOSE (Ign.): Generating or shedding tears; tearful.

LACHRYMATION (Eupr., Nat.m., Sabad.): The secretion and discharge of tears.

LACTATION (Caul.): The production and release of milk by mammary gland; the period of breastfeeding after childbirth.

LAIN (Pyr.): Past participle form of lie i.e.to be in or move into a horizontal position on a surface.

LAME (Abrot., Phyt., Ruta.): Physically disabled or limb defect, esp. foot or leg; incapable of normal locomotion; crippled.

LANGUID (Mag.p., Puls., Taren.): Exhausted; slow; sluggish; dropping or flagging from exhaustion.

LANGUOR (Helon., Med.): Slackness; lacking vigour or energy; tiredness or laziness of mind and body; lassitude.

LAPAROTOMY (Bis.): Cutting of abdominal wall for access to cavity of abdomen.

LARDACEOUS BASE (Mer., Mer.s.): Lard or fat like degenerated tissue at the bottom (of an ulcer).

LARYNGEAL POLYP (Sang.): A polyp attached to the vocal cords and extending to the air passageway.

LARYNGISMUS STRIDULUS: A spasmodic closure of glottis, lasting a few seconds, followed by noisy inspiration. Usually occur in children.

LARYNGITIS (Sel.): Laryngeal catarrh; inflammation of the mucous membrane of larynx.

TUBERCULAR LARYNGITIS (Sel.): A chronic form of inflammation of larynx due to tuberculous ulceration of the larynx; Inflammation of larynx secondary to pulmonary tuberculosis.

LASCIVIOUS (Hyos., Ver.): Feeling, expressing or causing excessive desire for sexual activity; lustful; sexual mania; lewd.

LASSITUDE (Benz.ac., Coc., Plb.): Extreme weakness; languor; debility.

LATENT (Sang.): Not manifest; concealed; dormant; hidden; present, but not yet active, developed or obvious.

LATENT PYOGENIC PROCESS (Pyr.): A pyogenic process which is hidden or concealed, and not actively manifesting.

LAUDABLE PUS (Nit.ac.): Pus that indicates healthy granulation of the ulcer. A term formerly used to describe pus, under the belief that it was nice to have it in a wound. Laudable means commendable, praiseworthy.

LAUREL BERRIS (Alum.): Small roundish fruit of Laurel tree (Bay-fruit).

LAX (Act., Agar., Kali c., Mag.c., Mer., Op., Sec., Sil., Spong.): Without tension; loose and not easily controlled; not of close texture; of the bowels, loose, open.

LEAN (Act, Coff., Kreos., Sulph.): Thin; without flesh; Not plump; Lacking nutritive quality.

LEMONADE (Sec., Sel.): A beverage of lemon juice mixed with water and sweetened.

LETS UP WITH A SNAP (Puls.): Diminishes or ceases after reaching the maximum point with a sudden terrible, unbearable pain.

LEUCOPHLEGMATIC (Calc., Cyc.): Flabby, calm, apathetic, slow to act or react; unexcitable.

LEUCORRHOEA Mag.m., Mer., Mill., Nux.m., Sang., Sanic., Sec., Syph., Thlapsi.): A discharge from the vagina of a white or yellowish, more or less viscid fluid, containing mucous and pus cells.

LEWD THOUGHTS (Sel., Ver.): Obscene thoughts; sexual thoughts in an obvious and socially unacceptable way.

LIABILITY (Bell., Calc., Kali bi., Nat.m.): Tendency; proneness.

LIENTERIA (Abort.): Loose watery in which stool containing undigested food.

LIES LIKE A LOG (Phos.ac.): Very much weak and lies without the power or strength to move or doing anything.

LIGHT HAIR (Sul.ac.): thin haired.

LIMBERGER CHEESE (Sanic.): A semi-hard, unpressed cheese originally made in the Belgian province of Limburg, has a peculiar, unpleasant odour and characteristic nutty flavour.

LINEA NASALIS (Aeth): A long narrow line on either sides of the nose.

LINEN (Mez.): Thread or cloth made of flax or hemp; clothing.

LIQUOR (Lyc., Med., Nux.m., Sul.ac.): An alcoholic drink, especially that has been distilled such as brandy, whisky, wine etc.

LISTLESS (Lil., Phos.ac.): Languid; having no energy, vitality or enthusiasm.

LITHOTOMY (Staph.): A cutting operation for removal of stone, especially from bladder.

LIVELY TO SERENE (Nux.m.): From joyful mood to serious mood.

LIVER SPOTS (Plb): Whitish spot which later changes into dark brown said to be due to liver diseases.

LIVID (Aster., Camph., Samb., Sul.ac.): A purple or dark blue or bluish-grey colour.

LOATHING (Ant.c., Colch.): Extreme disgust; a feeling of aversion.

LOCALIZATION (Acon.): Limitation to a definite area; the determination of the location of a morbid process.

LOCHIA (Caul., Kreos., Pyr.): The discharge from the vagina, of mucus, blood, and tissue debris following childbirth. At first pure blood, it later becomes paler, diminishes in quantity and finally ceases.

LONGING (Ant.c., Arg.n., Asar., Calc., Carb.ac., Chin., Coca): An eager desire; strong feeling for something; craving.

LOQUACITY (Can.ind., Lach., Pod.): Too much talkative;the quality, state or instance of being loquacious.

LOQUACIOUS (Stram.): Talkative; chattering.

LOUD SNORING (Op.): A rough rattling inspiratory noise produced by vibration of the pendulous palate or vocal cords during sleep or coma.

LOW SPIRITED (Kali br., Lach.): Weak, low strength or energy, especially in mental condition.

LUMBAGO (Nux.): A general non-specific term for dull, aching pain in the lumber region of the back.

LUMBRICI (Spig., Stan., Tereb.): Relating to or resembling an earthworm; vermiform; lumbricoid.

LUMP (Merc.b.iod., Psor., Rum.): A piece or mass of indefinite or irregular shape; a protuberance as a swelling or excrescent growth.

LUSTRELESS (Psor.): Dull; lack of lustre; lack of shine, glossiness, smoothness.

LYING-IN-PERIOD (Iod.): The period of time during which a woman staying in bed after child-birth.

LYMPHATIC (Cal ars): Pertaining to lymph; a vascular channel that transports lymph.

LYSSOPHOBIA (Lys.): Fear of becoming mad; a morbid fear of being affected with rabies. Imitative neurosis caused by such fear in person who have had a dog bite (*Lyssa- old term for rabies*).

MACULA: A small discoloured patch or spot on the skin, not elevated above the general surface, 1 cm or less in diameter.

MAGNETIZED (Calc., Phos., Sil.): Massaged, rubbed or stroked lightly in one direction only.

MALAISE (Bap.): A general feeling of uneasiness, discomfort, depression or despondency, often the first indication of an infection or other disease.

MALAR BONES (Stan.): Cheek bone; zygomatic bone.

MALICIOUS (Anac., Lyc., Nux.m.): Bearing ill will or spite; moved by hatred or ill will; mischievous; disposition to injure or harm others.

MALIGNANCY (Med.): The quality or state of being malignant.

MALIGNANT (Act., Am.c., Anthr., Arum., Carb.an., Con., Diph., Lach., Med., Sil.): Tending to become worse and leading to a gradual severe course, spreading and deteriorating rapidly and threatening to cause death, specially cancerous; in reference to a neoplasm having the property of locally invasive, and destructive growth and metastasis.

> **MALIGNANT AFFECTION (Kreos., Mur.ac.):** Cancerous diseases.
>
> **MALIGNANT DIPHTHERIA (Act., Merc.cy.):** An often fatal form of diphtheria beginning with rigors and marked

by massive swelling in the neck (bull neck) along with tonsillar enlargement and sometimes purpura.

MALIGNANT ERYSIPELAS (Anthr.): An acute contagious febrile disease associated with a local, intense, reddish inflammation of the skin and subcutaneous tissue that have tendency to become worse and leading to an ingravescent course, spreading and deteriorating rapidly and threatening to cause death.

MALIGNANT GROWTH (Sulph.): Growth, usuallyreference to a tumour having the property of locally invasive and destructive in nature and later metastasized.

MALIGNANT PUSTULES (Anthr., Lach.): Pustules which is very severe or tending to become fatal; a small round elevation of skin containing pus having an inflamed base which is very severe and which may show the severity towards been fatal.

MALIGNANT SCARLATINA (Am.c., Arum., Carb. ac.): A severe scarlet fever with the intensity to become fatal.

MALIGNANT ULCER (Anthr., Taren.): Ulceration tending to become progressively worse and to result in death having the properties of anaplasia, invasion and metastasis.

MALIGNANT TENDENCY (Kreos., Med., Tereb.): Tendency to develop malignant orcancerous affection or disease.

MALTREATED ORCHITIS (Spong.): Badly or roughly treated inflammation of testis.

MALTREATED STRICTURE (Mer.dul.): A narrowing or constriction of the ureter or urethra, which has not been treated properly or badly treated.

MAMMAE (Mer.): Breasts; mammary glands.

MAMMARY ABSCESS (Phyt.): Abscess forming in mammary gland.

MAMMILLARY (Aster.): Pertaining to or shaped like a nipple.

MANIA (Stram., Tar., Ver.): A mental illness characterized by exalted feeling, delusion of grandeur, elevation of mood, hyperactivity, over production of ideas, excessively rapid speech and violent, destructive actions; the elated phase of manic-depressive psychosis; excessive or unreasonable desire; a craze.

MANIACAL (Sel.): Relating to or affected with mania; wild; furious.

MAPPED TONGUE (Mer., Nat.m., Tar.): A patched-looking tongue, with patches surrounded by raised edges.

MARASMUS (Abrot., Act, Arg.n., Ars., Iod., Op., sanic., Tub.): A form of protein calorie malnutrition chiefly occurring in young children characterized by growth retardation and progressive wasting of subcutaneous fat and muscle, but usually with retention of the appetite and mental alertness.

MASHED (Hyper.): To beat or crush into a pulpy mass.

MASTICATING (Nit.ac.): Chewing; grinding or crushing with the teeth and prepare for swallowing and digestion, as food.

MASTURBATE (Phos.ac.): To practice masturbation.

MASTURBATION (Nux.): To induce sexual self-excitement through manipulation of the genital organs or other erogenous areas usually to orgasm, by some means other than sexual intercourse.

MATERIALIST (Vario.): The person who bears the philosophical opinion that physical matter is the only reality and that everything in the universe including emotion, thoughts, the mind, even the will, can be explain using physical laws.

MATRICES OF NAILS (Hyper.): (Pl. *of matrix*) The formative portion of a nail; the tissue lying beneath the root of a fingernail or toenail, and from which it develops.

MATTED (Mez.): To become, or make something become, tangled or interwoven into a dense untidy mass.

MEASLES (Apis., Camph., Carbo v., Dros., Eup., Psor., Vario.): (Syn. of *rubeola*)An acute, contagious febrile disease, caused by an RNA virus, commencing with coryza, cough, conjunctivitis and appearance of an eruption of distinct red circular spot on 4th day at buccal mucous membrane (koplik's spot) and few days later chills, fever and red maculopapular eruptions appear first on the face or behind the ears, then three days later the eruptions fade and is followed by a branny desquamation. One attack confers immunity.

MEATUS (Mer.s.): An opening or a passage, especially the external opening of a canal; a general term for an opening or passageway in the body such as meatus of nose, ear or urethra.

MECHANICAL AID (Sel.): Help or support by manual labor or by a machine or with tools.

MEDICINE (Nux.): Any substance or preparation used in treating diseases i.e. the drug or remedy.

> **AROMATIC MEDICINE (Nux.):** Having an agreeable, somewhat pungent, spicy odour; one of a group of vegetable drugs having a fragrant odour and slightly stimulant properties.
>
> **HOT MEDICINE (Nux.):** Stimulants.
>
> **PATENT MEDICINE (Nux.):** A medicinal preparation of known or unknown composition that is sold as a specific for a disease or certain diseased condition and often advertised to the public with false or extravagant claims.

MEIBOMIAN GLAND: Sebaceous gland on the margin of the eyelids which secrete a lubricating fluid.

MELANCHOLY (Agnus., Ars., Asar., Aur., Caps., Caul., Caust., Coca., Croc., Hell., Helon., Lach., Lyc., Murex., Nat.c., Nux., Tub.): A mental disorder characterised by extreme depression, apathy and indifference to one's surroundings, gloom, fear, brooding and painful delusion; sadness, low spirits, sluggishness.

MELTING SNOW AGGRAVATES (Calc.p.): Aggravation at the time (at the end of winter) when snow melts.

MEMORY (Carbo.v., Con., Kali.br.): The mental registration, retention, and recollection of past experiences, sensations, or thoughts; the power or function of reproducing and identifying what has been learnt or experienced.

MENARCHE: The commencing of the menstrual function or cycle in a young girl.

MENIERE'S DISEASE (Ther.): A recurrent and usually progressive group of symptoms including progressive deafness, ringing in the ears, dizziness, vertigo, nausea, vomiting and a sensation of fullness or pressure in the ears.First described by the French Physician P. Meniere (1799-1862).

MENINGITIS (Glon.): Inflammation of the meninges i.e. membranes of the brain or spinal cord, usually but not always caused by an infectious illness.

> **BASILAR MENINGITIS (Tub., Ver.v.):** Meningitis at the base of brain usually due to tuberculosis, syphilis or any low grade chronic granulomatous process.
>
> **CEREBROSPINAL MENINGITIS (Hell., Tub.):** Inflammation of the membranes of the brain or spinal cord.

SPINAL MENINGITIS (Nat.m.): Inflammation of the meninges of the spinal cord.

TUBERCULAR MENINGITIS (Hell.): Meningitis resulting from the spread of *Mycobacterium tuberculosis* to the central nervous system, usually from a primary focus of infection in the lungs.

MENOPAUSE (Amyl., Calc.ars., Crot., Lach.): (Syn: *Climaxis*) Permanent cessation of menstruation for more than 6 consecutive months, occurring usually between the 45 and 50 years of age.

MENORRHAGIA (Sab., Sep., Sulph, Trill.): Excessive flow of blood, more than 80 ml. during menstruation (the excess being either in number of days or amount or both).

MENSES (Alum.): Menstruation or menses is the periodic discharge of blood along with other materials (including one unfertilized ovum) from the female genital tract.

MENTAL DISTRACTION (Agnus.): A thing that takes attention away from what you are doing or thinking about; impossibility of concentration or fixation of mind.

MENTAL EXALTATION (Coff.): A mental state characterised by feeling of grandeur, excessive joy and optimism.

MENTAL EXERTION (Arg.n., Coffe., Colc.): Mental labor or effort.

MENTAL LABOUR (Arg.n.): Excessive mental work.

MENTAL TAXATION (Arg.n.): Heavy mental workload; any work or task that demands heavy mental exertion.

MENTAL TRAUMATISM (Nat.s.): A disease like condition as disordered feeling or behaviour (usually without pathological changes) caused after mental shock or trauma.

MERCURIAL (Phyt., Sel.): A medical or chemical preparation containing mercury;often changing or reacting in way that is unexpected.

MERCURIAL AMALGUM FILLINGS (Mer.dul.): Filling of teeth by a mixture of any metal with mercury.

MERCURIAL INHALATION (Nux.m.): Inhalation of vapours of mercury, specially of those persons who work with this metal or for any medicinal purpose.

MERELY (Sabad.): Only; simply; purely; absolutely; entirely.

MESENTERIC: Relating to or pertaining to mesentery which is a double layer of serous sac lining the abdominal cavity, and enclosing in its fold the different internal organs.

METALIC TASTING SALIVA (Mer.): Saliva having the taste of metals.

METASTASIS (Cup., Puls.): The transfer of location or its manifestation of a disease from one organ or part to another not directly connected with it. It may be due to either the transfer of pathogenic micro-organisms or due to transfer of cells, as in malignant tumours.

METEORISM (Tereb.): Distension of the abdomen or intestine due to the presence of gas;

METRORRHAGIA (Acet.ac., Apoc., Arg.n., Crot., Kali.c., Mag.m., Med., Phos., Plat., Stram., Thlaspi., Thuja.): Irregular, acyclic bleeding of any amount from the uterus between periods.

MICTURATION: Urination.

MIGRATING (Apis.): To pass from one part to another in an organ or in the body; to wander.

MILD (Puls.): Not violent, severe or extreme.

MILIARY RASH (Am. c.): Eruptions that are characterised by the formation of lesions resembling millet seeds (about 2 mm.), as in milliary tuberculosis.

MILLER'S ASTHMA (Samb.): A condition of the lungs found in millers caused by the inhalation of cereal dust. It usually attacks suddenly, usually in the middle of the night, producing difficulty of breathing, hoarse cough, a deep, harsh sounding voice, great anxiety, and apparent suffocation. Fits of vomiting, sneezing or coughing may occur, and then the patient may sleep briefly only to reawaken with a recurrence of symptoms.

MINUTE GUN COUGH (Dros.): Rapid coughs in short paroxysms.

MISCARRIAGE (Millf., Nit.ac., Sab., Sulph., Thlaspi.): Abortion.

MISCHIEF (Can.ind., Helon.): Bad behaviour that is annoying but that does not cause any serious damage or harm.

MISDEED (Colch.): An act that is bad or criminal or evil.

MISERABLE (Acon., Aesc., Puls.): Very unhappy, uncomfortable or causing much unhappiness.

MISERLY (Lyc., Sep.): Great desires to possess money, hates spending it and to spend as little as possible.

MIST (Ran.b.): A cloud of very small drops of water in the air just above the groundthat makes it difficult to see like a fog.

MITRAL REGURGITATION: Reflux of blood through an incompetent mitral valve.

MIXTURE (Nux.): A medicine of two or more components with known or unknown properties given to the patient in liquid form, which was very common at the time of Hahnemann.

MOANING (Can.ind., Cham., Kali br., Mur.ac., Pod.): Act of lamentation; Making a low mournful sound indicative of grief or pain or unhappiness.

MODELERS (Calc.): Someone who makes shapes or figures out of substances such as wood or clay.

MOISTURE (Sulph.): Very small drops of water that are present in the air, on a surface or in a substance.

MOLASSES (Ipec): A thick, dark brown sweet syrup, the residue left after crystallization of sugar.

MOLES (Sab.): A fleshy mass or tumour formed in the uterus by the degeneration or abortive development of the product of conception. The term is also used to designate a congenital discolouredraised spot or lump on the skin.

MOLLUSK (Murex.): Any member of the phylum *Mollusca*. *(Mollusca–* a phylum of animals containing nails, slugs, mussels, oysters, clams, octopuses, nautiluses, squids, cuttlefish, etc.)

MOODY (Ign.): Feelings and behaviour change frequently, and in particularly that they often become depressed or angry without any warning.

MORAL (Acon.): Dealing with, or concerned with establishing or disseminating, principles of right or wrong in conduct or behaviour; ethical.

MORBID (Nit.ac.): Diseased, unhealthy.

MORNING SICKNESS (Graph., Lob., Mer., Sep.): Nausea and vomiting in the morning, common in the early months of pregnancy.

MOROSE (Con., Cyc., Tub.): Sour tempered; gloomy; sullen; ill-humoured.

MORTIFICATION (Aur., Bry., Colch., Ign., Lyc., Nat.m., Staph.): Humiliation or indignation; a mortifying, or state of being mortified.

MORTIFYING (Lys.): Affecting with vexation, chagrin, or humiliation.

MOTH SPOT (Caul.): Black or dark discoloured spots. (Also called *liver spot or chloasma*)

MOTTLED (Hydr): Marked with areas of different colours in an irregular pattern; spotted.

MUCO LYMPH (Arg.n.): Pale yellowish-green fluid containing mucus membrane of intestine.

MUCO PURULENT (Arg.n.): Referring to an exudate which contain chiefly pus but also mucous material.

MUCOUS (Aloe., Ant.t., Arg.m., Arg.n., Can.ind., Canth., Carbo v., Hep., Stan.): A viscid, slippery secretion produced by mucous membranes, consisting of mucin, epithelial cells, leucocytes and various inorganic salts, and moisten and protect the membrane.

>**GLAIRY (Ipec.):** Mucous resembling the white of an egg; shining.

>**ROAPY (Kali bi.):** Tenacious, viscous mucous; capable of being drawn into a thread.

>**STRINGY (Kali bi.):** Mucous containing long, thin pieces of epithelial cells, leucocytes etc.

>**TENACIOUS (Canth.):** Mucous of adhesive character; clinging to another surface.

>**VISCID (Kali bi., Kali c.):** Sticky, slimy and thick adhesive mucous.

MUCOUS CONDYLOMATA (Thuja.): Wart like excrescence on the outer skin or the adjoining mucous membrane usually near the anus and genital organs, oozing moisture.

MUCOUS MEMBRANE (Aesc.): Lining membrane of the passages and the cavities of the body which communicate directly or indirectly with the exterior, as the alimentary, respiratory, and genito-urinary tract.

MUCOUS PILES (Ant.c.): Dilated blood vessels in the rectal mucosa forming a vascular tumour from which mucus is oozing.

MUDDLE (Nux.m.): State of being confused or disordered; intellectual cloudiness; to render muddy.

MUMPS (Mer., Puls.): (Syn. *Epidemic parotitis, parotiditis*) An acute, contagious, febrile disease characterized by non-suppurative inflammation and swelling of the parotid glands and sometimes of other salivary glands with fever, pain below the ear, malaise, headache etc. and caused by para-myxovirus.

MURMUR: Adventitious or abnormal cardiac sound produced by circulatory sequences through the valves, great vessels of abnormal opening when there is an abnormal turbulence in the flowing blood.

MUSK (Agnus.): A substance having a penetrating odour, obtained from a sacabout the size of an egg (musk bag) situated under the skin of the abdomen of the male musk deer.

MUSTY (Nat.c., Stan.): Having a moldy, stale, foul, fetid or sour odour or taste.

MUTTERING (Mur.ac.): To utter words in a low, indistinct voice;to sound with a low rumbling; grumbling.

MYALGIC (Ran.b.): Myalgia like (*Myalgia* means tenderness or pain in the muscles).

MYELITIS: Inflammation of spinal cord and/or bone marrow.

MYOPIA: Short sightedness, near sightedness; an error in refraction in which light rays are focused in front of the retina, enabling the person to see distinctly on only a short distance.

MYOSITIS: Inflammatory disease of muscle tissue.

NAEVUS (Fluor.ac.): A birth mark; a circumscribed stable discolouration of the skin caused by pigmentation containing aggregation of melanocytes or by hyperplasia of blood vessels, which is not due to external causes and therefore presumed to be of hereditary origin; a mole.

NAPKIN (Pod., Syph.): A disposable absorbent thick piece of cloth material that is used in between the legs and fastened at the waist for absorption of discharges like menstrual blood, urine, faeces, etc.

NARCOTICS (Cham., Nux., Thuja): A drug that in moderate doses depresses the central nervous system, thus relieving pain and producing sleep, but in excessive doses produces unconsciousness, stupor, coma and possibly death. Most of such drugs are habit forming. Examples – opium, morphine, heroin etc.

NARES (Caps., Mer.dul., Nat.c.): The external orifices of the nose, called also nostrils.

NASAL CATARRH (Calc., Kali bi.): Inflammation of the mucous membranes lining the nose and throat, causing an excessive discharge of thick mucus.

NASAL POLYP (All.c., Sang.): A projecting mass of swollen and hypertrophied mucous membrane, as in the nasal cavity or one of its accessory sinuses, caused by chronic inflammation.

NATIS (Lac.c.): Buttocks; the prominences formed by the gluteal muscles on either side with a covering of fat and skin on the lower part of the back.

NAUSEA (Act., Aloe., Ant.t., Apoc., Coc.): A subjective unpleasant wave-like sensation in the back of the throat, epigastrium or abdomen that may or may not lead to the urge or need to vomit, either by a reflex (e.g. irritation of stomach nerves) or conditioned (e.g. smell) stimulus.

NAUSEATES (Sep.): To become affected with nausea.

NECROSIS (Fluor.ac., Phos.ac., Phos., Ther.): The local death of living cells, tissues, or organs due to loss of blood supply, physical agents (e.g. trauma, radiant energy), chemical agents etc.

NERVES 'WORN OUT' (Ambr.): Thoroughly tired and exhausted nerves.

NERVOUS (Acon., Ambr., Amyl., Apis., Arg.n.): Easily agitated, excited, tensed or frightened; anxious; pertaining to nerves.

>**NERVOUS AFFECTION (Ambr., Gels.):** Any pathological condition of the nervous system.
>
>**NERVOUS COUGH (Caps.):** Cough that is produced due to stimulation or irritation of the nerves.
>
>**NERVOUS DEBILITY (Agnus.):** (Syn; *Neurasthenia*) Nervous fatigue with resultant physical exhaustion and weakness.
>
>**NERVOUS ERITHISM (Arg.n.):** A state of excessive excitement or irritability of nerves.
>
>**NERVOUS EXCITEMENT (Act.):** Easily excited.

NERVOUS EXHAUSION (Coca): State of extreme fatigue or weariness or inability to response to stimuli; loss of vital powers.

NERVOUS HEADACHE (Arg.n., Med., Spig., Ver.v): Headache that is produced due to overexertion or irritation of the nerves.

NERVOUS ORGANISATION (Mag.p.): Nervous person.

NERVOUS PROSTRATION (Pic.ac.): Nervous fatigue leading to physical exhaustion

NERVOUS WEAKNESS (Dig., Kali.br., Nat.m., Sabd., Staph.): Easily fatigue or loss of strength of nervous origin.

NETTLE RASH: (Syn.*Urticaria*) Multiple swollen raised areas on the skin characterized by sudden general eruption of papules or wheals associated with severe itching.

NEURALGIA (Act., Cact., CheL., Kali.bi., Kalm., Mag. p., Med., Phyt., Sang., Sars., Stan.): Pain of a severe character occurring along the course or distribution of a nerve.

NEURALGIA INTERCOSTAL (Ran.b.): Pain in the chest wall due to neuralgia of one or more of the intercostal nerves.

NEURALGIC (Mag.p., Ran.b., Sulph.): Subject to neuralgia.

NEURALGIA OF STUMP (All.c.): Pain due to irritation of nerves at the site of an amputation.

NEURASTHENIA (Pic.ac.): A term previously used for persons with unexplained chronic fatigue and lassitude, associated with nervousness, irritability, and lack of energy, feeling of inadequacy, anxiety, depression, headache, insomnia and sexual disorders.

NEURITIS (All.c., Calen.): Inflammation of nerves; a morbid condition characterized by pain and tenderness over the nerves, anaesthesia and paresthesia, paralysis, wasting, and disappearance of the reflexes. The condition is usually associated with a degenerative process.

NEUROMA (Calen.): A former term for any type of tumour composed of nerve cell, now it is pertaining to the cytologic and histologic characteristic, such neoplasm are now classified in more specific category, e.g. ganglioneuroma, neurilemmoma etc.

> **IDIOPATHIC NEUROMA (Calen.):** Neuroma occurs due to unknown cause.
>
> **TRAUMATIC NEUROMA (Calen.):** Neuroma develops as a result of any trauma or injury to the nerve cells.

NEW MOON (Alum., Sil., Sulph.): The moon when it first appear as thin curved shaped at the start of its four week cycle. The new moon is also the time of the month when the moon appears in this way.

NIGHT TERRORS: An emotional episode (usually in young children) in which the person awakens in terror with feelings of anxiety and fear but is unable to remember any incident that might have provoked those feelings.

NIGHT WATCHING: Not sleeping and awaking at night.

NOCTURNAL (Dros., Hyos.): Happening at night; belonging or relating to the night.

NOCTURNAL ENURESIS (Caust.): Bed-wetting at night; involuntary passage of urine usually occurring at night or during sleep.

NODDING (Ver.v.): Involuntary movement of head.

NODOSITIES (Benz.ac., Led., Phyt., Staph.): Having numerous protuberance or knot-like swelling; condition of having nodes.

NUMB (Cham., Kali br., Kal., Petr., Pic.ac., Plat., Pod.): To deprive completely, or to some degree, of the power of sensation or motion; insensible.

NOURISHED (Kreos.): To supply with whatever promotes growth, development, etc, or keeps in good health; to feed.

NURSING (Crot., Phyt.): To look after (sick or injured people) especially in a hospital; to breastfeed a baby; tending and taking care of a child.

NURSING CHILDREN (Alum.): Children who take breast milk.

NURSHING WOMEN (Cham.): Women who nurse child with her breast milk.

NOSTRIL (Ant.t.): Either of the two external apertures in the nose, through which one breathes and smells, etc.

NOSTRUMS (Nux.): A quack, patent, or secret remedy which have no effectiveness or has not been tested in proper scientific way.

NOT TO BE ALLAYED (Acon.): Not be considered of less value.

NOXIOUS EFFLUVIA (Crot.): Harmful or injurious and foul odours, fumes or exhalations from decayed matter.

NYMPHOMANIA (Murex, Plat.): Abnormally excessive sexual desire in female.

NYSTAGMUS (Phys.): An involuntary, constant rapid, movement of the eyeballs, which may be horizontal, vertical, rotatory, or mixed and it occurs normally with dizziness during and after bodily rotation, injury to the cerebellum etc or may be of nervous origin.

OBESITY (Calc., Graph., Kali br., Kali c., Lac.d.): Fatness; corpulent; an abnormal increase of fat in the subcutaneous connective tissue; having a body mass index more than 30 kg/m^2.

OBLIGED TO (Sel.): To force or make it expected for to do something.

OBSCENE THINGHS (Lil.): Lewd things; things which are offensive to one's sense of modesty.

OBSCURATION (Ruta): Darkness; vague: not clear; to hide from view.

OBSCURE (Coca.): To darken; to make dim; to conceal or hide, as by covering.

OBSTINATE (Fluor.ac., Plat., Sanic., Sep., Sil.): Blindly or excessive firm; unyielding to reason, argument, or other means; not easily subdued or remedied; hard to control or cure.

OBSTINACY (Sul.ac.): Quality or state of being obstinate; fixedness in will, opinion, resolution; stubbornness; unyieldingness.

OBSTRUCTED (Samb., Plb., Pyr.): Blocked up; to stopped up.

OBTUSED BODY (Symph.): Not pointed or acute; dull or blunt substance or thing.

OCEAN VOYAGE (Nat.m.): Travel or journey by sea.

ODOUR (Stan.): That property of a substance which effect the sense of smell.

> **CARRION LIKE ODOUR (Psor., Pyr., Sil.):** Smell as of dead or decaying flesh.
>
> **MOULDY ODOUR (Stan.):** A typical smell produced due to formation of mould on any damp substance (*Mould:* a superficial often woolly growth produced especially on damp or decaying organic matter or on living organisms by a fungus).
>
> **MUSTY ODOUR (Stan.):** Damp and unpleasant smell because lack of fresh air.
>
> **ODOUR OF VIOLETS (Tereb.):** Sweet smell like that of violet.

OEDEMA (Apis., Crot., KalI.bi.): An accumulation of an excessive amount of fluid in cells, tissues, or serous cavities.

OEDEMATOUS (Phos., Samb.): Marked by oedema.

OFFENCE (Nat.m.): An illegal act; crime that breaks a particular lawand requires a particular punishment.

OFFENDED (Coc., Colc., Petr.): To cause to be upset or to hurt the feelings of (someone), especially by being rude or showing a lack of respect.

OFFENSIVE (Aloe.): Extremely unpleasant; foul; repugnant; obnoxious.

OLD DRUNKARDS (Bar., Benz.ac.): Aged person who frequently drinks to excess; a habitual drinker.

OLD LOOKING PATIENT (Arg.n.): Patient looks like old or aged; patients who look older than their real age because of their long sufferings.

OLD MAIDS (Con.): Aged woman who works as a servant in a hotel or private house.

OLD SINNERS (Agnus.): Old persons who have been indulging in morally wrong activities since long, like excessive drinking, immoral sex, etc.

OLD TOPPERS (Carbo v.): Persons who are addicted to alcoholic beverages especially whisky for a long time; chronic drinkers.

OLFACTION (Ars.): The act, process, or faculty of smelling; the sense of smell.

OLIVE GREEN (Carbo.ac.): A medium dark yellowish green colour, like colour of olive.

OLIVES (Aster., Pyr.): The small green or black oily fruit of an evergreen tree with leathery leaves and hard yellow wood; a member of the genus, *Olena* (family *Oleaecaea*).

ONANISM (Arg.m., Calad., Lach., Lyc., Phos.ac., Plat., Staph.): Incomplete coitus; coitus interruptus; withdrawal of penis before ejaculation during coition. The term was previously used wrongly to mean masturbation. (Onanism is so named because it was practiced by the biblical character Onan, Son of Judah.)

ONANIST (Coc., Gels.): One who practices or is addicted to onanism.

ONYCHIA: (Syn. *Matrixitis, onychitis*)Inflammation of the nail bed with suppuration and shedding or loss of the nail.

OOZING (Ant.c., Calc.p, Carbo. v., Caul., Graph., Kreos., Med., Nit.ac., Psor., Sel., Staph.): Very slow flow of thick liquid in small quantity; exuding moisture

OPAQUE (Arg.n.): Not reflecting or giving out light, not shining; not transparent; dark.

OPEN SUTURE (Apoc., Calc.): Unclosed suture which is a stitch that joins the edges of a wound, surgical incision, etc. together.

OPISTHOTONOS (Cic., Nat.s., Ver.v.): (Syn.*Emprosthotonos*; *pleurothotonos*) A tetanic spasm in which the spine and extremities are bent with convexity forward, the body resting on head and on the heel. This is usually seen in strychnine poisoning, tetanus, epilepsy, the convulsion of rabies and in severe cases of meningitis.

OPPOSITION (Lyc.): The act of strongly disagreeing, especially with the aim of preventing something from happening.

OPPRESSION (Cact., Coca., Glon., Mill., Sep.): A feeling of distress or sense of heaviness in the body or mind or, of being weighed down by force or spirit; dullness of spirit; depression; lassitude.

OPPRESSED BREATHING (Ipec.): Sensation of distress or obstruction during breathing.

OPTHALMIA NEONATORUM (Arg.n., Thuja, Syph.): (Syn. *Blennorrheaneonatorum*) Gonococcal conjunctivitis in the newborn.

ORATOR (Arum.): A public speaker; one who delivers a lecture often.

ORBITAL NEURALGIA (Chel.): Pain of a severe throbbing or stabbing character in the course or distribution of the nerves supplying to orbits; severe sharp pains in and around the eyes.

ORCHITIS (Spong., Rhod.): Inflammation of testis.

ORGANIC AFFECTION (Dig., Lil.): Same as Organic Disease.

ORGANIC DISEASE (Apoc.): A disease associated with observable or detectable structural changes in the organs or tissues of the body. (As opposed to *functional diseases*, in which the function of the organ changes but not necessarily its structure).

ORGANIC HEART DISEASE (Lac.d.): Any pathological condition in which structural changes has taken place of the coronary vessels, heart valves, myocardium, pericardium or electrical conduction system of the heart.

ORGANIC LESION (Med., Psor., Tereb.): An abnormal or injurious change in an organ or tissue which is observable or detectable.

ORGASM (Calad.): A state of physical and emotional excitement, especially that which occurs at the height (climax) of sexual intercourse. In the male it is accompanied by the ejaculation of semen.

OSSIFICATION (Calc.): (Syn. *Osteogenesis*)The formation of bone matrix; the replacement of other tissue by bone, especially during foetal development.

OTORRHOEA (Mer.s., Psor.): A mucopurulent discharge from the ear.

OVARIOTOMY (Staph.): (Syn. *Oophorectomy, ovariectomy.*) Partial or complete excision or removal of an ovary;

OVARITIS (Med.): Acute or chronic inflammation of an ovary.

OVER EXERTION (Nux., Ruta.): Excessive mental or physical effort.

OVERGROWN (Kreos.): Abnormally, disproportionately, or excessively grown.

OVERHEATED (Bry.): Hotter than what is necessary or desirable; to become too hot.

OVERLIFTING (Pod.): Unusual or excessive lifting or movement beyond the capacity.

OVERSENSITIVE (Cham., Coff., Hep., Ign., Ipec., Nux.m., Nux., Phos., Sil.): Very quick feeling or responding to a stimulus; too easily upset or offended.

OVERTAXED (Hell.): To do or want to do more than the ability of an individual.

OYSTER (Puls.): A large flat shellfish of genus *ostrea* or family *ostreidae*, some of which can be eaten and other types of which produce pearls.

OZAENA (Am.c., Nit.ac.): A disease of the nose, of varying etiology, associated with atrophy of the turbinates and mucus membrane accompanied by considerable crusting, discharge and a very offensive odour.

PAIN: Suffering, either physical or mental; an impression on the sensory nerves causing distress, unpleasant, uncomfortable feeling or, when extreme, agony; one of the uterine contractions occurring in childbirth.

ACHING (Act., Agar., Eup., Helon., Lac c., Lyc., Mag.c., Med., Nux., Rat., Ruta., Stan.): Pain that is persistent rather than sudden or spasmodic, it may be dull or severe.

AGONIZING (Coloc.): Extreme or severe nature of pain.

ARTHRITIC (Coloc., Med., Sab.): Pain in one or more inflammatory joints of the body due to infectious, metabolic, or constitutional causes.

ATROCIOUS (Spig.): Very bad or unpleasant, extremely violent pain.

BEARING DOWN (Agar., Ham.): Pain like to push or press downwards with steady pressure on something.

BITING (All.c., Can.s., Petros.,): Pain as if bitten by any animals or insects.

BORING (Phos.ac.): Piercing, used to describe pain felt deep within the body.

BURNING (All.c., Apis., Can.s., Canth., Caps., Colch., Cyc., Equis., Ham., Graph., Kreos., Led., Mez., Petros., Phos.ac., Phos., Phyt., Pic.ac., Rat., Ran.b., Pyr., Spig.,

Tereb.): Pain that is very strong and feeling of burning present..

BURSTING (Gels., Glon., Lach., Lil., Nat.m., Sep.): Pain like to break open something or apart suddenly.

CARDIAC (Mag.m.): Pain relating to heart disease.

COLICY (Mer.cor.): Pain occurring due to spasm of any hollow or tubular soft organ.

CONSTRICTING (Mag.p., Med.): Pain with feeling of binding, squeezing or narrowing.

CONTRACTING (Spong.): Pain of becoming smaller, shorter or pressed together or like a tightening of the muscles.

CRAMPING (Act., Coloc., Mag.p.): A pain usually sudden and intermittent, of almost any area of the body, specially abdominal or pelvic viscera.

CRUSHING (Nat.s.): Pain as if the suffering part will be destroyed or broken into small pieces.

CUTTING (Aloe., Canth., Carbo.an., Coloc., Equis., Hydr, Ipec., Iod., Mag.c., Mag.p., Mer.cor., Nat.m., Nit. ac., Psor.): Sharply penetrating, shearing or piercing.

DARTING (Act., Cact ., Coloc., Kali c., Kal., Mag.p.): Rapid, sudden and swift, with or without changing direction.

DIGGING (Phos.ac.): Pain like push up or pressingforcefully thrusting against or making hole in the part by any tool.

DRAWING (Cinch., Colch., Cyc., Crot.t., Lyc., Petr., Phos.ac., Puls., Rhod., Sab., Tereb.): Pulling or stiffening up like pain.

DULL (Mez.): A mild discomfort, often difficult to describe.

ELECTRIC LIKE (Act., Phyt.): Sudden, violent, electric-shock like pain.

ERRATIC (Caul., Puls.): Pain that is changing places suddenly and unexpectedly and not happening at regular times; roving or wandering.

EXCRUCIATING (Aloe., Hyper., Rat., Sang., Sars.): Intense or extremely painful; torturing.

GNAWING (Nat.s.): Chewing or eroding in a persistent manner.

GRIPING (Aloe., Am.m., Dios.): A sudden, sharp pain in stomach or bowels.

HAMMERING (Fer.): Feeling as if hitting by a hammer.

HARD (Nux): Severe pain.

INTERMITTENT (Mag.p.): Pain which is stopping and starting over a period of time, but not regularly.

JERKING (Pod.): Sudden, short, sharp jerk like pain.

LABOR-LIKE (Mag.c., Med., Sab., Sec.,): Rhythmical, intermittent, uncomfortable pain like labor pain.

LACERATING (Mer.): Pain as like to cut, tear or separating flesh.

LANCINATING (Act., Carboan., Nit.ac., Phyt., Sep. Syph.): Piercing, stabbing, shooting or sharply cutting pain.

LIGHTENING (Cact., Coloc., Mag.c., Mag.p.): (Syn. *Fulgurant pain*) A sudden sharp pain spreading and appearing and disappearing quickly, that may be repetitive, usually in the legs, but may be at any location. It is associated with tabesdorsalis or other neurological disorder.

MYALGIC (Ran.b.): Pain like myalgia that is tenderness or pain in the muscles.

NEURALGIC (All.c., Am.m., Mag.c., Mez., Ran.b.): Pain as of a severe throbbing or stabbing character occurring along the course or distribution of a nerve.

PERIOSTEAL (Am.c., Symph, Sars.): Pain in periosteum of bones.

PIERCING (Agar.): A sharp, strong pain as if penetrating to the skin or body tissue.

PRESSING (Cact., Colch.., Kal., Lach., Sep.): Pain as if pushing firmly against something.

PRESSIVE (Agr.n., Cyc., Kali bi., Mag.m., Petr., Spig.): Pain as if being pressed by something.

PRICKING (Aesc., Caul., Ham., Nit.ac., Symph., Taren.): Pain caused by a sharp points like needles.

PULSATING (Cact, Croc., Glon., Fer., Mer., Petr., Spig.): Pain occurring rhythmically.

RHEUMATIC (Act., Cham., Med., Ran.b., Sang.): Pain in the body due to rheumatism.

SHARP (Act., Hydr, Lil., Mag.p., Ran.b., Spig.): Pain of rapid, very strong or sudden in character, often like being cut or wounded.

SHOOTING (Act., Coloc., Kal., Lach., Mag.p., Mer., Phyt., Ran.b.): *Pain passing* through swiftly, rapidly or suddenly; darting; piercing.

SMARTING (All.c., Am.m., Caps., Kreos., Nat.m., Ran.b.): Severe, sharp, vigorous stinging pain.

SPASMODIC (Act., Caul., Cham., Nit.ac., Nux., Tab., Sep.): Pain like a spasm that is a sudden involuntary, uncontrollable contraction of a muscle or muscles or of a hollow organ.

SPLINTER-LIKE (Nit.ac.): Pain as if a slender, sharp pieces of material piercing or embedded in the skin or subcutaneous tissue.

SPRINGING (Cact.): Pain appearing or coming or developing quickly and/or suddenly.

STABBING (Mag.p., Merc.s., Spig.): Very sharp, sudden and strong pain like being pierced with a sharp pointed weapon.

STICKING (Kali c., Kalm., Led., Nit.ac., Nux., Spig., Rat.): Pain as if pushing (something pointed) into or through something.

STINGING (Aesc., All.c., Am.m., Apis., Graph., Ham.): Sharp, quick pain with a burning smarting feeling as if caused by poisonous or irritating stings of bees, nettles, etc.

STITCHING (Act., Carboan., Ign., Ipec., Kali c., Kal., Lach., Mag.p., Naja., Nat.m., Ran.b., Spig.): Sudden, acute, sharp, tearing, pricking pain, like that caused by piercing with a needle, usually of momentary duration.

TEARING (Can.s., Cinch., Colch., Cyc., Led., Mer., Merc.s., Nit.ac., Phos.ac., Psor., Puls., Rhod., Spig.): Pain as if pulling apart or away from something by force; pain after injury to a muscle, etc. by stretching it too much.

TINGLING (Nux., Petros., Sec.): A slight stinging, prickling, thrilling or uncomfortable feeling or pain.

TEDIOUS (Act.): Slow, tiring, exhaustive, repetitious pain of long duration.

THROBBING (Cact., Croc., Glon., Kali c., Spig.): A feeling of pain that is experienced as a series of strong beats.

VIOLENT (Nat.s., Nit.ac., Nux., Spig.): Very strong, sudden, severe, extreme intense pain.

PAINTER'S COLIC (Alum., Am. c.): Colic due to lead poisonings. Lead was a very common component of the colours and paints used. During the process of painting it was a common practice to hold the brush in mouth or to wet it by applying saliva, hence lead was ingested and cause colic.

PALATINE (Aur.): Pertaining to the palate., the portion separating the nasal and oral cavities.

PALATINE ARCH (Diph.): Two arch like folds of mucous membrane that form the lateral margins of faucial and pharyngeal isthmuses. They are continuous above with the soft palate.

PALE (Acet.ac., Calc., Carbo. v., Carb. ac., Cina., Cham., Cinch., Cyc., Dig., Fer., Graph., Iod., Ipec., Kal., Kreos., Lac d., Lyc., Nat.c., Rheum., Plat., Plum., Puls., Psor., Pyr., Sec.): Deficient in colour or in intensity or depth of colour; not bright or brilliant; of a faint lustre.

PALE SICKLY COMPLEXION (Phos.ac.): Pale appearance of the face like a sick person; pale withered face.

PALLID (Amyl.): Of a pale appearance; lack of colour or spirit.

PALLIATES (Psor., Tub.): To relieve temporarily without curing; to ease or reduce effect or intensity of a disease.

PALLIATIVE (Amyl.): Which palliates; a palliative agent.

PALLOR (Lob., Tab.): Paleness; absence of the skin colouration.

PALPITATION (Act., Am.c., Apoc., Cact., Cal.ars., Coca., Collin., Glon., Iod., Lil., Lac c., Mag.m., Mill., Mur.ac., Naja., Spong., Spig., Tab., Trill.): Forcible pulsation of the heart, perceptible to the patient, usually with an increase in frequency, with or without irregularity in rhythm as when excited by violent exertion, strong emotion or disease.

PANARATIA (All.c., Am.c., Sel.): A whitlow; a painful inflammation of a finger or toe, especially near or around the nail. Also called felon.

PANNUS (Aur. Met., Kali bich.-Boericke): A superficial vascular inflammation of the cornea causing opacity. A patch of greyish, membrane-like vascularized tissue covering the upper half of (sometimes the entire) cornea. This condition may be seen in trachoma, acne rosacea, eczema etc.; a condition in which a layer of vascular fibrous tissue covers an organ.

PAPESCENT (Bis.): Having the consistence of pap which means any soft food, as bread soaked in milk.

PAPILLAE (Ant.t., Tereb.): A small nipple shaped projection or elevation.

PARALYSIS (Anac., Ant.t., Caust., Coc., Cup., Equis., Hell., Kali br., Kali c., Med., Mur.ac., Nat.m., Op., Pic.ac., Plum., Sel., Sil., Syph., Zinc.): Akinesia; loss of power of voluntary movement in a muscle through injury or disease of its nerve supply;palsy.

> **PARALYSIS AGITANS (Mer.s.):** Parkinson's disease; shaking palsy; a neurological disorder caused by post-inflammatory or degenerative disease of basal ganglia, associated with rigidity, rhythmical tremor, mask like facies, poverty of movement, festinating gait.
>
> **MOTOR PARALYSIS (Gels.):** Loss of power of muscular contraction.
>
> **THREATENED PARALYSIS (Am.c., Naja.):** There is chance or possibility of being affected with paralysis.

PARALYSIS OF RECTUM (Tab.): Loss of power of rectum.

PARALYTIC (Ign.): Affected with paralysis.

PARALYTIC FEELING (Aesc.): Feeling or sensation of loss of power of voluntary movement though there is no such disease present.

PARALYSIS OF BRAIN (Op.): Loss of functioning of brain. Hence, a comatose, semi-comatose or stuporous condition may be produced.

PARALYSIS BLADDER (Hyos., Op.): Loss of urinary reflex, hence manifested by loss of urge even when the bladder is full.

PARALYSIS OF SPHINCTER (Op.): Paralytic affection of sphincter vesical, manifested by incontinence, involuntary or dribbling of urination.

PARAPHYMOSIS (Mer.s.): Constriction or strangulation of the glans penis, due to retraction of narrowed or inflamed foreskin.

PARCHMENT (Ars., Sabad.): Extremely dry or thin piece (like membrane of skin).

PARESIS (Op., Psor., Rhus.): Partial or incomplete paralysis; often used alone to mean general paresis.

PARONYCHIA (Dios.): (Syn. *Felon, Whitlow*) Inflammation involving the folds of tissue surrounding the fingernail. (The term, years ago, was considered synonymous with whitlow, felon, panaritium, but today has a different meaning. Here the fold of the nail is damaged and the cuticle is lost. Bacteria, yeasts, etc. can enter the pocket between the nail fold and nail plate, producing chronic infections such as *Candida albicans*. The area is tender. Malformations and hyper-pigmentation of the nail can occur.)

PAROTID GLAND (Merc.p.iod.): The largest of the salivary glands, located below and in front of the ear.

PAROXYSM (Ambr., Apoc., Cact., Caps., Caul., Cina., Cinch., Con., Crot.t., Cup., Dios., Dros., Lach., Nat.m., Pod., Ran.b., Sabad., Sab., Samb., Tab.): A sudden, periodic attack or recurrence of symptoms of a disease such as the chills and rigor of malaria; a sharp spasm or convulsion.

> **SPASMODIC PAROXYSM (Sabad.):** Recurrent attacks of spasms or convulsions.

PARTURITION (Caul., Kali br., Pod., Rhus.): The act or process of giving birth to a child; childbirth.

PASSION (Nat.m.): A powerful emotion or its expression, esp. the emotion of love, anger, or hate.

PAVED STREETS (Nit. ac.)/ PAVEMENTS (Calc.): A footway, by the side of a street (footpath).

PEACHES (All.c.): A round fruit of a tree, *Prunuspersica* with sweet, juicy, yellow flesh, soft red and yellow skin, and a large seed in its center.

PEARLS (Nat.m.): Smooth, rounded concretions of aragonite or calcite with conchiolin, formed within the shells of certain mollusks to enclose irritating foreign objects, and valued as a gem when lustrous and finely coloured.

PEARS (Puls.): A sweet, juicy, yellow or green fruit with a round base and slightly pointed top and belongs to genus *Pyrus*, especially *P.communis*.

PEDICULATED (Staph.): Provided with a pedicle or stem. Pedicle means a foot-like, stem-like, or narrow basal part or structure, as the stalk by which a non-sessile tumour is attached to normal tissue, or the narrow strip of flap tissue, through which it receives its blood supply

PEDUNCULATED (Caust., Nit.ac., Thuja.): Same as the meaning of pediculated.

PEELS OFF (Tereb.): (Syn. *Desquamation*) Shedding of the surface layer of the skin.

PEEVISH (Ant.c., Ars., Cham., Cyc., Hep.s., Lyc., Med., Mur. ac., Rheum., Tub.): Easily annoyed by unimportant things; discontent, obstinate, ill tempered.

PELVIC CELLULITIS (Med.): Inflammation of cellular or connective tissue in pelvic region.

PENDENTS SHREDS (Aur.): A scrap, or torn small pieces, (esp. narrow and long pieces, as of cloth or leather) hanging or suspended.

PENETRATING (Calen., Merc.s., Ther.): Having the power of entering, piercing or pervading into or through something; shrill.

PERCEIVE (Ign.): To become or be aware of through the senses; to get knowledge of by the mind.

PERCEPTION (Phos., Plb.): An awareness or consciousness of things through the senses; the observation or receipt of sensory information.

PERCEPTIBLE (Camph.): That can be seen, heard, felt, tasted, smelled, or noticed.

PERFORATING (Mur.ac.): Making an opening in a hollow organ or viscus.

PERIODIC (Cact., Chel., Cina., Cup.m.): Recurrence at regular intervals of time.

PERIODICITY (Cinch.): The state of being regularly recurrent.

PERIOSTEUM (Mez.): The thick fibrous membrane covering the entire surface of a bone except its articular surface. Its outer fibrous layer furnishes attachment for muscles and inner layer furnishes osteoblasts and contains blood vessels by which bone is nourished.

PERIOSTITIS (Ruta.): Inflammation of the periosteum characterised by pain, fever, sweat, leucocytosis and rigidity of overlying muscle.

PERISTALTIC (Anac.): The worm-like movement of the intestine or other tubular structure; a wave of alternate circular contraction and relaxation of the tube by which the contents are propelled onward.

PERNICIOUS (Nat.s., Pic. ac., Ver.): Injurious, hurtful; causing great harm, destructive; deadly or fatal.

PERSISTENT (Nat.m., Pyr.): Existing or happening continuously or for a long time; tenacious of position or purpose.

PERSPIRATION (Aloe., Med., Mer.): Sweating; the excretion of fluid by the sweat gland of the skin. It consists of water containing NaCl, phosphates, urea, ammonia, creatinine, fat and other waste products.

PERSPIRE (Nux m.): To produce or excrete sweat on the body.

PERTUSSIS (Caust., Carbo v., Cina., Dros., Euph., Lob., Vario.): (Syn. *Whooping cough*) An acute infectious disease caused by *Bordetella pertussis*, and marked by recurrent attack of spasmodic coughing continued until the breath is exhausted, then ending with a deep noisy inspiration producing a "whoop" sound.

PERVERSION (Petros.): A deviation from the normal course; (A morbid alteration of function which may occur in emotional, intellectual. Or it can be psychiatric or sexual deviation).

PERVERTED (Petros.): One who practices perversion.

PESSARIES (Nux m.): An instrument inserted into the vagina to support the uterus or to correct any displacement.

PETECHIA (Sul. ac.): A pinpoint to pinhead size, not raised, perfectly round, purplish red spot on the skin caused by intradermal or sub mucous haemorrhage.

PETTISH (Fer.): Peevish, petulant, childishly bad tempered or impatient, especially about unimportant things; irritable.

PETULANT (Cham., Nit. ac., Staph., Thuja.): Peevish; irritable; fretful; bad tempered and unreasonable angry.

PHAGEDENIC ULCERATION (Mer.cy.): Rapidly spreading destructive eroding ulceration.

PHLEBITIS (All.c., Ham.): Inflammation of a vein

PHLEGM: Thick, viscid, stringy mucus, secreted by the mucosa of the upper air passages; one of the four humors of humoral theory of medicine.

PHLEGMATIC HABBIT (Aloe., Ant.t.): Sluggish or dull temperament; apathetic (one who is not easily excited to action or display or emotion).

PHLEGMONOUS (Graph.): Related to inflammation of the subcutaneous connective tissues.

PHOTOPHOBIA (Con., Nat.s., Psor.): Abnormal intolerance or sensitiveness of light; morbid dread of light.

PHTHISIS (Acet.ac., Diph., Dros., Mill., Phos.ac., Puls., Ruta., Sang., Trill.): A progressive wasting disease of the body. An old term for consumption or tuberculosis of lungs with subsequent emaciation and loss of strength.

    LARYNGEAL PHTHISIS (Dros.): Tuberculosis of the larynx.

PHTHISIS FLORIDA (Ther.): Acute fulminant tuberculosis, galloping consumption. An active case of tuberculosis or consumption of the lungs.

PHYMOSIS (Mer. s.): Stenosis or narrowness of the opening of the prepuce so that the foreskin cannot be pushed back over the glans penis.

PHYSOMETRA (Brom., Lyc., Nux m.): Distension of the uterine cavity with air or gas and subsequent passing of gas or flatus through vagina.

PICKS (Cina, Hell., Hyos., Op.): Remove or pull something from a place with fingers or hand.

PILES (Collin., Ham., Ign., Lach., Lyc., Nit.ac., Sulph., Thuja.): Haemorrhoids.

PIMPLES (Con., Hep., Led.): A papule or pustule of the skin especially seen in adolescent.

PINCHED (Sec., Tab.): Pale and thin, anxious, especially because of illness, cold or worry.

PINNING BOYS (Aur.): Boys with lean, thin, emaciated look who are low in energy, avoiding physical and mental exertion.

PITEOUS (Cham.): Pitiable; exciting pity or compassionate; sad.

PITIFUL (Cina., Plat.): Full of pity; tender hearted; eliciting compassion; lamentable.

PIT OF STOMACH (Calc., Tab.): The depression at the end of the xiphoid process.

PLETHORA (Acon., Aloe., Cact.): Over fullness of blood vessels or of the total quantity of any fluid in the body.

PLETHORIC (Amyl., Calc., Glon., Kali br., Sulph., Zinc.): Pertaining to or characterized by plethora.

PLETHORIC HABIT (Acon., Cact., Caps.): Tendency of a person to develop plethora easily.

PLEURISY (Abrot., Carbo an., Ran.b., Sabad.): Inflammation of the pleura with or without effusion marked by pain in chest or side, fever, etc.; may be primary or secondary; unilateral, bilateral, or local; acute or chronic; fibrinous, serofibrinous, or purulent; pleuritis.

PLICA POLONICA (Psor., Tub.): A matted condition of the hair caused by filth and the presence of parasites.

PLUGGED (Anac.): A mass obstructing a hole or intended to close an orifice.

PNEUMOGASTRIC NERVE (Agar.): Vagus nerve; 10th pair of cranial nerve supplying mainly lungs and stomach. It is a mixed nerve having both motor and sensory function.

PNEUMONIA (Ant.t., Chel., Hyos., Lyc., Ran.b., Sang., Sulph.): A disease characterized by inflammation of the lung with exudation into the lung tissue and resulting solidification of the tissue; pneumonitis.

> **MALTREATED PNEUMONIA (Lyc.):** Pneumonia which is not properly or wrongly treated resulting in incomplete healing or suppression.
>
> **NEGLECTED PNEUMONIA (Carbo v., Lyc.):** A case of pneumonia in which the proper treatment was delayed or was not treated at all due to negligence
>
> **SYCOTIC PNEUMONIA (Nat.s.):** Pneumonia having sycotic base or sycotic background.

POLYPI (Mer.s., Thuja., Sang.): (Pl. of *Polypus*)*Polyp* means a morbid excrescence, or protruding growth, from mucous membrane, commonly found in vascular organs such as the nose, uterus, colon and rectum.

PORK (Puls.): Meat from swine eaten as food.

PORTAL CIRCULATION (Aloe.): Blood flow from the abdominal organ that passes through portal vein, the sinusoids of the liver and into the hepatic vein before returning to the heart from the inferior vena cava.

PORTAL CONGETION (Collin.): The accumulation of an abnormal amount of blood in the portal system.

PORTAL SYSTEM (Sulph.): A system of vessels in which blood passes through a capillary network, large vessels, and then another capillary network before returning to the systemic circulation.

POST CLIMACTERIC (Agar): Occurring after menopause.

POST MORTEM (Lach.): Medical examination performed after death in order to find out the cause of the death; autopsy; necropsy.

POSTERIOR NARES (Ant.c., Hydr, Med., Nat.c.): The posterior opening of the nasal fossa on either side.

POST-PARTUM (Nit. ac., Op.): After childbirth or after delivery. **POTBELLIEDNESS (Sep.):** Deposition of adipose tissue (fat) in the abdominal subcutaneous tissue. Common in middle-aged persons of sedentary habits.

POULTICES (Am.c.): A hot, moist, usually medicated mass that is placed between cloth sheets and applied to the skin to relieve pain, soothe injured tissues, stimulate the circulation and act as a counterirritant.

POURING AWAY (Phos.): To making a liquid or other substance flow in a continuous stream.

PRAYING (Stram.): To make supplication to God; to ask someone to do something.

PRECEDED (Aloe., Mill., Phos.): To be, go, or come before in arrangement or sequence or in order of time; to be earlier than.

PRECISELY (Ign.): Of a clearly determined manner; exactly.

PRECOCIOUS (Tub.): Exceptionally early or prematurely development; Mental or physical development earlier than would be expected.

PREDISPOSING (Lyc.): Conferring a tendency to disease; making susceptible to a disease; previous inclination, tendency, or propensity.

PRETTY (Sulph.): Look nice and attractive.

PREGNANCY (Act., Alum., Apoc.): The condition of having a developing embryo or fetus in the body after successful conception. The average duration of it is 280 days; gestation; gravidity.

PREJUDICE (Lac c.): To prepossess with opinion formed without due knowledge or examination; to bias the mind.

PREMATURE OLD AGE (Fluor.ac.): Looking like old person at young age.

PREPUCE (Thuja.): The fore skin or fold of skin over the glans penis in male.

PRESERVE (Hyper.): To keep in existence or intact; to save from decomposition, as by refrigeration, curing, or treating with a preservative.

PRESSED ASUNDER (Asar.): Pressed into parts or apart.

PREVENTING (Aloe., Sep., Vario.): Stopping of something from happening or someone from doing something; hindering the progress, appearance, or fulfilment of.

PRIAPISM (Canth., Pic.ac., Sel.): Persistent abnormal erection of the penis, usually without sexual desire, and accompanied by pain and tenderness. It is seen in diseases and injuries of the spinal cord, and may be caused by vesical calculus and certain injuries to the penis and due to excess androgen.

PRIDE (Staph.): Quality or state of being proud; inordinate self-esteem; an unreasonable conceit of superiority in talents, beauty, wealth, rank, etc.

PROFUSE (Mer., Nat.c., Nat.m., Nux., Sab., Sanic., Sec.,): In large amounts; excessive.

PROGRESSIVE (Lyc., Sanic.): Continuous or gradually advancing; unfavourable course.

PROJECTED (Apoc.): To stick out above or beyond the edge or surface.

PROLAPSE (Helon., Ign., Mur.ac., Nat.m., Sep.): The falling down, or dropping down of an organ or internal part (such as the uterus or rectum).

> **PROLAPSE ANI:** The falling downward or displacement downward of the anus (proctoptosia).
>
> **PROLAPSE OFRECTUM (Fer., Ign., Med., Pod., Ruta., Stan., Tab.):** Protrusion of the rectal mucosa or full thickness of rectum (procedentia).
>
> **PROLAPSUS (Sep.):** Prolapse.
>
> **PROLAPSUS UTERI (Aesc., Agar., Arg.m., Kali bi., Lys., Pod.):** The dropping down of the uterus into the vagina resulting from laxity and atony of the muscular and fascial structures of the pelvic floor, usually resulting from injuries of childbirth or advanced age.

PROLONG (Nat.m., Sec.): To lengthen in time; to extend the duration; to draw out; to continue.

PROMOTES (Sab., Sil.): To contribute to the growth, enlargement of something in course; to advance from a given grade or course.

PROMPTLY (Lac d., Stram.): Done quickly and without delay, or acting quickly or arriving at an arranged time.

PRONE TO (Anac.): Having a tendency, propensity, or inclination; predisposed to.

PROPHETIC PERCEPTION (Lach.): Power of predicting or understanding what will be happening in future as is found in prophets.

PROPHYLACTIC (Diph., Mer. cy., Tereb.): An agent or regimen that contribute to the prevention of infection and disease.

PROSOPALGIA (Spig.): Neuralgic pain in face, the course of trigeminal nerve and its branches.

PROSTRATIC FLUID (Sel.): A thinurethral discharge coming from the penis, originating from the prostate.

PROSTRATITIS (Thuja.): Inflammation of the prostate gland.

PROSTRATING (Phos.ac., Sulph.): Exhausting.

PROSTRATION (Abrot., Aeth., Aloe., Amyl., Anthr., Ant.t., Camph., Ver.): Extreme exhaustion or powerlessness or weakness or lack of energy mental or physical.

PROTRACTED (Caul., Helon., Kreos., Lac d., Mill., Murex., Puls., Sab., Sulph.): Lasts a long time, especially longer than the usual time.

PROTRUDE (Lach., Lyc., Med., Mur.ac., Rat., Sanic.): To project outward; to thrust or push out or forward; to obtrude.

PROTRUDES AND RECEDS (Op.): To project or push forward and move back away into the former position.

PROUD (Plat.): Feeling or manifesting pride; possessing or showing too great self-esteem; arrogant; haughty.

PROVOCATIVE (Lac c.): That which excites, provoke or stimulate; stimulating.

PROVOKE (Taren.): Excite or call into action, stimulate; bring about; to excite with anger or sexual desire; to annoy or exasperate.

PRURITUS (Calad., Collin., Hydr, Mer., Plat.): Itching.

> **PRURITUS VULVAE (Med., Taren.):** Itching of the external genital organ.

PRUSSIC ACID (Camph.): Hydrocyanic acid, hydrogen cyanide. This acid exists in a great variety of combination in the vegetable kingdom as in bitter almond, cherry laurel, kernels of fruits. This rapidly acting poison speedily undergoes decomposition.

PSEUDO (Mur.ac.): Pretended; false; closely resembling.

PSEUDOMEMBRANOUS (Kallbi.): A leaf or shelf-like exudate made of inflammatory debris and fibrin that may form on epithelial surfaces like a false membrane, found in such as pharyngitis caused by *Corynebacterium diphtheria*in Diphtheria.

PSORA (Thuja.): One of the three fundamental miasms of Hahnemann responsible for occurrence of true chronic diseases with primary manifestations.

PSORIC AFFECTION (Kali bi., Kreos.): Persons affected due to psora.

PSORIC CHILDREN (Hell.): Children with prominent psoric constitution.

PSORIC DISEASE (Sulph.): Diseases caused by psora.

PSORIC PERSON (Cal ars., Caust., Diph.): Persons who may or may not manifest the secondary manifestations of psora, but with significant presence of latent manifestations of psora.

PSORIC PATIENT (Mer.s., Psor.): Persons manifesting pathological diseased symptoms (hence they are patient) which have their origin in psora.

PTOMAINE (Pyr.): One of a nonspecific and vague class of toxic (nitrogenous organic) bases of unpleasant taste and odour formed by the action of putrefactive bacteria on proteins and amino acidsand formerly thought to cause food poisoning.

PTOSIS (Caust., Rhus., Syph.): Drooping of an organ or part, as the upper eyelid from paralysis of the levatorpalpebrae muscle due to affection of third cranial nerve or from sympathetic innervation or the visceral organ from weakness of the abdominal muscle.

PTYALISM (Dul., Kreos., Mer. s.): (Syn. *Xerostomia)* Excessive secretion of saliva, seen in chronic mercury poisoning, pregnancy, stomatitis, rabies, epilepsy, etc.

PUBERTY (Cal.p., Caul., Graph., Hell., Lyc., Puls., Ther.): The stage of life at which both the sexes become functionally capable of reproduction. The changes occur between the ages of 13 to 15 years in boys and 9 to 16 years in girls.

PUBLIC SPEAKERS (Arg.m.): A person who gives a speech at a public event.

PUCKER (Hydr): To draw up into folds or wrinkles.

PUDENDA (Kreos.): The external genital organs, especially of female.

PUERPERAL (All.c., Hyos., Pyr.): Relating to puerperium, the period from the termination of labor to complete involution of the uterus, usually defined as 6 weeks.

> **PUERPERAL CONVULSION (Amyl.):** Puerperal eclampsia; convulsion occurring immediately after childbirth.

PUERPERAL MANIA (Act.): A form of mental disorder marked by excessive excitement, passion, elevation of mood, and psychomotor over activity following childbirth.

PUFFY (Apis., Med., Op., Phos.): Distended, inflated; swollen.

PULSATING (Pyr.): Characterized by rhythmic beat.

PULSATIONS (Lil.): A throb or rhythmical beat, as of the heart.

PULSE (Ant.t., Apoc.): It is the lateral expansion of the arterial wall imparted by the column of arterial blood due to contraction of the left ventricle.

PUNGENT (Caps.): Very strong, sharp in smell or taste, sometimes unpleasant.

PUNY (Lyc., Mag.m.): Small or inferior (as in power, significance etc.); Stunted; Feeble.

PURGATIVE (Nux., Op.): Cathartic, an agent that will stimulate the production of bowel movements.

PURGING (Ver.): Causing a free evacuation of the bowel by cathartics.

PURPLE (Phyt.): A colour formed by mixture of the blue and red, between crimson or violet.

PURPURA HAEMORRHAGICA (Crot., Sul.ac., Tereb.): A disease characterized by small haemorrhagic spots in the skin or mucous membrane due to petechial haemorrhage without any injury, with bleeding from the mucous membranes and great tiredness and prostration. It is a systemic disease in which there is reduction in the number of platelets in the blood.

PURRING (Pyr.): Making a soft, low, continuous, vibratory sound.

PURSUING (Anac.): To follow with enmity; to follow eagerly, or with haste; to follow with a view to overtake.

PURULENT (Arg.n., Dros., Trill.): Consisting of or containing pus; associated with the formation of or caused by pus.

PUS (Calen., Can.s., Kali c., Mer., Mez., Nat.s.): A protein rich fluid containing white blood cells, specially neutrophils, and cell debris and tissue elements liquefied by proteolytic and histolytic enzyme commonly caused by infection with pyogenic bacteria such as streptococcus, staphylococcus, etc.

PUSH (Staph.): To put a continuing force against something to cause it to move forward or away from body.

PUSILLANIMOUS (Lyc.): Wanting firmness of mind; mean spirited; cowardly.

PUSTULE (Cic., Hep., Kali bi.): A small elevated skin lesion filled with lymph or pus.

PUTRESCENCE (Sec., Trill.): Rottenness; decay.

PUTRID (Am.c., Carb.ac., Chel., Colch., Mer.cy., Mer.dul., Sec., Stan., Thuja.): Rotten or decayed.

PYROSIS (Bis., Nux.): Heartburn; water-brash; a burning sensation in the epigastric, sternal region or in the throat with raising of sour, acid liquid from the stomach.

QUACK (Nux.): One who fraudulently misrepresents his ability and experience in the diagnosis and treatment of disease or the effects to be achieved by the treatment he offers; a pretender to medical knowledge or skill.

QUACK REMEDIES (Nux., Psor.): A remedy used by quacks.

QUARRELSOME (Con., Fer., Ign., Nux., Petr.): Argumentative; likes arguing or often starts arguing to be unfriendly, angry or violently disputative.

QUININE (Nat.m.): A white, flaky, odourless bitter powder, very slightly soluble in water. It is the most important of the alkaloids derived from cinchona and an effective anti-malarial.

QUICK TEMPERED (Sulph.): Easily angered.

QUINSY (Bar., Benz.ac., Hep., Psor.): Peri-tonsillar abscess; extension of tonsillar infection beyond the capsule with abscess formation usually above and behind the tonsil due to bacterial inflammation.

RABID (Lys.): Having rabies i.e. a highly fatal infectious disease transmitted almost exclusively by the bite of carnivorous animals (dogs, cats, wolves etc.) characterised by profound disturbance of nervous system, excitement, aggressiveness, and madness and followed by paralysis and death.

RACHITIC (Clc. Phos., Mag. m., Sil.) Pertaining to or affected with rickets i.e. a disease of bone formation of children, most commonly the results of vitamin D deficiency, marked by inadequate mineralization of developing cartilage and newly formed bone, causing abnormalities in the shape, structure and strength of the skeleton.

RACHITIS (Cal.p., Cic., Mag.m., Med., Phos., Phos.ac., Sil., Ther.): Rickets.

RAGE (Apis., Croc., Hyos., Lac c): A state of violent anger.

RAKES (Coc.): A debauched, immoral man or dissolute person, an idler or loafer.

RANULA (Ambr., Thuja): A small, soft, fluctuating, cystic and semi-transparent tumour which forms under the tongue on either side of the fraenum; a retention cyst of the submandibular or sublingual ducts.

RASH (Dul., Sars.,): (Syn. *Exanthem*) A general term for any cutaneous eruption, that may be localized or generalized.

RASPING (Spong.): A harsh, rough grating sound or feeling.

RATTLING (Brom., Hep., Ipec., Kali bi., Kali c., Spong.): Coarse, crackling sound in the chest due to excessive airway secretions.

RATTLE OF WAGON (Nit.ac.): A sharp, clattering sounds produced by wagon (strong vehicle with four wheels, usually pulled by horses or oxen, for carrying heavy loads) when going through the streets.

RAVE (Agar., Stram.): To talk as if mad; to talk wildly or incoherently or irrationally.

RAW (Aesc., All. c., Arg. m., Arg.n., Calc., Canth., Caust., Ham., Lac c., Mer., Mer.s., Nat.m., Nit.ac., Phos., Tar., Tub.,): Not processed or treated; in or nearly in its natural state or condition; crude; deprived of skin; a sensitive spot; not cooked.

REACTIVE FORCE (Caps.): The physical, often violent, strength or power to react any stimulus.

REACTIVE POWER (Sulph.): Same as the reactive force.

RECEDES (Sanic., Sil., Thuja.): Moves back away into the former position.

RECOVARY (Psor.): Restoration from sickness, weakness, or the like, or from a condition of misfortune, fright, evil force, depression, etc.

RECTUM (Aesc.): The lower part of the large intestine, about 5 inch long, between the sigmoid colon and anal canal.

RECUMBENT POSITION (Acon.): Lying down, wholly or partly; reclining.

RED STRAND (Canth.): Strand is a single, thin length of wire, thread etc., especially as twisted together with others; an element that parts of complex whole. It denotes here an important unit within a large structural whole. The use of the word red strand in this context denotes guiding symptom.

REFLEX (Act., Caust., Kali br., Lac.d.): A reaction; an involuntary movement of exercise of function in a part, excited in response to a stimulus applied to the periphery and transmitted to the nervous center in the brain or spinal cord.

REFLEX SYMPTOM (Act., Caul.): A symptom occurring in a part remote from that which is affected by the disease.

REFRACTION (Ruta.): Deflection from a straight part, as of light rays as they pass through media of different densities; the act of determining the nature and the degree of the refractive errors in the eye and correction of the same by lenses.

REFRACTORY (Caps.): Resistant to ordinary treatment; not yielding to stimulus; obstinate.

REFRESHING THINGS (Phos., Ver.): Vigour restoring things; things (food) which revives, freshen up and gives energy.

REGURGITATION (Aeth., Fer., Phos.,): A backward flowing, as the casting up of undigested food to the mouth from the stomach, or the backward flowing of blood into the heart, or between the chambers of the heart when a valve is incompetent.

RELAPSE (Phos.ac.): Recurrence of a disease or symptoms after apparent recovery.

RELAPSING (Sulph.): Recurring, said of a disease returns in new attack after convalescence has begun.

RELAXATION OF STOMACH (Tab.): Dilatation or lengthening or lessening of tension of stomach.

RELIGIOUS (Ver.): Manifesting devotion to, or the influence of religion; concerned with religion; belonging to or followed by an order of religious monk.

RELIGIOUS MELANCHOLY (Melil., Psor.): Extreme depression and sadness associated with brooding over religious matter.

RELISH (Cic.): To eat or drink with pleasure and gratification; a characteristic flavour, especially pleasing or zestful flavour.

RENDERED (Acon, Lys., Op.): Surrendering; giving or submitting for approval.

RENEWED (Cac., Chel., Cic., Chin., Stram.): To begin again; to recommence; to resume; to come back, as to a fresh attack.

REPOSE (Mag.c., Nux m., Rhus.): Tolay in a position of rest; to lie at rest.

REPRESS (Lil.): To keep under restrain or control; to block the expression; suppress.

REPRIMANDS (Graph., Ign., Stram.): Toscold or correct angrily, specially publicly or officially.

REPUGNANT (Cyc., Nux., Rheum.): Offensive to taste or feeling.

RESEMBLES (Acon., Nit.ac., Sec.): To be like; to be like each other.

RESERVED DISPLEASURE (Aur., Ign., Lyc., Nat.m., Staph.): An annoyance or displeasure or dislike which has not been expressed.

RESPIRATION (Ant.t.): Act or process of breathing i.e. inhalation and expiration.

DEFFECTIVE RESPIRATION (Ant.t.): Impaired respiration due to any respiratory disease.

    SAWING RESPIRATION (Iod.): Sound of respiration as like produced of by cutting a wood.

WHEEZING RESPIRATION (Iod.): To breathe with a husky, whistling sound.

RESTLESS (Acon., Nat.c., Tar., Mur.ac., Phos.): Deprived of rest or sleep; uneasy; characterized by or manifesting unrest, especially of mind.

RESTORATIVE (Pic.ac.): A remedy that aids in restoring health, strength, or consciousness.

RESUSCITATION (Amyl.): Restoration to life after apparent death.

RETAIN (Apis., Bis., Chel., Op., Pyr., Ruta., Sab., Stram., Sulph.): To hold or continue to hold in possession or use; to keep as in fixed place or condition.

RETAINED PLACENTA (Sab., Stram.): The placenta is said to be retained when it is not expelled out even 30 minutes after the birth of the baby.

RETARDED (Graph., Plb.): Slow in development or progress; to delay or impede the progress, course, or event of something.

RETARDED EMISSION (Nat.m.): Delayed or impeded, slow seminal emission.

RETCHING (Dros.): Make an unsuccessful effort to vomit.

RETENTION (Can. Ind., Hyos., Op., Tereb.): The persistent keeping within the body of materials normally excreted, such as urine, faeces; memory or recall.

RETIRING (Mag. c., Mer. cor., Nux., Zinc.): To go to bed; to go into retreat.

RETRACTED (Ver.v.): Shortened; drawn backward; shrinked.

RETRACTION (Cup., Sars.): A shortening; the act of drawing backward or the condition of being drawn back.

RETROCESSON (Op.): Going backward; metastasis of a condition from the surface to internal organs.

RETROVERSION (Lil.): The displacement of an entire organ backward; bending backward of uterus and cervix.

RHAGADES (Sars.): Fissures, cracks, or fine linear scars in the skin, especially such lesions around the mouth, anus or other regions subjected to frequent movement. Such cracks are usually painful.

RHEUMATIC CARDITIS (Naja.): Inflammation of cardiac tissue as a result of acute rheumatic fever, characterized by formation of Aschoff bodies in the cardiac interstitial tissue, may be associated with acute cardiac failure, endocarditis with small fibrin vegetation on the margin of closure of valve cusps on fibrinous pericarditis.

RHEUMATISM (Abrot., Act., Cal. p., Caul., Caust., Colch., Dulc., Kali bi., Kal., Led., Med., Nux.m., Phyt., Rhod., Sars.,): Any of a variety of disorders marked by inflammation, degeneration, or metabolic derangement of the connective tissue structures of the body, especially the joints and related structures, including muscle, bursa, tendons and fibrous tissue and attended by pain, stiffness, or limitation of motion. It may be acute or chronic.

ACUTE RHEUMATISM (Ver.v.): Acute and severe pain and inflammation of the joints and other connective tissue of the body.

ARTICULAR RHEUMATISM (Ham.): Inflammation and pain of joints only.

CATARRHAL RHEUMATISM (Dulc.): Pain and inflammation of joints associated with excessive discharge from serous membrane.

INTERCOSTAL RHEUMATISM (Ran.b): Rheumaticpain, tenderness. Soreness and spasm of intercostal muscles.

MUSCULAR RHEUMATISM (Ham.): One of several muscular conditions marked by tenderness, soreness, pain and local spasm, including fibromyalgia, myositis, polymyalgia and torticollis.

RIDING (Nit.ac., Nux.m): Travelling on horse-back, carriage on car.

RIGG'S DISEASE: Progressive necrosis of alveoli and looseness of the teeth.

RIGID (Acon., Act., Caul., Caust., Con., Cup., Nit.ac., Plat.): Inflexibly fixed or set in opinion, conduct, etc.; unyielding; not lax or indulgent.

RINGING (Acon., Chin., Fer., Spong.): The sound clearly and resonantly, as a bell or other metallic sonorous body.

RING WORM (Nat.m., Sanic., Tub.): (Syn. *Tinea*) Contagious skin affection caused by fungi of the genera *Mycrosporum* or *Trichophyton* characterized by well-defined red rash, with an elevated, wavy or worm shaped border.

RIPPLES (Sulph.): A small wave or undulation on the surface of water or any liquid.

RISUS SARDONICUS (Stram.): Abnormal sustained spasm of the facial muscle that appears to produce a grinning usually occurring in tetanus.

ROARING (Ign., Kreos.): Any loud, rough, whistling sound as of wind or waves, caused by unilateral or bilateral paralysis of certain laryngeal muscles due to injury of the recurrent laryngeal nerve.

ROBUST (Cinch., Colch., Samb.): Stout, strong, and sturdy; constitutionally healthy; vigorous; thick-set; characterized by great strength and endurance.

ROCKING (Kali. c.): To sway to and fro, tilt from side to side.

ROLLING (Hell., Lach., Pod., Zinc.): Rotating on or as if on an axis, or moving along a surface by rotation.

ROSE COLD (Sang.): Allergic rhinitis (inflammation of nasal mucous membrane) occurring in spring and in early summer.

ROTTEN (Cham., Mag.m): Putrid; decayed;

ROUGHNESS (Aecs.): Coarseness; not even or smooth.

ROUSE (Kreos., Sulph.): To wake up from sleep or repose; to excite to physical, mental or spiritual activity from a state of idealness, languor.

ROWING (Rhus.): An act of rowing, i.e. using oars, sweeps in propelling a boat.

RUB (All. c., Cina., Crot.t. Sec., Zinc): To cause a body to move with pressure and friction along a surface.

RUDDY (Aur.): Red; reddish; the colour of the skin in high health.

RUMBLING (Alum., Crot.t., Graph.): A low, heavy, continuous rolling sound

S

SACCHARINE (Helon.): Relating to or containing sugar.

SADDLE (Sep.): Flattened bridge of the nose;leather seat for riding on horse.

SADNESS (Ambr. Ant.c., Caust., Coca., Cyc., Graph., Lach., Nat.s., Phos.ac., Plat.): Feeling unhappy or sorrowful; expressing or suggesting unhappiness.

SAGO LIKE PARTICLES (Phos.): Particles like sago that is the grain substance obtained from the trunk of a type of palm tree, used for making sweet pudding.

SALIVATION (Acet.ac., Lac.ac., Mer.s.): The secretion of saliva especially in excess often accompanied with soreness of mouth and gums. (*saliva*: the enzyme containing secretion of salivary glands).

SALPINGITIS (Med.): Inflammation of the Fallopian tube or sometime that of the Eustachian tube also.

SALVATION (Lil., Psor.): Liberation or saving of man from the influence of sin, and its consequences for his soul; the act of saving them from harm, destruction, or an unpleasant situation.

SANDY HAIR (Puls.): Light orange-brown coloured hair.

SANGUINE MAN (Ign.): The person having excess amount of blood, plethoric; having a red complexion, light hair and eyes and a quick but not lasting temper.

SANIOUS (Phyt.): Thin and seropurulent, with a slightly bloody tinge.

SANIOUS LIQUID BLOOD (Sec.): Thin, foetid, seropurulent bloody discharge from wound or ulcer.

SAPRAEMIA (Pyr.): (Syn. *Septicaemia*)A toxic state resulting from the presence in the blood of toxic products of putrefactive bacteria and often accompanying gangrene of a part of the body.

SATIETY (Cyc., Lyc., Nat.s., Plat.): Sufficiency, or satisfaction as full gratification of appetite or thirst, with abolition of the desire to ingest food or liquids; excessive gratification of a desire.

SATYRIASIS (Pic.ac.): Abnormal, excessive, insatiable sexual desire in the male.

SAUSAGE (Ars., Puls.): A mass of chopped or minced seasoned meat, especially pork or beef, sometimes mixed with fat, cereal, vegetables, etc., and stuffed into a tube of gut.

SAVIN (Sab.): The evergreen shrub, juniperus Sabina. The leaves and tops afford acrid volatile oil, which is used in dysmenorrhoea, gout, and rheumatism, and is used locally as an application to ulcers, condylomas, and carious teeth

SCABIES (Caust.): A contagious infestation of the skin with the itch mite, Sarcpotesscabiei, female of the species burrows into the skin, typically presents as an intensely pruritic rash, composed of scaly papules, insect burrows and secondarily infected lesions distributed in the webs between fingers and on the waistline, trunk (esp. the axillae), penis, and arms. It readily spreads in households, among playmates and between sexual partners- that is among people having close physical contact.

SCABS (Cic., Mez.): A crust formed by coagulation of blood, pus, serum or a combination of these, on the surface of an ulcer, erosion or other type of wound.

SCALES (Graph., Tub.): A small dry flake, shed from the upper layers of skin. Some shedding of skin is normal, increases in diseases like pityriasisrosea, psoriasis, teniapedis etc.

SCALDS (Apis., Caust., Psor., Sulph., Ver.v.): Injure or burn with hot liquid or steam.

SCALY (Psor., Sanic.): Covered or abounding with scales or scale.

SCAR (Calen., Graph., Kali br.): (Syn. *Cicatrix*) A mark left in the skin or an internal organ by the healing of a wound, sore or injury or surgical operation because of replacement by connective tissue of the injured tissue.

SCARCELY (Alum., Camph., Kal., Ver., Thlaspi.): Only just; hardly ever; not really.

SCARLATINA (Am.c., Apis., Apoc., Camph., Crot., Dig., Hell., Hyos., Mur.ac., Psor., Sang., Tereb.): Scarlet fever; an acute exanthematous disease, caused by bacterial infection and marked by fever and other constitutional disturbances and a generalized eruptions of closely aggregated points or small macules of a bright red colour followed by desquamation.

SCARLET RED (Arg.n., Bell.): Deep red.

SCARMBLED EGGS (Sanic.): To cook an egg by mixing white and yellow parts together and heating them, sometimes with butter and milk.

SCIATICA (Coloc., Rhus., Staph., Val.): Intense and intermittent pain in the lower back, buttocks and backs of the thighs caused by compression, inflammation or reflex mechanism of the sciatic nerve or due to herniated lumber discs.

SCIRRHOUS (Apis., Med., Spig.): A hard swelling, especially a hard cancer; obsolete term for any fibrous indurated area, especially an indurated carcinoma.

SCIRRHOUS CARCINOMA (Med.): (Syn. *Fibrocarcinoma*) A hard cancer in which induration has occurred through overgrowth of fibrous connective tissue in the stroma.

SCLEROSIS (Plb.): Pathological hardening of chronic inflammatory origin, especially, of nerves and other structures by hyperplasia of interstitial fibrous connective tissues.

SCOLDED (Ign.): Person who have been criticized angrily due to anything donewrong.

SCORBUTIC (Kreos.): Pertaining to or affected with scurvy, a disease caused by inadequate intake of ascorbic acid marked by fatigue, anemia, bleeding in the skin, gum and in the joints, a spongy condition sometimes with ulceration of the gums, impaired wound healing, dry skin, oedema of lower extremities, follicular hyperkeratosis and coiling of body hairs.

SCORBUTIC CACHEXIA (Staph.): A general emaciation occurring when suffering from scurvy.

SCRAMBLED EGGS (Sanic.): Eggs of which the whites and yolks are stirred together while cooking or eggs beaten slightly, often with a little milk and stirred while cooking.

SCRAPED (Phos.ac.): To remove something by rubbing something rough or sharp against it, or to rub any part of the body against something rough that tears away or injures the skin.

SCRAPING (Canth., Carb.ac.): A small amount of something produced by scratching a surface.

SCRAPINGS OF INTESTINE (Ant.c., Colch.): Decidual products of intestine.

SCRAPINGS OF MUCUS MEMBRANE (Carb.ac.): Decidual products of mucous membrane.

SCRATCH (Alum., Sulph.): To draw a sharp or pointed object across a surface, causing damage or making marks; to rub the skin with the fingernails, especially to relieve itching.

SCRAWNY (Arg.n., Sec.): Unhealthily thin and bony; ill-nourished.

SCREAM (Acon., Apis., Co., Colch., Hell., Kali br., Lac c., Lyc., Rheum., Op., Psor., Sars., Tub.): To cry out in a loud high-pitched, shrill voice, as in fear, pain or anger.

SCREWING (Arg.n.Coloc.): The turning or twisting of a screw; pushing or pulling with a twisting action.

SCROFULA (Nit.ac.): Itis a glandular swelling, the former name for tuberculosis of the lymph nodes, especially of the neck.

SCROFULOUS (Bar., Brom., Cal.p., Con., Diph., Iod., Kreos., Mer.s., Nit.ac., Phos.ac., Ruta., Samb., Sil., Spig., Sulph., Ther.): Relating to scrofula.

SCROFULOUS EXOSTOSIS (Ruta): A hard (like bone) glandular swelling.

SCROFULOUS OPTHALMIA (Bar.): Purulent conjunctivitis of a scrofulous diathetic person.

SCUM (Mag.c., Sanic.): Dirt or waste matter floating on the surface of a liquid, especially in the form of foam or froth.

SCURF (Psor.): Small flakes or scales of dead skin, especially on the scalp; dandruff; branny desquamation.

SEASICKNESS (Carb.ac., Coc., Petr., Tab., Ther.): A disorder of equilibrium occurring in ship due to the stimulation of the semi-circular canals by the unaccustomed movements of the body presenting with giddiness, malaise, nausea and vomiting.

SECOND CHILDHOOD (Bar., Op.): Old age.

SECUNDINE (Pyr.): The placenta and membranes expelled after childbirth, which constitutes the third stage of labor; afterbirth.

SEDENTARY HABBIT (Nux.): Involving little exercise or physical activity.

SEDENTARY LIFE (Acon., Aloe., Am.c., Anac., Con., Nux., Ran.b., Sep., Tab.): A person inclined by nature or driven by occupation, spends most of the parts of his daily life in sitting position or taking little exercise.

SEDIMENT (Colch., Lob., Mer.cor., Pod., Sil., Sep., Tereb.): Solid material, such as dirt or minerals, that falls to the bottom of a liquid.

SEEDY (Thuja.): Abounding with seeds.

SEIZE (Amyl., Gels.): To take or grab or affect suddenly, eagerly or forcibly.

SEIZED WITH DESIRE TO URINATE (Petros.): Sudden urging or desire to urinate.

SELF ABUSE (Murex., Phos.ac.): Masturbation; self-pollution.

SELF-CONTEMPT (Agnus.): Feeling of no value or disrespect of oneself.

SEMI DROPSICAL (Lyc.): Swelling or puffiness not fully developed but to a certain level.

SEMI STUPID (Diph.): State of semi-conscious condition.

SEEMINGLY (Kali br.): In a way that appears to be true but may in fact not be; apparently.

SENSATION (Aesc., Agar, Ambr.Cact. etc.): An awareness of an external or internal stimulus, e.g. heat, pain or emotions, as a result of its perception by the senses.

ALL GONESENSATION (Murex., Phos., Puls., Sep., Stan.): Sensation of emptiness.

BANDSENSATION (Gels.): Sensation of a thin, flat strip of material has been tightened the part strongly.

SCRAPING SENSATION (Dros.): Sensation of scratching or rubbing by something in the mucous membrane or skin.

RAW SENSATION (Rum.): Sore, painful sensation.

SWASHING SENSATION (Crot.t.): Sensation as if pouring or moving with a splashing sound.

SENSIBILITY (Kali br.): The ability to experience and understand deep feelings; tendency to become easily offended or influenced by others.

SENSITIVE (Aesc., Agar., Amyl., Ant.c., Apis., Mag.m.): Feeling or responding to a stimulus readily, strongly or painfully.

SENSORIUM CLOUDED (Hyos.): Confused senses.

SENTIENT NERVES (Calen., Hyper.): Nerves capable of carrying sensation.

SEPSIS (Pyr.): A toxic condition due to presence of various pus forming and other pathogenic microorganism or their toxin in the blood or tissues.

SEPTICAEMIA (Pyr.): Systemic disease caused by the spread of micro-organism and their toxins via the circulating blood. (Formerly called blood-poisoning)

SEPTIC FEVER (Anthr., Pyr.): Fever due to septicaemic condition of the body.

SEPTIC GERMS (Calen.): A very small organism or microbe or microorganism that causes sepsis.

SEPTIC MATTERS (Crot.): Toxic materials or substances which may lead to sepsis.

SEQUELAE (Camph., Diph., Kal., Med., Vario.): A morbid condition following as a consequence of another disease.

SERENE (Nux m.): Calm and quite; at peace.

SEROUS EXUDATION (Mez.): Thin or watery rather than syrupy, thick or vicious exudation.

SERRATED (Syph.): Having a saw like edge.

SERVICEABLE (Lac.c.): Able or willing to serve; capable of rendering long service; useful.

SEWER GAS (Pyr.): Foul gas coming out of a large underground pipe or channel for carrying away sewage from drains and water from road surfaces.

SEXUAL ERETHISM (Murex.): An abnormal state of sexual excitement or irritation.

SEXUAL INDULGENCE (Samb.): Sexual gratification or satisfaction.

SHATTERING (Stan.): To break into tiny fragments, usually suddenly or with force; wrecking.

SHINGLES (Ran.b.): The disease herpes zoster, caused by the chickenpox virus, in which acute inflammation of spinal nerve ganglia produces pain and then a series of blisters along the path of the nerve, especially in the area of the waist and ribs, but sometimes around the head and face.

SHIVERS (Act.): To quiver or tremble; an involuntary muscular movement in response to the cold, fright, excitement etc.

SHOCK (Acet.ac., Camph., Cic., Glon., Hyp., Pod., Sep.): A state of profound depression of the vital processes of the body due to failure of the circulatory system to maintain adequate perfusion of vital organ and usually characterized by pallor, low blood pressure, a weak thready rapid pulse, rapid and shallow respiration, diminished urine output, subnormal temperature, restlessness, anxiety and mental dullness resulting from severe esp. crushing injuries, haemorrhage, burns, major surgery or other causes.

SHORE (Brom., Murex., Nat.m.): The land along the edge of the sea or ocean, a lake or another large area of water.

SHOT (Crot.t.): To fire a gun or other weapon, or to hit, injure, or kill.

SHREDDY STRIPS (Arg.n.): To cut or tear something into small pieces.

SHRIEKS (Hell., Hyos.): A loud, high cry as occurs during any excitement, after fright or in pain.

SHRILL (Apis., Ther.): High-pitched and piercing sound.

SHRINKING LOOK (Stram.): Collapsed condition due to fear.

SHRIVEL (Sars., Sec.): To make or become shrunken and wrinkled, especially as a result of drying out due to heat, cold or being old.

SHRUB FLOWERS (Ham.): Flowers of a plant with a wooden stem and many small branches that usually does not grow very tall.

SHRUNKEN. (Sabad.): Reduced in size or contents; shrivelled; atrophied.

SHUDDERING (Caps., Sep., Spig.): Shaking suddenly and briefly, especially because of an unpleasant thought or feeling as fear, horror or after becoming cold.

SIBILANT (Spong.): Similar to, having or pronounced with a hissing or whistling sound.

SICK (Sab., Staph.): Affected with disease; physically or mentally ill; not well or healthy.

SICKLY (Cina., Lac d., Psor.): Disposed to illness; weak and unhealthy; not looking healthy or strong.

SICKLY BODY (Lyc.): Weak, feeble and sick state of the body.

SIGHING (Arn., Cal.p., Dig., Ign., Samb.): To let out slowly and audibly a deeply drawn breath specially as the involuntary expression of weariness, dejection, grief, regret, sadness, longing or relief.

SIMILIMUM (Pyr.): Most similar.

SIMULATES (Stram.): To create conditions or processes similar to something that exists.

SINKING (Acet.ac., Caust., Crot., Dig., Lac c., Murex., Pod., Sep., Stan., Ver.): Becoming submerged, wholly or partly; falling or dropping to a lower level or state.

SINKS (Carbo an., Lach.): To fall or move to a lower level; to move below the surface of water.

SINUSES (Lyc.): Any of the hollow spaces in the bones or other tissues; a dilated channel for venous blood; a fistula or tract leading to a suppurative cavity.

SLENDER (Calc., Bry., Phos.): Thin built.

SLEEPLESSNESS (Ka!i br., Psor.): Inability to sleep; insomnia.

SLIMY (Chel., Mer., Mer.cor., Puls., Sars., Tab.): Viscous; glutinous; pertaining or resembling or of the nature of slime (*Slime:* any unpleasant thick liquid substance.)

SLOUGHING (Anthr., Calc., Carb.ac., Hyper., Med.): A mass of dead tissue separating from an ulcer or living tissues or skin.

SLUGGISH (Am.m., Op., Phos.): Unenergetic; habitually lazy or inactive.

SMALL POX (Vario.): Variola; an acute eruptive contagious disease and frequently fatal viral illness caused by the variola virus and marked at the onset by chills, high fever, backache and headache. In 2 to 5 days the constitutional symptoms subside and the eruption appears, first papular, then vesicular and pustule. Pustules are dry and forms scabs which on falling off leave a permanent marking of the skin (pock marks).

SMELLING BOTTLES (Am.c.): A bottle containing Ammonium carbonate used for smelling. Earlier faint hearted ladies used to carry it and used to smell from it, whenever they felt giddy or faint.

SNAPPISH (Cham): Speaks in a sharp, unfriendly manner; cross; petulant.

SNEEZING (Arg.m., Cina., Mer., Phos., Sabad.): To make a sudden, violent, spasmodic, audible expiration of breath through the nose and mouth usually as a reflex act following irritation of nasal mucous membrane.

SNORING (Op.): A rough, rattling, inspiratory noise produced by vibration of the pendulous palate, or sometimes of the vocal cords, during sleep or coma.

SNUFFLES (Am.c., Nux., Lyc.): The act of breathing heavily through the nose (as when the nose is blocked or congested due to polyp, congenital syphilis).

SOAPY (Mer.): Smeared or covered with; leathered; soft, smooth as soap.

SOLITUDE (Coca., Cyc., Lyc., Stram.): The situation or state of being alone, often by choice that is peaceful and pleasant.

SOOTY (Hell.): Like black powder that is produced when wood, coal etc.is burnt.

SOMNAMBULISM (Kali br., Sil.): Sleep walking; a state of dissociated consciousness in which action of walking or performance of other motor acts occur while asleep and the actions are not recalled after waking and this is considered as normal in children, but as an illness in adults having a hysterical basis.

SOMNOLENCE: Sleepiness or drowsiness.

SOPOR (Cinch., Diph., Hell., Op.): Stupor; an unnaturally deep sleep.

SORDES (Hyos.): A dark brown or blackish crust-like debris, especially of the encrustations of food, epithelial matter and bacteria that collects on the lips, teeth and gums of a person suffering from prolong fever or chronic debilitating disease.

SORE (Abrot., Act., Aesc., Agar., All.c., Aloe., Am.c., Am.m., Ant.c., Apis., Arg.m., Arg.n., Bap., Phos.): A popular term for almost any type of tender or painful lesion or ulcer of the skin or mucous membrane; any place in an animal body where the skin and flesh are ruptured or bruised and tender or painful.

SORE THROAT (Phyt.): Inflammation of the tonsils, pharynx or larynx.

CLERGYMAN'S SORE THROAT (Dros.): (Syn. *Angina granulsa, granular pharyngitis*) Inflammation of the mucous membrane and underlying parts of the pharynx whereby the lymph follicles are enlarged, studding the surface and forming minute nodules or granules; sore throat of religious preacher.

SORROW (Caust., Lach., Phos.ac.): A feeling of great sadness or regret, or something that causes this feeling; uneasiness or pain of mind due to loss of any good, real or supposed; grief.

SOUR KROUT (Bry., Petr.): Dried leaves of cabbage, soaked in saline water.

SPARE (Alum., Cal.p., Chel.): Lean, thin.

SPASM (Act., Aeth., Cic., Cina., Cup., Hyos., Ign., Kali br., Lys., Mag.m., Mag.p., Med., Op., Pic.ac., Plat., Samb., Ruta., Ver.v.): A sudden involuntary, uncontrollable contraction of a muscle or muscles or of a hollow organ.

> **CATALEPTIC SPASM (Cup.):** Spasm relating to catalepsy, the condition where body becomes stiff and the person temporarily become unconscious.
>
> **CLONIC SPASM (Cup., plb.):** Alternate involuntary contraction and relaxation of muscles.
>
> **SPASM OF SPHINCTER (Tab.):** Sudden involuntary contraction of sphincter (sphincter vesicae- sphincter of bladder)
>
> **EPILEPTIC SPASM (Act., Aeth.):** Spasms occurs during an epileptic attack.
>
> **HYSTERICAL SPASM (Act.):** Spasm occurring during hysterical attack.
>
> **INFANTILE SPASM (Melil.):** Seizure activity marked by momentary flexion or extension of the neck, trunk, extremities or any combination with onset occurring in the first year of life.
>
> **TONIC SPASM (Plb.):** Continuous involuntary muscle contraction.

SPASMODIC (Ant.t., Croc., Crot.t., Kali c., Mag.c., Puls.): Relating to or characterised by a spasm.

SPASMODIC RETENTION (Tereb.): Retention of urine in urinary bladder due to its spasm.

SPERMATORRHOEA (Staph.): An involuntary discharge of semen, without orgasm.

SPHACELUS: Moist gangrene, a slough, necrotic matter.

SPICED (Nux.): Flavoured with or tasting or smelling of spices; pungent.

SPINA BIFIDA: A developmental anomaly marked by defective closure of vertebral arch, through which the meninges may or may not protrude, resulting in various degrees of disability, with severe cases manifesting permanent paralysis of the legs and mental retardation.

SPINAL IRRITATION (Nat.m., Ran.b., Zinc.): A condition characterized by tenderness along the spinal column, numbness and tingling in the limbs, and susceptibility to fatigue.

SPIRIT (Asar., Lach., Lil., Nux., Pod., Murex.): The vital principle or animating force within living things.

SPIRITOUS LIQUORS (Lyc., Nux.m., Sel.): An aqueous solution of ethyl alcohol that has been distilled.

SPITEFUL (Nux., Cham.): Full of spite; desirous to vex or injure or annoy; malicious.

SPLENDID (Vario.): Excellent, very good or fine.

SPLINTERS (Cic., Hep., Hyper., Nit.ac., Rat.): A slender, sharp piece of material piercing or embedded in the skin or subcutaneous tissue.

SPONGE (Spong.): The elastic fibrous skeleton of certain marine animals; used mainly as an absorbent; a very light soft substance with lots of little holes in it, which can be either artificial or natural and used to clean things or as a soft layer.

SPONGY GUM (Kreos.): Sponge-like texture of gum, causing haemorrhage as in scurvy.

SPRAIN (Can.s., Carbo an., Caust., Led., Nat.c., Psor., Rhus., Ruta.): A joint injury in which some of the fibres of a supporting ligament are ruptured but the continuity of the ligament remains intact.

SPUTA (Nat.s., Psor., Trill.): (Pl. of Sputum) A mixture of saliva, mucus and/or pus that is coughed up from the bronchial passages, and is indicative of an inflammatory disorder, especially in smoking-related conditions and other pulmonary conditions such as bronchitis, etc. Also called phlegm.

> **PURULENT SPUTA (Dros.):** Sputa containing pus found in some diseases of air passages such as lung abscess etc.

SQUEEZE (Iod., Ipec., Spong.): To grasp or embrace tightly; to exert pressure specially on opposite sides.

SQUINT: Abnormal alignment of one or both eyes; strabismus.

SQUIRMING SENSATION (Nat.m.): Wriggling or crawling sensation (like that of a worm).

STAGGERRING (Kali br.): Walking with unsteady steps, as if going to fall.

STAGNATED (Carbo an.,): Not active or brisk; dull; stopped in developing or making progress; still; standing

STAINNING LINEN (Sep.): A mark on cloth that is difficult to remove.

STAMMERING (Cup., Spig., Stram.,): Stuttering; act or condition of one who stammers by making involuntary stops in uttering syllables and words.

STARCHY (Sel.): Consisting of starch or resembling starch or something starched.

STARTING (Hell.): To move suddenly and quickly after being surprised or afraid.

STARTLES (Acon., Calad., Psor.): To move suddenly and violent from a state of stillness or rest or sleep due to fear, surprise or shock.

STENCH (Sars.): A strong and extremely unpleasant smell.

STENOSIS: Stricture; an abnormal narrowing or contraction of a duct or canal.

STERCORACEOUS (Pyr.): Faecal; containing, consisting of or relating to feces.

STERILITY (Arg.n., Nat.c.): Infertility; unproductiveness; barrenness.

STERTOR (Arn.): A noisy inspiration occurring in coma or deep sleep, sometimes due to obstruction of larynx or upper airways; loud snoring sound.

STERTOROUS BREATHING (Am.c., Nux.m., Op.): A breathing characterised by stertor.

STICKING (Rat): Pushing something usually a sharp object into something.

STIFF (Act., Ipec., Kal., Med.): Not easily bent or folded; rigid.

STIFFEN (Kreos, .Nux.m.): To make or become stiff or stiffer.

STIMULANTS (Coloc., Con., Op.): An agent (as a drug) that produces a temporary increase of the functional activity or efficiency of an organism or any of its parts and promotes a sense of well-being.

STINGS

STINGS (Anthr., Ars., Crot., Led., Mer.): Act of stinging esp. of insects, plants, and animals to produce a small but painful injury by making a very small hole in the skin; the sharp pointed part of insect or creature that go into the skin leaving a small, painful and sometimes poisonous wound.

STOMATITIS: Generalised inflammation of oral mucosa.

STOOL (Aesc., Aloe., Alum., Ambr.): Solid waste matter passed out from body through bowels; feces.

- **CADAVEROUS STOOL (Kreos.):** Stool resembling, especially having the colour or appearance of a dead body.

- **FERMENTED STOOL (Ipec.):** Stool as chemically changed through the action of living substances, such as yeast or bacteria often changing sugar to alcohol.

- **FOAMY STOOL (Ipec.):** Stool like mass of small, usually white, bubbles formed on the surface of a liquid or consists of mass of bubbles.

- **LUMPY STOOL (Plb.):** Stool contains lumps (solid mass without a regular shape).

- **KNOTTY STOOL (Mag.m., Sep., Sulph.):** Lumpy.

- **PASTY STOOL (Chel.):** Stool like a small pie that consists of pastry folded around meat, vegetables or cheese.

- **PIPE STEM STOOL (Dig.):** Stool resembling the shape of a pipe stem, seen in stricture of the lower rectum.

- **SHEEP-DUNG STOOL (Plb.):** Small ball like feces of sheep.

- **RIBBON LIKE STOOL (Arn.):** Long and narrow strip-like or tape-like stool.

SLIMY STOOL (Am.m., Chel., Mer.): Slippery, viscous, glutinous stool.

UNDIGESTED STOOL (Fer.): Stool containing food particles which has not been digested.

STOOPING (Am.c.Kal., Lach., Phos., Ruta.): To bend the upper part of the body forward and down.

STORMY WEATHER (Psor.): An extreme weather condition with strong winds and heavy rain or snow

STOUT (Am.c., Caps., Cinch.): Physically strong, vigorous and powerful; well-built; hard-wearing; robust.

STRABISMUS (Tab.): Squint; the condition of having one or both eyes set slightly off-center due to in-coordinated action of the muscles of the eye ball, that preventing parallel vision.

STRAIN (Alum., Carbo an., Coca., Cinch., Lac d., Med., Nat.m., Nit.ac., Phos., Pod., Rat., Rhus., Ruta., Sanic.): To stretch; to make tight; to draw with force.

STRANGE (Thuja., Tub.): Unusual or unexpected and makes you feel slightly nervous or afraid; not familiar.

STRANGE TEMPER (Anac.): An unpredictable or unusual or odd state of mind, mood or humour that is not known or experienced before.

STRANGLING (Hep., Stan., Ipec.): The act of suffocating (someone) by constricting the windpipe.

STRANGULATED (Lach.): Constricted so as to prevent the passage of air or so as to cut off the blood supply or any part encircled by a tight band.

STRANGULATED HERNIA (Nux., Plb.): hernia not reducible by ordinary means.

STRANGURY (Berb., Canth., Tereb.): A slow and painful discharge of urine drop by drop produced by spasmodic muscular contraction of the urethra and bladder.

STREAKES OF BLOOD (Canth): A line, stria or stripe of blood especially one that is more or less indistinct or evanescent.

STRETCHING (Amyl.): To straighten and extend the body or part of the body, example: when waking or reaching out or during sleep.

STRICTURES (Petros., Syph.): A narrowing or constriction of the lumen of a tube, duct or hollow organ such as the oesophagus, ureter or urethra, it may be temporary or permanent.

STRIDULOUS: Making a shrill, harsh unpleasant sound.

STRINGS (Croc., Kali bi.): Material made of several threads twisted together; a small cord or slender strip of leather or the like.

STRINGY (Croc., Hydr, Lac c., Mag.p., Mer.): Consisting of string, or small threads; capable of being drawn out to form a string, as a glutinous substance; ropy; viscid.

STUBBING A TOE (Colch.): Striking toe against something hard eg. stone etc.

STUDDED (Mur.ac.): Having a lot of something on or in it.

STUFFED UP (Lac c.): Filled or plugged with some material or substance; to obstruct by filling up; to stopped up.

STUMBLES (Agar., Phos.ac.): To lose one's footing in walking or running so as to stagger or fall.

STUMBLING BLOCK (Vario.): An obstacle to progress.

STUMP (Phos. ac.): The distal end of the part of the limb left in amputation.

STUNTED (Med.): Check or prevent the growth or development.

STUPIFIED (Nat.c., Phos.ac.): To make physically stupid, dull or insensible; to surprise or shock as to make someone unable to think clearly.

STUPID (Mur.ac., Op., Phos.ac.): Wanting or lacking in understanding, intelligence or reasoning power; foolish; dull.

STUPOR (Bap., Diph., Lach., Nux.m., Op., Phos.ac.): A physical or mental condition characterised by great diminution or suspension of sense or feeling like inability to think, hear etc. and often its resulting from stress, shock, drugs and alcohol.

STYE (Puls., Staph., Thuja.): (Syn. *Hordeolum*) A localized, purulent, inflammatory staphylococcal infection of one or more sebaceous glands of the eyelids.

SUBDUED (Staph.): Quiet, shy, restrained or in low spirits; passive; toned down.

SUBINVOLUTION (Lil., Pod., Psor.): Incomplete involution failure of a part to return to its normal size and condition after enlargement due to functional activity as subinvolution of the uterus after delivery of a baby.

SUBSULTUS TENDINUM (Hyos.): A twitching of the tendons especially noticeable at the wrist, occurring in low, asthenic fever, e.g. typhoid fever.

SUCCEEDED (Kal.): To came next after something and took their place or position; to follow another thing in order.

SUCCESSION (Gels., Phos.ac.): A series of things coming one after another in time or order; the regular pattern of one thing following another thing.

SUFFOCATING (Acon., Act., Crot.t., Cup., Lac d., Puls., Spong.): Make unable to breathe because of heat and lack of air or by other causes; subject to an oppressive feeling in normal breathing.

SUFFUSED (All.c.): To spread over or through in the manner of fluid, light, colour etc.

SUGGILLATION (Ham.): Ecchymosis; bruise specially one that develops post mortem.

SUICIDAL THOUGHTS (Psor.): Thoughts or intension about killing oneself.

SUICIDAL INSANITY (Naja.): Derangement of the mind manifesting in constantly thinking or attempting to kill oneself.

SULKY (Ant.c., Plat., Tub.): Bad-tempered or unwilling to speak because of anger or unsociable from ill temper; to be sullen.

SULTRY (Sep.): Very hot, humid and uncomfortable weather.

SUMMERSAULT (Lyc.): A leap or roll in which the whole body turns a complete circle forwards or backwards, leading with the head in the ground or air.

SUNBURN (Ant.c., Canth.): Injury to the skin, with erythema, tenderness, and sometimes blistering after excessive exposure to sunlight produced by unfiltered UV rays (usually within the range of 260-320 nm in sunlight).

SUNKEN (Cal.p., Cinch., Mur.ac., Phos. ac., Plb., Staph., Tab., Ver.): Hollow and deep as a result of disease., getting old or not having proper nutrition.

SUNKEN COUNTENANCE (Lach., Sec.): Face with deep and hollow eyes and cheeks with prominent malar bone as a result of disease, or getting old, or not having enough food.

SUNSTROKE (Glon., Nat.c., Ver.v.): (Syn. *Heatstroke*) A condition of final stage of heat exhaustion brought on by over-exposure to the sun, marked by hyperpyrexia, weakness, headache, convulsion, coma and death may ensue.

SUPPLANTS (Ant.t): To take the place of someone or something.

SUPRESSION (Acon., Mill., Nat.m., Op., Psor.): Holding back, repressing, , restraining or arresting; the act of checking.

SUPPRESSED ACUTE EXANTHEMA (Bry.): Suppression of acute skin eruption.

SUPPRESSED DISCHARGE (Bry., Mer.s.): Suppression of any natural discharges from the body.

SUPPRESSED ERUPTION (Aloe., Agar., Ant.c., Bry., Caust., Cic., Dulc., Hep., Sulph., Zinc.): Arrest or suppression of appearance of eruption.

SUPPRESSED FOOT SWEAT (Cup., Mill., Sec., Sil., Zinc.): Suppress or arrest of natural perspiration of foot.

SUPPRESSION BY QUININE (Gels., Ipec., Lach.,): Suppression of malarial fever or any other diseases by large doses of quinine.

SUPPURATION (Calen., Cinch., Mer.s., Mer.p.iod., Petr., Phyt., Sil., Staph.): The formation of pus; pyogenesis.

SUPPURATION BENIGN (Carboan.): Mild suppuration.

SUPPURATING ERUPTION (Psor.): Eruption suppurative or pus forming in nature.

SUSPENDED (Cyc., Kali c.): Hanging; held in suspension; temporarily inactive.

SUTURE (Sil.): A type of fibrous joint in which the opposite surfaces are closely united by fibrous membrane continuous with the periosteum as in the skull; a stitch that joins the edges of a wound, surgical incision, etc together.

SWALLOW (Sabad.): To cause or enable the passage of something from the mouth through the throat and oesophagus into the stomach; deglutition.

SWARTHY PERSON (Cinch.): Dark complexioned person.

SWEAR (Anac., Lac c.): To use rude or offensive or indecent language; to assert something solemnly or earnestly, sometimes with an oath.

SWEETEN THE STOMACH (Mar.c.): Magnesium carbonicum taken in crude form to neutralize the acidity of stomach in order to make less painful.

SYCOSIS MENTI (Cic.): Barber's itch (Skin diseases of bearded part of face); a chronic inflammatory disease involving the hair follicles specially of the bearded area of face and marked by papules, pustules and tubercles perforated by hairs with crusting.

SYDENHAM (Bell.): A celebrated English physician Thomas Sydenham, sometimes called the "English Hippocrates".

SYDENHAM SCARLET FEVER (Bell.): An infectious fever, usually marked by sore throat and scarlet rash.

SYMPATHY (Caust.): The feeling of being sorry for someone; a feeling or expression of understanding and caring for someone else who is suffering or has problems that make them unhappy.

SYNCHONDROSES (Trill.): (Pl. of *Synchondrosis*) A type of cartilaginous joint that is formed by hyaline cartilage or fibrocartilage and usually temporary, and later converted into bone before adult life.

SYNCHRONOUS (Glon., Spig.): Occurring or existing simultaneously.

SYNCOPE (Dig.): Transient and usually sudden loss of consciousness, accompanied by an inability to maintain an upright posture.

SYPHILIS (Fer., Mer.s., Nat.s., Nit. ac., Phyt., Sars., Thuja.,): An acute and chronic infectious disease caused by *Treponemapallidum* and transmitted by direct contact, usually through sexual intercourse. characterized by painless ulcers (chancre) on the genitals, fever and a faint red rash, which if left untreated may eventually result in heart damage, blindness, paralysis and death.

SYPHILITIC AFFECTION (Kali bi., Mer.cor., Nit.ac., Phos. ac., Phyt.): Diseases of syphilitic origin.

SYPHILITIC ANGINA (Hydr): Sore throat marked by spasmodic attacks of intense suffocative pain having syphilitic base or background.

SYPHILITIC DYSCRASIA (Flour.ac., Nit.ac., Phos.ac., Syph.): A general morbid condition associated with ulceration and destruction of tissues. A patient of syphilitic miasm is dull, stupid, stubborn, sullen, morose and usually suspicious; Melancholic and condemn themselves; very silent; wants to commit suicide; Forgetful and slow comprehensive. Complaints are aggravated at night, becomes restless and anxious. Complaints are aggravated at summer and ameliorated in winter. Ulceration and discharge of pus with offensive odour but it ameliorates the complaints. Eruptions crusty and oozing pus, skin greasy and sweaty; much offensive odour; sweat does not relieve. Hair tends to fall out. Desires cold food and aversion to meat.

SYPHILITIC MERCURIAL DYSCRASIA (Flour.ac.): Diseases which has a syphilitic origin but is made complex and mixed with the symptom produced due to overuse of large doses of mercurial medication.

TABES: A progressive wasting disorder, usually signifying tabesdorsalis meanslocomotor ataxia. Symptoms are ataxia or muscular incoordination, anaesthesia, neuralgia, lancinating pain, muscular atrophy, later paralysis; a disease of middle age, a sequel of syphilis.

TABES MESENTERICA (Bac.): Emaciation and malnutrition caused by engorgement and tubercular degeneration of mesenteric glands.

TACHYCARDIA: Abnormally rapid heart rate, more than 100 beats per minute in adults.

TACITURN (Aur., Bell., Cinch., Plat., Tuber.): Disinclined to speak; reserved in speech; in the habit of saying very little.

TALLOW-LIKE MASSES (Mag. c.): Fat-like lump.

TANGLED (Bor., Psor.): A confused interwoven mass; twisted together in an untidy way; to interweave or interlock as threads.

TAPE WORM (Tereb.): A parasitic intestinal cestode worm having a flattened band-like form.

TARDY (Bell., Bov., Thlaspi., Tub.): Sluggish; slow.

TARSAL (Arg.m.): The thin elongated plates of dense connective tissue found in each eyelid, contributing to its form and support; tarsal cartilage of the eyelid.

TARSAL TUMOUR (Thuja): Tumour on the tarsipalpebra of eyes; Tumour of the tarsus or supporting plate (outer edge) of the eyelid.

TARTAR: An incrustation on the teeth consisting of plaque that has become hardened by the deposition of mineral salts (as calcium carbonate).

TASTING OF INGESTA (Ant.c.): Taste of what has been eaten (ingested).

TEASING (Graph.): To intentionally annoy a person or animal by laughing at them or pretending to do something, often in a playful way; irritating.

TEDIOUS (Act.): Tiresome from continuance; tiring, esp. because long or repetitious;wearisome; fatiguing.

TEETH ON THE EDGE (Sul. ac.): Extremely unpleasant or irritating.

TELL TALE FACE (Sep.): The face that tells the story of the suffering.

TEMPER (Aesc.): The state of mind or feelings; the way that someone feels at a particular time; disposition or frame of mind, particularly with regard to the passion and affection as calm or fiery temper.

TEMPERAMENT (Chel., Lob.): The peculiar physical and mental character of an individual; the physical organization peculiar to the individual, which influences one's metabolic process, manner of thought and action, and general views of life; that aspect of personality which denotes a person's emotional disposition.

> **BILIOUS TEMPERAMENT (Pod.):** Bitter, ill-humoured, resentful, discontented, irritable; peevish, ill-natured person.

BILIOUS SANGUINE TEMPERAMENT (Nux.): Plethoric persons who are irritable, peevish, ill-humoured in nature.

CHOLERIC TEMPERAMENT (Coff., Lach.): One marked by more or less general pigmentation, high blood pressure, slow pulse, well developed muscle, strong appetites, tenacity of purpose.

EXCITABLE TEMPERAMENT (Cham.): Easily stimulated and roused to activity of any sort and have strong feelings, especially of happiness and enthusiasm.

HYSTERICAL NERVOUS TEMPERAMENT (Nux.m., Val.): Extremely sensitive, excitable mentally unstable person.

IMPATIENT TEMPERAMENT (Nux.): Persons are not willing to wait for something to happen and becoming annoyed at delays; restlessly or eagerly desirous; anxious.

IRRITABLE TEMPERAMENT (Aster., Nux., Sec., Sil.): Getting annoyed easily; bad-tempered.

LYMPHATIC TEMPERAMENT (Bap., Thuja.): Pertaining to lymph; a vascular channel that transports lymph. Flabby, pale, sluggish *(qualities formally attributed to excess of lymph).*

MELANCHOLIC TEMPERAMENT (Murex., Lach.): Characterised by extreme depression, apathy and indifference to one's surroundings, gloom, fear, brooding and painful delusion; sadness, low spirits, sluggishness.

NERVOUS TEMPERAMENT (Gels., Glon., Ign., Mag.c., Nit.ac., Sec., Sil., Sulph.): Characterized by lack of confidence, indecisive, hesitant, bashful and started easily.

NERVOUS SANGUINE TEMPERAMENT (Ver.): The person having excess amount of blood and having indecisive, hesitant, bashful character.

PHLEGMATIC TEMPERAMENT (Mez., Puls.): Sluggish or dull temperament; apathetic (one who is not easily excited to action or display of emotion).

SANGUINE TEMPERAMENT (Coff., Fer., Hyos., Phos., Plat., Sil.): The person having excess amount of blood; plethoric; having a red complexion, light hair and eyes and a quick but not lasting temper.

TEMPLE (Act., Arg.n., Carbo.ac., Dulc., Fluor.ac., Lach., Spig.): Areaon the side of the head above the zygoma, in front of the ear, one on each side.

TENDENCY TO CAKE (Phyt.): To form or harden into a mass.

TENDER (Cham., Crot., Hello., Lach., Med., Petr.): Fragile or delicate, so as to be easily injured, hurt or affected; gentle, sensitive or feeble in nature.

TENACIOUS (Canth., Croc., Dros., Hell., Med., Mer., Nux.): Strongly cohesive; unwilling to accept defeat or stop doing or having something; keeping a firm hold on property, principles, life etc.; adhesive, sticky.

TENDO-ACHILLES: The cord-like tendon, on the back of each foot just above the heel. It is situated at the lower end of the gastrocnemius muscle inserted into the oscalcis and is the strongest and thickest tendon.

TENESMUS (Aloe., Canth., Carb.ac., Collin., Coloc.Med., Mer., Mer. cor., Tereb.): Spasmodic contraction of anal or vesicle sphincter with pain and persistent desire to empty the bowel or bladder, with involuntary ineffectual straining efforts.

TENSION (Meny., Nat.c., Puls.): Process or act of stretching, straining or tensing; pressure, force; mental strain, anxiety.

TERMINI OF NERVES (Tar.): The end part of nerves.

TERRIBLE (Carbo.ac., Med., Mer.c., Nat.s., Rat., Pyr., Tab., Syph.): Very unpleasant or serious or bad; causing great harm or injury.

TERRIFIC (Sep., Syph.): Used to emphasize the great amount or degree of something; very good or enjoyable; extreme; tremendous.

TERROR (Kali br.): Intense fright; over whelming, extreme fear; violent action that causes fear.

TESTICLE (Apis., Arg.m.): One of the two male reproductive glands in which the spermatozoa develop.

TETANUS (Cic., Hyper.): An acute infectious disease marked by painful tonic muscular contraction and often, respiratory and autonomic failure, caused due to toxin of tetanus bacillus, *Clostridium tetani*, growing anaerobically at the site of injury.

> **IDIOPATHIC TETANUS (Phys.):** Tetanus occurring without any visible wound to serve as a portal of entry for the specific bacillus.
>
> **TRAUMATIC TETANUS (Phys.):** Tetanus produced after injury caused by infection of a wound.

TETANIC CONVULSION (Ver.v.): A tonic spasm with constant muscular contraction.

TETTERY (Alum., Bov.): Scaly, eczematous skin eruption; popularly applied to eczema and occasionally to other eruptions such as herpes, eczema, pemphigus, and psoriasis.

THEORIZING (Can.ind.): To form opinions solely by theories; speculating; guessing.

THIN, SPARE SUBJECTS: (Alum., Ambra., Arg.m., Mag.p., Sec.): Lean and thin persons.

THREAD OF CONVERSATION (Med.): A sequence of ideas or events, which continues from beginning to end, and that serves to connect all parts and details during talking between two or more people.

THREATENING EFFUSION (Hell.): The possibility of affected with effusion or impending, harmful effusion.

THREATENING MALIGNANCY (Con.): Tending to or possibility of become worse and leading to malignancy.

THREATENING SUFFOCATION (Hep., Ipec, Lob.): Risk of development of difficulty to breathe due to deprivation of air exchange in different pathological conditions of lungs.

THREATENED (Ver.v.): Expressed a threat of harm or violence; endangered.

THREATENED IDIOCY (Bar.): The possibilities of development of congenital mental deficiency due to affection during intra-uterine life or from any genetic cause.

THRILL (Sel.): A strong feeling of excitement, pleasure or fear.

THRIVE (Nat. s.): To grow; to grow healthy and vigorously.

THROAT PIT (Rum.): Depression present in mucous membrane of throat.

THROBBING (Glon., Lac d., Pyr.): A beat or sound with a strong, regular rhythm.

THROBBING OF CAROTIDS (Mell.): A strong, pulsating carotid pulse, found in some diseases like congestive carotid failure.

THROMBOSIS: The formation, development or existence of a blood clot or thrombus within the vascular system. (*Thrombus is a* blood clot that obstructs a blood vessel or a cavity of the heart.)

THRUSH (Symph.): Infection of oral mucous membrane, characterised by white patches, ulcerations and occasionally by fever and gastrointestinal inflammation and caused by *Candida albicans*.

THUNDERSTORM (Agar., Med., Nat.c., Petr., Phos., Psor., Sep., Rhod.): A rain storm with thunder and lightning.

TIC DOULOUREX: A neuralgic pain of the face, marked by severe lancinating pain of short duration.

TICKLING (Am.c., Petros., Rumex., Tereb.): A slight irritating, uncomfortable feeling in a sensitive part of the body.

TIMBRE OF VOICE (Arg.m.): The resonance quality of voice or sound.

TIMID (Calc., Coca., Graph., Lil.t., Puls.): Inclined to fear; wanting courage; faint-hearted.

TINNITUS: Subjective ringing, buzzing or hissing sound in the ear.

TITILLATION (Dros.): The act or sensation of tickling; to excite pleasurably.

TOBACCO HEART (Tab.): A heart showing irregularity of action attributed to excessive use of tobacco.

TONIC: A state of continuous unremitting muscular contraction; a medicine that increase strength and tone.

TONICITY (Caul.): Healthy elasticity of muscles, etc.; state of normal tension or partial contraction of muscle fibres while at rest.

TONSILITIS (Caps., Lach., Lac c., Mer., Sabad.): Inflammation of tonsils, especially of the palatine tonsil.

TOOTHACHE (Cham., Coff., Kali c., Mag.c., Mag.m., Mer., Mez., Puls., Rat., Rhod., Ther.): Pain in the teeth.

TOO UGLY TO LIVE (Cham.): Very unpleasant, loathsome, and repulsive to live.

TOPICAL MEDICATED APPLICATION (Rhus.): Local application of medicines in the form of various ointments, lotion, liniments, etc.

TORMENTED (Caul., Lil.): To torture; to put to extreme pain; severe and persistent bodily or mental suffering.

TORNADO (Carbo.an.): A whirling wind of exceptional force and violence accompanied by a funnel shaped cloud marking the narrow path of greatest destruction; any destructive or violent windstorm.

TORN (Nat.m., Nit.ac.): To damage something by pulling it apart or into pieces or by cutting it on something sharp.

TORN AND LACERATED MEMBER (Hyper.): Damaged, torn parts of the body, specially limb or extremity.

TORPID (Ant.t., Hep., Mer. sol., Sulph.): Sluggish; slow to act or respond; apathetic; spiritless; dull.

TORPOR (Plb.): Complete or partial lack of response to normal or ordinary stimuli; apathy; listlessness; dullness.

TORTICOLLIS, WRY NECK: Stiffness of the neck as a result of shortening or spasmodic contraction of neck muscles.

TOSSING (Acon, Coff., Puls., Rheu.): To roll about restlessly from side to side or up and down.

TOTTERING (Alum.): Walking unsteadily.

TRANSLUCENT (Phyt.): Transmitting light, but diffusing it so that objects beyond are not clearly distinguished; allowing the passage of light but not permitting a clear view of any object.

TRANSPERANT (Sel.): Transmitting light rays so that objects are visible through the substance.

TRANSUDATION (Crot.t.): The passage of serum or other body fluid through a membrane (may not be the result of inflammation).

TRAUMATIC NEUROMA (Calen.): An unorganized bulbous or nodular mass of nerve fibres and Schwann cells produced by hyperplasia of nerve fibres and their supporting tissues after accidental or purposeful incision of the nerve.

TRAUMATIC (Ham., Hyper., Petros., Psor.): Caused by or relating to an injury.

TRAUMATISM (Acon., Calen., Led., Nat.s.): The physical or psychic state resulting from an injury or wound.

TREADING ON NAILS (Hyper.): To step or walk over nails or some pointed object.

TREMBLING (Agar., Camph., Caust., Cinch., Coc., Gels., Lach., Phos., Phos. ac., Plat., Phys, Sabad., Staph., Sul.ac., Tab., Ver.v., Zinc.): Shaking involuntarily, as from fear, cold or weakness; to vibrate or move slightly.

TREMOR (Phys.): An involuntary trembling or quivering; an involuntary movement of a part or parts of the body resulting from alternate contractions of opposing muscles.

TRICKLING (Thuja.): To flow slowly in thin stream and without force.

TRIFLES (Caps., Coc., Hep., Med., Mez., Nat.m., Petr., Plat.): Thing, fact, or circumstance, of little or no value and importance.

TRIFILING (Nux., Plat.): Of small value, importance, or amount; trivial; insignificant.

TRISMUS (Cic.): (Syn. *Lockjaw*)Tonic spasm of the muscles of mastication, causing difficulty in opening the mouth; a firm closing of the jaw due to tonic spasm of the muscles or mastication from disease of the motor branch of the trigeminal nerve, usually associated with and due to general tetanus.

TRIVIAL (Acon.): Negligible; insignificant; of little value or importance.

TUBERCLES (Led.): Any small, rounded nodule produced by infection with *Mycobacterium tuberculosis*; a nodule, or small eminence such as a rough, rounded eminence on a bone.

TUBERCULAR PERSON (Calc.ars., Diph.): Persons of a tubercular (psoro-syphilitic) state.

TUBERCULAR PHARYNGITIS (Merc. b. iod.): Inflammation of pharynx resulting or secondary to from tubercular infection.

TUBERCULOSIS (Dros.): An infectious disease caused by the tubercle bacilli, *Mycobacterium tuberculosis* and characterised by inflammatory infiltration, formation of tubercles, caseation, necrosis, fibrosis and calcification, most commonly affect the respiratory system but other parts of the body such as gastro-intestinal tract, genitourinary tract, lymphnodes, bones, joints and skin may also be infected.

TUBERCULOUS PARENTAGE (Mag.c.): History of tuberculosis in family members.

TUMEFIED (Phyt.): Swollen; puffed up; inflated.

TUMOUR (Con., Mez., Plb., Sulph.): Any swelling or tumefaction; an abnormal growth, mass or proliferation that is independent of neighbouring tissue, may be benign or malignant.

TUMULTOUS HEART ACTION (Amyl., Phyt.): Irregular and violent contraction and relaxation of cardiac muscles manifested by violent disorderly palpitation.

TURBID (Cina., Nit. ac.): Cloudy, showing turbidity as with sediment; muddy or opaque; dense.

TURPENTINE (Nux m., Tereb.): The resinous, oily liquid obtained from *pinuspalustris* and other species of pinus. It contains a volatile oil, having characteristic odour and pungent bitter taste and is widely used in the arts, as in paints, varnishes and also in medicine.

TWILIGHT (Syph.): The faint light or the period of time at the end of the day or late in the day, after the sun has gone down, just before the darkness of night.

TWITCH (Acon., Agar., Cros., Hyos., Ign., Kali br., Phoys., Sab., Stram., Tarax., Zinc.): A momentary spasmodic contraction of a muscle fibre; to make a short and sudden movement.

TYMPANITES (Tereb.): Distention of the abdomen or intestine due to the presence of gas or air in the intestine or in the peritoneal cavity, as in peritonitis and typhoid fever.

TYMPANITIC: A state of swelling of the abdomen from gas.

TYMPANITIS (Tereb.): (Syn. *Otitis media*) Inflammation of the middle ear.

TYPHILITIS: Inflammation of the caecum (beginning of large intestine and appendix attached to it). An old term to mean appendicitis.

TYPHUS (Acet.ac, Apoc., Bap., Caust., Crot., Lach., Mur. ac., Nit. ac., Pyr., Sel.): Any of a group of acute infectious, contagious disease caused by *Rickettsia*, transmitted to man by body lice (tics) or rat fleas and characterized by great prostration, sustained high fever, chills, severe headache, stupor alternating with delirium, generalized maculo-papular red coloured rash and usually progressive neurological involvement ending in a crisis in 10 -14 days.

UGLINESS (Lac c., Lyc.): Unpleasantness; quality or state of being ugly.

ULCER (Calen., Carbo v., Chel., Fluor.ac., Hep., Hydr, Kali bi., Lach., Lac c., Med., Mer., Mer.b.iod., Mer cor., Mez., Nat.m., Nit.ac., Pyr., Sars., Sil.): A lesion of the skin or mucous membranes marked by inflammation, necrosis and sloughing of damaged tissue.

ANGRY ULCER (Phyt.): Severely inflamed and painful ulcer.

SYPHILITIC ULCER (Kali bi.): In the first stage of syphilis, hard chancre appears on the external genitalia which is painless and possesses a characteristic indurated base. In the second stage the mucous patches which are small, round, white and form superficial erosion particularly in the mouth and coalesce to form snail-track ulcer, and gummatous ulcers occur in tertiary syphilis, mostly seen over the subcutaneous bones (e.g. tibia, sternum, ulna), in the scrotum and the upper part of leg and marked by punched out indolent edge and yellowish grey gummatous tissue (wash-leather slough) in the floor.

ULCERATION (Am.c., Anthr. Arg.n., Carb.ac., Graph., Ham., Kali c., Kreos., Mur.ac., Tereb.): The process of forming of an ulcer.

GANGRENOUS ULCERATION (Am.c.): An ulceration with marked gangrenous changes (death of tissue).

PHAGEDENIC ULCERATION (Mer.cy.): A rapidly spreading ulceration attended by formation of more or less extensive sloughing.

UNBEARABLE (Acon., Ambr., Lac c., Led.): Too painful, annoying or unpleasant; unendurable; intolerable.

UNCONCIOUSNESS (Acon., Arg.n., Hell., Mur.ac., Nat.m., Op., Phos.ac.): A state of being partly or completely unaware of external stimuli, normally occurs in sleeps and pathologically as in syncope, shock, intoxication etc.; in Freudin psychiatry, that part of our personality consisting of a complex of feeling and drives of which we are unaware and that are not available to our consciousness.

UNCONQUERABLE (Cup., Nuxm.): Too strong to be defeated.

UNEASINESS (Lach.): The feeling of being worried or unhappy; restlessness or disturbance by pain, anxiety or the like.

UNION (Cal. p., Calen., Symp.): Growing together and joining of severed or broken parts, as of bones or edges of a wound.

UNION BY FIRST INTENTION (Calen.): The process by which edge of the wounds are closed for healing with little or no inflammatory reaction and in such a manner that little or no scar is left to reveal the site of injury (*Healing by second intention occurs when suppuration and / or granulation is present*).

UNMERITED INSULT (Staph.): Being insulted without any reason; insulting or being rude without any reason to somebody who does not deserve it.

UNMOVED BY APOLOGIES (Nit.ac.): A person who does not accept or responds to apologies offered or made by others.

UNQUENCHABLE (Ver.): Intense; insatiable.

UNRELIABLE (Sanic.): Undependable; untrustworthy.

UNSIGHTLY SCARS (Kali br.): Ugly looking scars.

UNUSUAL ORDEAL (Gels.): An unusual experience that is very painful, difficult, or tiring.

UNWIELDLY (Calc., Hyos.): Difficult to move, manage or control.

URAEMIA (Arum.): A toxic state of the body associated with renal insufficiency produced by the retention in the blood of nitrogenous substances which is normally excreted by the kidney.

URAEMIC (Calc.): Relating to or suffering from uraemia.

URETHRITIS (Can.s., Petros.): Inflammation of the urethra.

URGING (Aloe., Canth., Crot.t., Ham., Hyper., Kreos., Lach., Lil., Mer., Mer. s., Nat.s., Petros., Plat., Plb., Rheum., Ruta., Rum., Staph.,): Strong desire; a continuing impulse or tendency towards some activity or goal.

> **INEFFECTUAL URGING (Iod., Lyc.):** Inability to achieve or fulfill the desire activity as urging for stool or urine.

URINE: The fluid and the dissolve solutes including salts and nitrogen-containing waste products, which are eliminated from the body by the kidneys

> **ALBUMINOUS/ALBUMINURIA (Hell., Helon., Lac d.):** The presence of protein in urine, chiefly albumin but also globulin, usually indicates disease, but sometimes results from a temporary or transient dysfunction.

CLOUDY URINE (Lys.): Urine containing earthy phosphates in excess, giving it the unclear and non-transparent appearance.

MILKY URINE (Dul.): Presence of chyle in urine, giving it a whitish appearance; Chylous urine.

SACCHARINE (Helon): Presence of sugar in urine; glycosuria.

URTICARIA (Apis., Ars., Bov., Dul., Nat.m.): (Syn.*Hives, nettle rash*) Multiple swollen raised areas on the skin characterized by sudden general eruption of papules or wheals associated with severe itching, it may be due to a state of hypersensitivity to food or drugs, foci of infection or psychic stimuli.

USHERING (Nat. m.): Cause or mark the start or something new.

UTERINE INERTIA (Thlaspi.): An absence or weakness of uterine contractions in labor.

UTTER (Gels., Mer., Stram.): To say something or make a sound with your voice; pronounce; complete or extreme.

UTTERLY REGARDLESS (Phos.ac.): Complete or extreme inattentive or giving no importance or indifferent to anything though it is very necessary.

UVULA (Mer.): The small, soft, fleshy structure made up of muscle, connective tissue and mucous membrane, hanging from the free edge of soft palate in midline above the root of the tongue

VACCINATION (Ant.t., Crot., Mez., Thuja., Sil., Vario.): Inoculation with any vaccine or toxoid to establish resistance to a specific infectious disease; immunization.

VAGI (Tab.): Pl. of vagus. *Vagus:* Pneumogastric or 10th Cranial nerve.

VAGINISMUS (Mag. p., Plat.): Painful spasm of the vagina due to local hyperaesthesia during sexual activity preventing satisfactory coition.

VALVULAR (Calc.ars., Naja.): Any one of the various membranous structures in a hollow organ or passage that temporarily closes in order to permit flow of fluid in one direction only, e.g. Aortic valve, Bicuspid valve, Mitral Valve etc.

VARICELLA (Vario.): Chicken Pox. An acute infectious disease caused by *varicella zoster virus* marked by an eruption of papules, becoming vesicles and then pustules in clusters over the trunk, face, scalp, upper extremities and sometimes the thigh. There is usually a slight fever which lasts from a few days to a week. It transmitted by droplet infection and also direct contact with lesion.

VARICES: Pl. of varix. *Varix:* Enlarged and tortuous veins, arteries or lymphatic vessels.

VARICOCELE: Enlargement of the veins of the scrotum forming a soft, elastic swelling causing a boggy tumour of the scrotum. It feels like a collection of worms – may cause pain and a dragging sensation

VARICOSE ULCER (Calen., Ham.): An ulcer that is due to varicose veins; a stasis ulcer. It occurs usually in the leg afflicted with varicose veins resulting from stasis or infection.

VARICOSE VEIN (Calen., Fluor. ac., Ham., Pyr., Thuja., Vario.): Dilated, twisted superficial veins, the valves of which become incompetent so that blood flow may be reversed. Most commonly found in the lower limbs, rectum (haemorrhoids) or lower oesophagus.

VARIOLA (Carbo.ac., Vario.): Small Pox. An acute eruptive contagious disease marked at the onset by chills, high fever, backache, and headache. These symptoms subside within 2-5 days and then the skin eruptions appear first on the mouth, then face, and arms and then spread to the other body parts such as back and the chest. These are at first papular, then in turn become vesicular and then pustular, which dry, form scabs and fall off leaving permanent scars (pock-marks).

VARIOLOID (Vario.): A modified and mild form of smallpox occurring in a patient who is relatively immune as they had a previous attack or has been vaccinated; resembling small pox.

VARNISHED (Pyr.): Covering, coating or glaze given by the application of varnish; glossy. (Varnish: a substance consisting of resin dissolved in a liquid, applied to wood to give a hard, clear, shiny surface when dry.)

VEGETABLE PILLS (Nux.): Medicines in pills form of vegetable origin having tonic, stimulant effects or used for indigestion.

VEHEMENT (Bry.): Intensely emotional; marked by extreme intensity of feeling, emotion or conviction.

VEIL (Tab.): A piece of thin and light fabric, worn over the face or head for concealment, protection or ornament

VENEREAL DISEASE (Mez.): A term formerly used to describe any illness transmitted by intimate sexual contact with an infected person.

VENERATED (Plat.): Revered; respected.

VENOUS PLETHORA (Carbo.an.): Congestion or fullness causing fullness or distension of veins.

VENTRICLE: A small cavity; either of two lower chambers of heart; one of the cavities of the brain.

VERGE OF ANUS (Sanic., Mag.m.): The extreme edge or end of the anus.

VERGE OF SPASM (Ver.v.): End of spasmodic convulsion.

VERMIN (Mez.): An external animal parasite, animal ectoparasites collectively; parasitic insects like lice, bed bugs.

VERSES (Ant.c., Stram.): A single line of a poem; a group of lines or stanza in a poem.

VERTIGO (Coc., Coloc., Con., Cyc., Eup., Fer., Gels., Hyper., Kal., Nat.m., Phyt., Tab., Mez., Mur.ac., Petr., Ther., Thuja, Sil.): Dizziness or giddiness of the head; a sensation of moving around in space (subjective vertigo) or of having object move about the person (objective vertigo).

> **AURAL VERTIGO (Ther.):** Vertigo caused by disease of the internal ear or pressure of cerumen on the drum membrane.
>
> **LABYRINTHINE VERTIGO (Ther.):** Meniere's disease.
>
> **SPINAL VERTIGO (Sil.):** Vertigo due to any spinal disease such as in cervical spondylosis.

VERTEX (Act., Cact., Cal.p., Graph., Lach., Lil.): The topmost part on the head.

VESICAL SYMPTOMS (Canth.): Symptoms relating to urinary bladder.

VESICAL PARESIS (Psor.): A partial or incomplete paralysis of the urinary bladder.

VESICLE (Fluor.ac., Ran.b., Mez., Staph, Sulph..): A small blister like elevation on the skin containing serous fluid, may vary in diameter from a few millimeter to a centimeter.

VESICATION (Canth.): Process of formation of vesicle (a small swelling filled with liquid under the skin) in or beneath the skin.

VEXATION (Apis., Ars., Aur., Caust., Con., Cup., Ign., Lach., Lyc., Mez., Nat.m., Plat., Petr., Staph.): Anger produced by some annoying irritation;astate of being annoyed or worried (by petty irritation).

VICARIOUS (Acet.ac., Crot., Phos.): Acting as being a substitute; assumption of the function of one organ by another; occurring at an abnormal site.

VICARIOUS MENSTRUATION (Acet. ac., Bry., Crot., Ham., Phos.): Discharge of blood from an extra genital source such as haemorrhage from nose, breast, eyes etc. at the time menstrual period is normally expected.

VINDICTIVE (Nit. ac.): Revengeful; tendency to seek revenge.

VIOLENT (Abrot., Aloe., Ambr., Arg.n., Bry., Mez., Mill., Psor., Sep., Thuja., Ver., Zinc.): Characterized by extreme force; marked by abnormally sudden physical activity and intensity; extremely or intensely loud; unnaturally strong; produced or effected by force.

VIOLET (Tereb.): A perennial herb bearing irregular flowers usually of a bluish purple colour and with a typical pleasant fragrance.

VIRGIN (Plat.): A woman (or a man) who never had sexual intercourse.

VIRULENT POISON (Nit. ac.): Very strong poison.

VIRUS (Apis., Med., Syph.): One of a group of minute infectious agents with certain exceptions not seen in the light microscope, and characterized by a lack of independent metabolism and by the ability to replicate only within living host cells. (*Unknown to 19th and early 20th century medicine, it was archaically defined as a special contagion, imperceptible to our senses, which acts in exceedingly minute quantities to cause disease in the body.*)

VIS MEDICATRIX NATURAE (Zinc.): The healing power of nature; the power inherent in the organism which overcome the disease in its usual course without the help of any medicines.

VISCERA (Tereb.): Pl. of viscus which means Interior organ in any one of the three great cavities of the body, esp. in the abdomen.

VISCID (Arg.m., Cros., Hydr., Hyos., Kali c., Lac c., Lys., Med., Psor., Sanic.): Glutinous; sticky; thick and adhering.

VISE (Coloc.): A clamping device, usually of two jaws made to be closed together with a screw or lever and it is used to hold an object firmly while work is done on it.

VISE LIKE GRIP (Cact.): Grasped or held firmly so that it is not immovable as in a vise.

VISION: Act of seeing or viewing of external object; sight; sense by which light, colour, form, and contrast are apprehended.

    BLURRED VISION (Ruta.): Indistinct or unclear vision.

DIM VISION (Cyc., Gels., Phys., Psor., Ruta., Ver.): Indistinct vision.

DOUBLE VISION (Ver.v): Diplopia.

MISTY VISION (Ruta.): Blurred vision as in fog.

PARTIAL VISION (Ver.v): Incomplete vision; seeing only a part of an object or scene.

VITAL ACTIVITY (Pyr.): The necessary activities of a living body as respiration, circulation, excretion etc.

VITAL DEPRESSION (Apoc.): Lack of physical or mental energy and strength.

VITAL FLUIDS (Carbo.v., Cinch., Fer., Lach., Nat.m., Phos., Phos.ac., Staph.): Fluids which are contributing to or essential for life, e.g. blood, semen, etc.

VITAL FORCE (Ars., Camph., Carbo.v., Crot., Ver.): That form of energy which is manifested in the phenomena of life esp. when regarded as distinct from other forces of nature (mechanical, chemical etc.).

VITAL HEAT (Carbo.an., Led., Sab., Sep., Sil.): The heat, which is required to maintain the normal functions of body and is produced by the various physiological processes which are essential for life.

VITAL POWER (Carbo.v.): Energy or power required for survival of the organism for normal functioning.

VITAL REACTION (Diph., Op.): The power to react or respond against some external or internal stimuli, which is important for maintenance of health or survival.

VITALITY (Am.c., Carbo.v., Camph., Caul., Kreos., Zinc.): The state of being alive; physical or mental energy, strength; having an appearance of vigorous life; lively.

VIVID (Dios., Lach.): Very bright, strong (of colours); producing a sharp or clear impression on the senses.

VOICE (Stan.): The sound uttered by living beings, especially by human beings in speech or song, crying, shouting etc., and produced by vibration of vocal cord.

VOID (Carbo.v., Con., Hep., Phos., Ruta.): To evacuate the bowels or bladder; excrete or discharge from the body.

VOLUNTARY (Apoc.): Pertaining to or under control of will.

VOLUPTUOUS (Petrose., Sulph.): Sensual pleasure; producing sexual pleasure.

VOMITING (Acet.ac., Aeth., Am.m., Ant.t., Apoc.): Forcible ejection of contents of the stomach through the mouth; emesis.

> **BILIOUS VOMITING (Crot.):** Bile forced back into the stomach and ejected with vomited matter; bitter, greenish vomiting.
>
> **FAECAL VOMITING (Plb.):** The ejection of faecal matter, aspirated into the stomach from the intestine by the repeated spasmodic contraction of the gastric muscles.
>
> **OBSTINATE VOMITING (Psor.):** Vomiting which is difficult to control or cure.

VULVA (Am.c., Bell., Lil., Plat., Staph., Taren.): The external female genitals including the labia majora, labia minora, clitoris, and vestibule of the vagina.

WADING (Dul.): Walking through water, mud, snow, sand or any other substance that impedes free motion or offers resistance to movement.

WANDERING (Rhod.): Moving about here and there without any specific purpose; not fixed.

WANING (Iod.): Growing smaller or less; decreasing; fading.

WANT OF BODILY IRRITABILITY (Op.): A (weakened) state of body where reaction to stimuli is lacking.

WANT OF CONFIDENCE (in sphincter ani) (Aloe.): Loss of control of anal sphincter; Feeling as if stool would pass out involuntarily.

WANT OF VITAL HEAT (Sil.): Weak or exhausted state where normal bodily heat is lacking.

WART (Anac., Caust., Dul., Nat.m., Nit.ac., Ruta., Thuja.): A circumscribed cutaneous elevation resulting from hypertrophy of the papillae of the corium covered by thickened epidermis.

WART LIKE EXCRESCENCES (Thuja.): Any outgrowth of the skin surface looking like wart.

WASHER WOMEN REMEDY (Sep.): Remedies suitable for women who are in the profession of washing and cleaning cloths. Hence has to work water for a long period of time.

WASTING (Acet.ac): Gradual loss or decay with emaciation; destruction of body tissue; enfeebling; to wear away or impair gradually.

WATER-BRASH (Acet.ac., Lyc.): Pyrosis; a sudden gush into the mouth of acid fluids from the stomach, accompanied by burning sensation (heartburn) behind the sternum; rising of water from the stomach into mouth.

WAXY (Acet.ac., Apis.): Resembling wax in texture or appearance and especially denotes some combination of pliability, paleness, smoothness and lustre;soft.

WEAKNESS (Aeth., Aloe., Ambr., Arg.m.): Want of strength; lack of vigour; feebleness; debility.

WEANING (Cham.): To discontinue the breast-feeding of an infant, with substitution of other feeding habits.

WEARING OUT (Coca.): To feel extremely tired; to harass, tired, exhaust.

WEARY (Aloe., Bov. Phos.): Exhausted; having the strength much impaired by toil or exertion; mentally or spiritually fatigued.

WEARINESS (Cup., Mer.s., Phos., Pic.ac., Sil.): Tiredness; fatigue.

WEARINESS OF LIFE (Phos.): Dissatisfied or bored of life; sensation of being tired from living life.

WEARY PERSONS (Aloe., Pic. ac.): Tired, exhausted persons. The term is also used to denote dissatisfied or bored persons.

WEEPING (Ambr.): Shedding tears; lamenting; tending to cry easily; to expressing sorrow, grief or anguish by outcry.

WEN: A sebaceous cyst, especially one occurring on the scalp; a cyst containing oily matter.

WHEEZING (Hep., Iod., Ipec., Spong.): To breath with a husky, whistling sound.

WHINES (Ant.t): To utter high, nasal sound expressive of grief or distress; to complain in a childish way.

WHINNING RESTLESSNESS (Cham.): Uttering a low usually nasal, complaining cry or sound, (as from uneasiness) with restlessness.

WHISKERS (Sel.): Formerly the word was used to mean hair on the upper lip. But now usual hair (beard) on the side of face.

WHISTLE (Acon): A clear shrill musical sound produced by the forcing of air or steam against a thin edge or into a cavity (may be through a small hole between nearly closed lips).

WHITLOW: Paronychia; a deep usually suppurative inflammation of the finger or toe especially near the end or around the nail. Also called felon.

WICKEDNESS (Anac): Evil in character or principle which creates a desire to harm or put others in trouble; mischievous; devastating.

WIDOW (Apis., Arg.n.): A woman whose husband has died and who has not married again.

WILD (Kreos., Lil.): Living in a state of nature; uncivilized; impatient of, or not subjected to restrained or regulation; indicating strong emotion, excitement, elevation of the spirit or the like.

WILD HAIR (Bor.): Disorderly, uncontrolled hairs which cannot be smoothed even by repeated combing.

WILTED SKIN (Chel.): Withered, wrinkled skin.

WIND PIPE (Kali c.): The tubular structure through which air passes from the larynx to the lungs, i.e. trachea.

WINDGALL (Med.): A soft pulpy swelling in the synovial bursa in neighbourhood of the fetlock joint (the joint of the horse's leg above the hard part of the foot) of the horse varying in size from a pinhead to a large hen's egg; a soft and puffy tumour.

WIRY (Pyr.): Small but tense; resembling or having the feel of a wire.

WITHERED (Arg.n., Sars.): To lose vigour, power, force or strength; to fade or become lean, dry and shrivelled; to lose freshness.

WOEFUL (Hell.): Sorrowful or afflicted; bringing misery or calamity; full of great sorrow or distress.

WOMB (Helon., Murex): The uterus.

WORM (Cina., Hyos., Nat.m., Sabad., Spig., Stan., Sulph., Tereb.,): Any of the soft-bodied, elongated invertebrates of the phyla Platyhelminthes and Nemathelminthes, that live inside of the bodies of the humans or animals and causes illness. Formerly classified as Vermes.

WORN OUT (Ambr., Helon., Pic. ac.): Much injured or rendered useless by use; wearied, tired.

WORRY (Acon., Iod., Kali br., Psor.): To feel or express great care and anxiety; to keep thinking about unpleasant things that might happen or about existing problem.

WOUND (Led., Sec.): An injury or traumatism to any of the tissues of the body, caused by mechanical violence, with or without a solution of continuity.

    CONTUSED WOUND (Ham., Hyos.): An injury to the soft parts without a break in the skin like bruise, may be caused by blunt instrument.

    DISSECTING WOUND (Crot.): Wound caused by sharp instruments during dissection.

INCISED WOUND (Ham., Hyos.): A clean cut made with a sharp instrument.

JAGGED LOOKING WOUND (Calen.): Wound looking rough and uneven shape with sharp edges.

LACERATED WOUND (Calen., Carb.ac., Ham., Hyos., Lac d., Sul.ac.): A tear of the tissue.

POISON WOUND (Lach.): Injury to the tissue due to any poison.

PUNCTURED WOUND (Hyos., Led.): A wound made by a sharp pointed instrument such as a dagger, ice pick or needle.

WRAPPING (Bell., Hep., Iod., Mag.m., Nux m., Rhod., Rhus., Sil.): To enclose; to wind a covering around an object.

WRATH (Staph.): Extreme or violent anger; to become angry.

WRETCHEDNESS (Tab.): Very miserable; pitiable; distressingly bad; uneasiness of body and mind.

WRINKLED (Abrot., Kreos., Op., Sanic., Spig.): Small creased or furrowed or folded appearance on a surface; a crease or ridge in the skin or mucous membrane.

WRONG WAY (Can.s.): Going in wrong direction.

WRY NECK: Torticollis; stiff-neck.

XIPHOID: The sword-shaped lower end of the sternum or breastplate; breast bone.

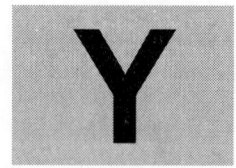

YARROW (Mill.): A strong-scented plant, *AchilleaMillefolium*, or similar species.

YAWNING (Am.c., Amyl., Asar., Eup.): Deep inspiration with mouth wide open. Yawning is induced by drowsiness, boredom or fatigue. (It usually stimulates observers to yawn).

YEAST LIKE VOMITING (Nat.c.): Vomitus containing yellowish frothy viscous substance.

YELLOW FEVER (Crot.): An acute infectious disease of tropical or subtropical regions caused by *group-B arbovirus* harboured by the *AedesAegypti* mosquito, characterized by fever, slow pulse, albuminuria, jaundice, congestion of face and haemorrhages, specially haematemesis (black vomiting). It is fatal in 5-10 % of the cases, otherwise recovery is complete.

YELLOW SADDLE (Sep.): A yellowish discoloration of the skin across the bridge of the nose resembling saddle.

ZEALOUS (Nux.): Devoted; enthusiastic and eager.

ZIG ZAG (Can.s., Nat.m., Nit.ac.): Not straight but with turns and curves.

ZIG ZAG DAZZLING LIKE LIGHTENING (Nat.m.): Vision overpowered or confused with flash of too bright light having sharp turns; flashes of light.

ZONA (Mez.): It is synonymous to Herpes zoster. *'Zona'* means 'a belt or sash'. It is an acute inflammatory viral disease, characterized by groups of small vesicles associated with neuralgic pain. Lesions usually occur along the course of cutaneous nerves. Though most common site is abdomen but may also be found on face and neck.

ZYGOMA, ZYGOMATIC: The long arch which joins zygomatic process of the temporal and malar bones on the sides of the skull. It forms the hard part of the check and lower lateral portion of rim of each orbit. Also called the *malar bone* or the *cheekbone*.

ZOSTER: Herpes zoster. (same as *Zona*).

ZYMOSIS: An archaic term for prostration and septicaemia; the process by which an infectious disease is said to develop; the term also means fermentation or an infectious disease.

ZYMOTIC (Crot.): Relating to zymosis, is an infectious or contagious disease; relating to or produced by fermentation. *(The Zymotic doctrine / theory was in vogue during the mid to late*

1800, and described infectious diseases as essentially fermentative process. The term was used to describe a vast member of epidemic, endemic and contagious diseases which acted in a similar way to the fermentative process.)

ZYMOTIC DISEASE (Crot.): An infection or contagious disease caused by the growth of microorganisms.

HELPS FOR FURTHER STUDY OF ALLEN'S KEYNOTES

CHILD

Intolerance of milk; cannot bear milk in any form - **AETH**

(*Diarrhea; the milk passes undigested in nursing children - MAG CARB*)

Aversion to milk; Diarrhea from it - NAT CARB

Constipation, with ineffectual urging >cold milk - IOD

Diarrhea from boiled milk - NUX MOS

Diarrhea from drinking milk - NAT CARB; CALC; SULPH)

Children who cannot bear milk - **AETH**

Children during dentition are unable to digest milk - **MAG MUR**

Diarrhea; the milk passes undigested in nursing children – **MAG CARB**

Diarrhea- during dentition - **CHAM**

Constipation of infants during dentition - **MAG MUR**

Oozing of bloody fluid from navel of infants – **CALC PHOS**

Oozing of urine from navel - **HYOS**

Asphyxia neonatorum; relieves the "death rattles"- **ANT TART** (TARENT)

Ophthalmia neonatorum - **ARG NIT**

Ophthalmia neonotorum, sycotic or syphilitic > warmth and covering; if uncovered, feels as if a cold stream of air were blowing out through them - **THUJA**

(*Eyes: as if cold wind blowing across the eyes- CROC SAT*)

Acute ophthalmia neonatorum > by cold bathing - **SYPH**

(When reading, sensation as if they would be pressed as under or outward; relieved by bathing them in cold water- ASAR)

Body painfully sensitive to touch; part touched feels chilly; touch sends shudder through the whole frame - **SPIG** (KALI CARB)

(Entire body painfully sensitive to slightest touch- CAMPH)

Child whines and cries if anyone touches him; will not let you feel the pulse- **ANT TART** (ANT CRUD; SANIC)

Child cannot bear to be touched or looked at; sulky, does not wish to speak or to be spoken to- **ANT CRUD** (ANT TART; IOD; SIL)

Solitude is unbearable: desires company, child holds on to its mother's hand for company - **BISM** (KALI CARB; LIL TIG; LYCO)

(Desires darkness and solitude - COCA)

Desires light and company; cannot bear to be alone - STRAM

Child: Cannot bear to be alone – Stram.; Bis.)

Child *wants abdomen uncovered relieves nausea and vomiting; coldness in abdomen – TAB (COLCH; ELAPS; LACH)*

(Coldness of single parts - CALC CARB

Sensation of coldness about the heart – PET

Coldness of vertex - SEP; VAL; VERT ALB

Cold feeling in abdomen - VERT ALB)

Scrofulous, rachitic children with long heads, open fontanel's and sutures, much sweating about the head (less than Calc.) - **SIL**

Head sweats profusely while sleeping wetting pillow far around - **CALC** (SIL; SANIC)

When laying the child down on a couch, or in the crib, cries and clings to the nurse - **BOR**

[*Diarrhea from downward motion*- *CHAM (BOR; SANIC)*]

Children fear of falling, grasp the crib or seize the nurse - **GELS** (BOR; SANIC)

Child is good, plays all day; restless, troublesome screaming all night – **PSOR** (JALAPA)

Baby cries all day, sleeps all right – **LYCO**

Enuresis, bed is wet almost as soon as the child goes to sleep; always during the first sleep - **SEP** (KREOS)

Urination during first sleep from which child is aroused with difficulty - **KREOS**

Enuresis during full moon, obstinate, with a family history of eczema - **PSOR**

Nocturnal enuresis –passes enormous quantity of ammoniacal urine in bed every night after over work or over play, extreme of heat or cold- **MEDO**

Enuresis nocturna of delicate children - **BENZ AC**

Enuresis diurna et nocturna; profuse watery urine, where habit is the only ascertainable cause - **EQUIS**

In children nocturnal enuresis with constipation - **CAUST**

MIND

Child is ill-natured, irritable, <u>cross</u> and despondent; violent, inhuman, would like to do something cruel- **ABROT**

Despondent, gloomy; very irritable; loses temper easily and gains control slowly; miserably cross – **AESC (CHAM)**

Child exceedingly irritable, fretful; quiet only when carried; impatient, wants this or that and becomes angry when refused, or when offered, petulantly rejects it (Bry., Cina, Kreos.); "too ugly to live;" cross, spiteful- **CHAM**

Patient cannot endure any one near him; is cross, cannot bear to be spoken to- **CHAM**

Adapted to children with dark hair, very cross, irritable, ill-humored, want to be carried, but carrying gives no relief- **CINA**

Cross, irritable; child cries and screams all the time, especially at night - **LAC CAN (JAL., NUX, PSOR.)**

Irritable; peevish and cross on waking- **LYCO**

Irritated at trifles; cross during the day, exhilarated at night- **MEDO**

Irritability: child cross when spoken to; crying from slightest cause- **NAT MUR**

The countenance is expressive of fear; the life is rendered miserable by fear; is sure his disease will prove fatal; predicts the day he will die; fear of death during pregnancy- **ACON**

Anxious fear of death; thinks it useless to take medicine, is incurable, is surely going to die; dread of death, when alone, or, going to bed- **ARS ALB**

Fear of imaginary things, wants to run away from them; hallucinations- **BELL**

Fear of death; believes disease incurable - **CACT G** (ARS)

Fears she will lose her reason or that people will observe her mental confusion - **CAL C** (ACT.)

Fear of death (Ars.); utter lack of courage- **GELS**

Fears: being alone; poison; being bitten; being sold; to eat or drink; to take what is offered; suspicious, of some plot- **HYOS**

Fears to be alone (Kali c.); of dying (Ars.); of becoming insane (Lil.); of falling down stairs (Bor.) - **LAC CAN**

Despondent; does not care to live; has no fear of death but is sure he is going to die- **LAC DEF**

Anxious: about the disease; fears the symptoms indicate an organic affection; marked in both sexes- **LIL TIG**

Great anxiety about his disease; constantly thinking about his past troubles; morbid fear of cholera (Ars.); depressed and anxious in the evening- **NIT AC**

Resembles: Ars. in morbid fear of cholera- **NIT AC**

Satiety of life, with taciturnity and fear of death – **PLAT** (ACON, ARS)

Anxious, full of fear; evil forebodings- **PSOR**

Despondent: fears he will die- **PSOR**

Great apprehension at night; fears he will die of being poisoned; cannot remain in bed- **RHUS TOX**

Anxiety: with fear, flushes of heat over face and head; about real or imaginary evils; toward evening- **SEP**

Ailments: from sudden emotions, fear, fright, joy (Coff., Gels.); from anger or vexation- **CAUST**

Bad effects from fright, fear, exciting news and sudden motions – **GELS** (IGN)

Bad effects from pleasant surprise- **COFF**

Ailments: the bad effects of sudden emotions or pleasurable surprises- **COFF** (CAUST)

Bad effects of mental excitement, fright, fear, mechanical injuries and their later consequences- **GLON**

Bad effects of unfortunate love; with jealousy, rage, incoherent speech or inclination to laugh at everything- **HYOS**

Bad effects of disappointed affection - **ANT C** (CAL. P)

Ailments from grief, disappointed love - **CAL P** (AUR, IGN, PHOS. AC)

Bad effects of unfortunate love; with jealousy, rage, incoherent speech or inclination to laugh at everything; often followed by epilepsy- **HYOS**

Aggravation- jealousy, unhappy love- **HYOS**

Bad effects of anger, grief, or disappointed love – **IGN** (CAL. P., HYOS.)

Ailments from long lasting grief; sorrow, fright, vexation, jealousy or disappointed love – **LACH** (AUR., IGN., PHOS. AC)

Solitude is unbearable: desires company, child holds on to its mother's hand for company – **BIS** (KALI C., LIL, LYC)

Great aversion to being alone - **KALI CARB** (ARS., BIS., LYC.)

Dreads being alone, yet avoids society - **CON MAC** (KALI C., LYC.)

Fears: being alone, insanity, heart disease; fears she is incurable; some impending calamity or disease- **LIL TIG**

Dread of men; of solitude, irritable and melancholy; fear of being alone – **LYCO** (BIS., KALI C., LIL.)

Desires light and company; cannot bear to be alone (Bis.); worse in the dark and solitude- **STRAM**

Dread of being alone; of men; of meeting friends; with uterine troubles- **SEP**

Desires to be let alone; wants to lie down and sleep- **CAPS**

Desire to be quiet, to be let alone; does not wish to speak or have any one near her, even if the person be silent – **GELS** (IGN)

Fears: being alone- **HYOS**

Desire to be alone- **IGN**

Desires to be alone- **IGN., NUX**

Fears to be alone - **LAC CAN** (KALI C.)

Aggravation -when alone- **STRAM**

Cannot bear to be left alone; yet persistently refuses to talk- **VER ALB**

Great sadness, sits for days, weeping- **AMBR**

Great sadness, with weeping- **ANT C**

Anxious lachrymose mood, the slightest thing affects her - **ANT C** (PULS)

Profound depression of spirits; Can hardly avoid weeping; is very timid, fearful and weeps much; indifferent about what is being done for her- **LIL TIG**

Great sadness and weeping- **SEP**

Weeping disposition; cannot help crying; discouraged, despondent – **APIS** (PULS.)

Melancholy mood: sad, hopeless; from care, grief, sorrow; with weeping, "the least thing makes the child cry."- **CAUST**

Weeping from delight; alternate laughing and weeping - **COFF**

Fits of uncontrollable weeping and profound melancholic delusions – **KALI BROM**

Cannot speak without weeping – **MEDO**

Marked disposition to weep; sad weeping mood without cause – **NAT MUR** (PULS.)

Weeps easily: almost impossible to detail her ailments without weeping (weeps when thanked, Lyc.) - **PULS**

Music is unbearable, makes her sad – ACON (SAB)

Music in intolerable: Produces nervousness goes through bone and marrow – **SAB**

Music is unbearable, makes her sad during menses – **NAT CARB**

Sad, despondent; music makes her weep – **GRAPH**

Music causes weeping – **THUJA**

Attacks of anxiety and restlessness during a thunderstorm (Phos.) < from music (Sabad.) – **NAT CARB**

Depressed; lively music makes her sad – **NAT SULPH**

Remedy of great contradicitions- **IGN**

Strange temper, laughs at serious matters and is serious over laughable things- **ANAC**

Changeable humor; are moment laughing the next crying; "sudden change from grave to gay, from lively to serene – **NUX MOS**

Frequent and extreme changes in sensations; sudden from greater hilarity to the deepest despondency – **CROC**

Mental conditions rapidly, in an almost incredibly short time, change from joy to sorrow, from laughing to weeping - **IGN**

Great loquacity; one word often leads into another story- **LACH**

Disposed to talks continually – **STRAM** (CIC., LACH)

Irritability: slight noises like crackling of paper drive him to despair – **FER MET** (ASAR., TARENT)

Oversensitiveness of nerves, scratching of linen or silk, crackling of paper is unbearable- **ASAR** (FERR)

- *Vertigo from any even least noise – THER*
- *Headache, neuralgia, < by noise, touch, strong light and ameliorated by rubbing head against the pillow.- TARENT*
- *Restless, fidgety; starts at least noise- SIL*

Sad weeping mood, without cause but consolation from other < her trouble - **NAT MUR**

Consolation < - **NAT MUR, HELL, LIL TIG**

Stormy weather he feels acutely feels restless for days before or during a thunderstorm - **PSOR**

Feels restless for days before or during thunderstorm – **PSOR; PHOS**

Attacks of anxiety and restlessness during a thunder aggravation. from music - **NAT CARB**

Ailments which are worse before and during thunderstorm - **PET**

Nervous persons who dread a storm and are particularly afraid of thunder storm especially electrical storm – **RHODO**

Lyssophobia; fear of becoming mad- **LYSS**

Hydrophobia: fear of water, with excessive aversion to liquids – **STRAM** (BELL., LYS.)

- *Diarrhea: choleric, from fear- PHOS AC*
- *Fears the terrific suffering from exhaustion on awakening – SYPHI (LACH.)*

Irresistible desire to curse and swear (Lac. c., Lil., Nit. ac - wants to pray continually, Stram.) - **ANACARD**

Disposed to curse, strike, to think obscene things - **LIL TIG**

VERTIGO

Vertigo as if intoxicated when rising in bed- COCC

Vertigo when lying down or turning is bed; turning the head to the left - **CON (COLOC)**

Vertigo when quickly turning head specially to left as if he would fall- **COLOCYNTH**

Vertigo sensation as if falling to the left- **EUP PERF**

Vertigo on seeing flowing water – **FER MET**

(The sight or sound of running water or pouring water aggravates all complaints-LYSSIN

Convulsions renewed by sight of bright light, of mirror or water- STRAM; BELL; LYSS)

Vertigo with sensation as if head became suddenly elongated – **HYPER**

(Headache with sense of expansion-ARG NIT)

Tooth feels elongated – Ratania

Vertigo at night with urging to urinate - **HYPER**

Vertigo when stooping, or when rising after stooping; on every change of position - **BELL (BRY)**

Vertigo when moving slowly, but not when taking violent exercise – **MILL**

(Sensation of congestion, pressure or weight in chest as if blood from extremities was filling it, > by rapid walking- LOB

Dyspnoea < sitting, after sleep, in room, > dancing or walking rapidly- SEP

Fears that unless on the move heart will cease beating – GELS
Sensation as if heart would stop beating if she moves– DIG (COCCAINE)

Vertigo on closing the eyes – **THER** (LACH; THUJA)
Sweat as soon as closing the eyes- CON MAC; THUJA; CHINA)

Vertigo on opening the eyes – **TAB**
(Sweet on opening the eyes – SAMB)

Vertigo as if one would fall forward, from looking up - **SIL, TAB** (PULS)

Vertigo as if one would fall forward from looking down - **KAL** (SPIG)

Vertigo from any even least noise – **THER**

Vertigo- death like pallor, on rising on looking backward — **TAB**

Every sound seems to penetrate through the whole body causing nausea and vertigo - **THER**

Vertigo, when standing or walking; worse when lying down - **RHUS TOX**

HEADACHE

Headache ceases during menses; returns when flow disappears – **ALL CEPA** (LACH; ZINC MET)

(Feels better every way as soon as the menses begins to flow; it relieves all her suffering –ZINC MET; LACH; CYCL)

Headache as if the skull would burst - **CINCH**

Headache when stooping, as if brain would burst through forehead - **BRY**

Amelioration. from heat in general except headache which is temporarily > by cold bathing – **ARS ALB** (SPIG)

Headache are worse from heat, better from cold application - **ALOE** (ARS ALB)

Headache from taking cold – **ANT CRUD**

(Diarrhea from cold – CHAM)

(Gastric and intestinal affection after over heating – Ant crud)

Cold bathing causes violent headache - **ANT CRUD**

Headache after river bathing –**ANT CRUD**

(Ailments lying on damp ground; too much summer bathing in lake or river – RHUSTOX)

Headache after sea bathing - **ARS ALB**

Headache relieved entirely when eating - **ANAC**

[Gastralgia whenever stomach is empty, relieved by constant eating – PETROLEUM (ANAC., CHEL. CEPA.)]

Eating little too much causes headache - **NUX MOS**

(At every attempt to eat, colic pains in abdomen- CALC PHOS)

Headache: always hungry during; > while eating – **PSOR** (KALI PHOS; ANAC)

Headache: in nape and occiput; extending to the spine; as if tightly bound by a cord; with nausea, as if at sea; at each menstrual period; < lying on back of head - **COCC** (IOD.; CACT.; LIL. TIG.; DIOSC.; GELS.,

Headache from suppressed eruption - **ANT CRUD**

[Asthma after suppressed eruption - HEP SULPH

Cough after suppressed itch, or eczema- PSOR

Epilepsy from suppressed eruptions- AGAR (PSOR; SULPH)

Diarrhea especially if eruption be suppressed- APIS; PET

Brain diseases from suppressed eruptions- CICUTA

Chorea from suppressed eruption; from fright- ZINC MET

Headache from suppressed eruption or menses – PSOR

Diarrhea from suppressed eruption – PSOR.)

Dropsy from suppressed exanthemata- Hell.)]

Headache ending in bilious vomiting - **ARG NIT**

(Fever: bitter vomiting at close of chill – Eup perf.)

Headache returning every year in winter – **BISMUTH**.

[Itch appears each year, as winter approaches- ALOE

Tips of fingers rough cracked, fissured, every winter- PET

Cough returns every winter- PSOR

Many complaints come on only in winter – AURUM MET

Erethitic chlorosis, worse in winter- FERR MET

Diseases occurring in winter – MERC

Dry, itch like eruptions, prone to appear in spring; become crusty – SARS

Croupy cough in winter alternating with sciatica in summer- STAPH

Spare, dry, thin subjects; dark complexion; mild, cheerful disposition; hypochondriacs; dry, tettery, itching eruption, worse in winter – ALUM (PETR)

Hay fever; in August every year; violent sneezing on rising from bed; from handling peaches – ALL CEPA

Headache alternates with Diarrhea; headache in winter and diarrhoea in summer – **PODO** (ALOE)

(Croupy cough in winter alternating with sciatica in summer – STAPH

Headache returning every winter; alternating with, or attended by gastralgia.- BISM

Fistula in ano, alternating with chest symptoms- CAL PHOS (BERB.; SIL.)

Chorea and hysteria with great hilarity, singing and dancing (Tar.);

Alternating with melancholy and rage – CROC SAT

Rheumatism alternating with gastric symptoms, one appearing in the fall and the other in the spring; rheumatism and dysentery alternate – KALI BI (ABROT)

Delirium alternating with colic – PLUMB

Constipation: alternating with diarrhea – SULPH

Rheumatism; alternates with haemorrhoids, with dysentery – **ABROT**

Alternate constipation and diarrhea – **CHEL; COLLIN; SULPH; VER**

Cerebral congestion, or alternate congestion of the head and heart – **GLON**

In heart diseases that have developed from rheumatism, or alternate with it – **KALMIA LAT**

Cough: periodic, returning spring and fall- CINA]

Headache alternating with or attended by gastralgia – **BISM**

Headache alternating with lumbago - **ALOE**

Headache from constipation - **BRY**

Headache from insufficient stool - **ALOE**

Headache > by pressure or tight bandaging - **ARG NIT; LAC DEF; BELL; SIL** (APIS, PULS)

Complaints occurring in hot weather- **KALI BI**

Headache of school girl- **CALC PHOS** (TUB)

Headache in anemic school girls- **NAT MUR**

Headache as if tornado in head - **CARB AN**

Sensation as of a hoop or band around a part- **ANAC** (CACT; CARB AC; SULPH)

Dull heavy frontal headache as if a rubber band were stretched tightly over the forehead from temple to temple- **CARB AC** (GELS; PLAT; SULPH)

Sensation of band around the head above eyes - **GELS** (CARB AC; SULPH)

Sensation as if a band around head - **SPIG** (CACT; CARB AC; SULPH)

Headache: as of an iron hoop round the head - **TUB** (ANAC; SULPH)

Epilepsy: headache follows attack - **KALI BR**

Sensation: of a band around head, around the bones - **NIT AC** (CARB AC; SULPH)

Chronic sick headache > by profuse urination - **SIL**

(Vertigo: at night with urging to urinate – HYPER)

American sick headache > copious, pale urine - **LAC DEF**

Headache preceded by blindness >by profuse urination- **GELS**

Headache blurred vision or blindness precedes the attack- **KALI BI**

Headache preceded, by flickering before eyes, by dimness of vision or blindness - **PSOR**

Headache beginning with blindness; with zig zag dazzling, like lightening in eyes- **NAT MUR**

American sick headache: intense throbbing, with nausea, vomiting, blindness and obstinate constipation- **LAC DEF**

American sick headache > by perfect quiet in a dark room- **SANG**

Cannot bear the heat of sun, worse from over exertion in sun, < from overheating near the fire, ailments from sun burn- **ANT CRUD**

Head troubles from working under gaslight when heat falls on head cannot bear heat almost the head, heat of stove or walking in the sun- **GLON**

Chronic effects of sunstrokes; headache from sun or working under gaslight- **NAT CARB**

Headache < afternoon until midnight- **LOB**

In headache could not lie down "the pillow would beat" – **GLON**

(Palpitation: violent, visible and audible- SPIGELIA)

Violent congestive headache epistaxis affords relief- **MEL** (PSOR; HAM; BUFO; FER PHOS; MAG SULPH)

Head: feels enormously large; as if skull were too small for brain - **GLON**

Headache with sense of expansion- **ARG NIT**

(Vertigo with sensation as if head became suddenly elongated – HYPER)

Headache-after a fall upon occiput - **HYPER**

Headache ameliorated by pressure and external heat - **MAG PHOS**

Headache < 10 to 11 am or 4 to 5 pm – **MAG PHOS**

Headache from slightest mental exertion - **NAT CARB**

Headache from pressure of hat – **NIT AC**

Headache from worms - **SABAD**

Pain on vertex as if hair were pulled – **MAG CARB**

Headache as if everything in the head were alive – **PETR**

Headache of students, teachers and over worked business men - **PIC AC**

Headache from too much thinking – **SABAD; COFF**

Nervous headache periodical beginning in morning at the base of brain spreading at temple of lt. side - **SPIG**

Headache begins in occiput spreads upwards and settles over rt. eye - **SANG**

Chronic sick headache ascending from nape of neck to the vertex as if coming from spine and locating in one eye epecially right - **SIL**

Headache, pressing like a heavy weight on vertex - **CACT**

Headache pressing in vertex from above downwards > by hard pressure with hand- **MENYAN**

Headache crushing weight on vertex - **PHOS AC**

Sensation of lump of ice on vertex - **VER ALB**

Coldness of vertex with headache - **SEP** (VER ALB)

[*Burning round spot on vertex- GRAPH (CALC)*

Sensation of burning on vertex- SULPH]

Sensation of great coldness in the head - **VAL**

Heat of vertex - **GRAPH; SULPH; CALC CARB**

Headache, neuralgia, < by noise, touch, strong light and ameliorated by rubbing head against the pillow - **TARENT**

Sick headache coming on in early morning, intolerable by noon, deathly nausea, violent vomiting - **TAB**

Sick-headache from carriage, boat or train riding – **COCC**

Complaints > by riding in a carriage – NIT AC

Hardness of hearing amel by carriage riding or train- GRAPH; NIT AC

Backache while riding in a carriage- NUX MOSCH

Nausea or vomiting from riding in carriage boat or railroad car- COCC)

Headache and diarrhea from jarring of cars - **MEDO**

Hairs falls off, on head, eyebrows, whiskers, genitals – **SELEN**

(Hair falls out in bunches, baldness of single spots – PHOS)

Brain feels loose when stepping or shaking the head; sensation of swashing in brain - **RHUSTOX**

(Swashing sensation in intestines – CROT TIG

Sensation as if the brain was loose in forehead and falling from side to side – SULPH AC)

Headache commencing at 4 P.M. - **SYPH**

Headache and periosteal pains generally from mercury, syphillis, or suppressed gonorrhoea - **SARS**

Head feels as if scattered about- **STRAM** (**BAPT**)

Headache as though thousands of little hammers were knocking in the brain during fever- **NAT MUR**

Headache: intense, as if thousands of needles were pricking in the brain- **TARENT**

Headache as if pressing with a convex button - **THUJA**

Headache as if nails were driven out through the side, relieved by lying on it - **IGN** (COFF; NUX VOM; THUJA)

Headache one sided, as if from a nail driven into the brain - **COFF** (IGN; NUX VOM)

Headache as if nails were driven into parietal bones - **THUJA** (COFF; IGN)

Headache: every 7th day - **SANG** (SABAD; SIL; SULPH)

Headache: every 8th day - **IRIS**

Headache: every six weeks, in forehead and around the eyes - **MAG MUR**

Headache: < by noise of running water or bright light - **LYSS**

Headache: every afternoon - **SEL**

Sick headache every week or every two weeks - **SULPH**

Headache: For two, three or four days every two or three weeks - **FERRUM MET**

Nervous or sick headache; congestion from suppressed menses; intense, almost apoplectic, with violent nausea and vomiting - **VER VIR**

Headache: from tea - **THUJA; SEL**

Headache: gastric, with nausea, vomiting and great prostration; following intoxication; < afternoon until midnight; sudden pallor with profuse sweat (Tab.); < by tobacco or tobacco smoke - **LOBELIA**

Coffea increases nervous headache– **ARG NIT**

(Constipation: in women who are habitual coffee drinkers – IGN)

"All-gone" sensation in stomach, in tea drinkers especially – PULS (LOB)

Is useful in bad effects from excessive tea drinking or abuse of chamomile tea, when haemorrhage results – CHINA

Flatulence after meals or after eating, especially of tea-drinkers – DIOS

Faintness, weakness and an indescribable feeling at epigastrium, from excessive use of tea or tobacco – LOB

Toothache from tea drinking – THUJA

Toothache from coffee – CHAM

Toothache from tobacco smoking – SPIG

Headache from beer – RHUS TOX

Aggravation: Of many symptoms from drinking wine, even a small quantity – ZINC (ALUM, CON)

All irritating things - salt, wine, vinegar, pepper - immediately produce cough – ALUM

Wine, which aggravates urinary gouty and rheumatic affections – BENZ AC

Gastric complaints: bad effects of beer – KALI BI

It antidoes mercurial inhalation, lead colic, oil of turpentine, spiritous liquors and especially the effects of bad beers – NUX MOS

EYE

Conjunctival or retinal haemorrhage. with extravasations from injuries and cough – **ARN** (LED; NUX VOM)

Contusion of eye and lids, especially with much extravasations of blood- **LED**

Pain in eye from a blow of an obtuse body; snow ball strikes the eye infants thrusts its fist into mother's eye- **SYMPH**

Periodic orbital neuralgia (right side) with excessive lachrymation; tears fairly gushes out- **CHEL**

Lachrymation of tears stream down the face whenever be cough - **NAT MUR**

Diplopia, one image seen below the other - **SYPH**

Dim – Sighted as sees as through a veil - **TAB**

Hemiopia, sees only the left half— **LITH CARB; LYCO**

Hemiopia – sees only the lower half – **AUR MET**

Ciliary neuralgia < going up stairs > lying down- **ACTEA**

Intolerable pressive pain in eyeballs could not turn the eyes without turning the whole body- **SPIG**

Severe stitching pain in rt. eye and orbit < when turning the eyes; begins at sunrise < at noon and leaves at sunset- **KAL** (NAT MUR)

Weak eyes-after coition, pollution, abortion, measles- **KALI CARB**

Eyeballs sore to touch pain as if they would be pulled back into head- **HEP** (OLEAN; PARIS)

Intense photophobia without inflammation of eyes - **CON MAC**

Intense photophobic with inflamed lids can't open the eyes, lies with face buried in the pillow - **PSOR**

Granular lids; like small blisters; green pus and terrible photophobia gonorrheal or sycotic - **NAT SULPH**

Cold air or cold water pleasant to the eye-relieved by bathing in cold water- **ASAR**

Ophthalmia neonatorum, large granulation, like warts or blisters: > by warmth and covering; if uncovered, feels as if a cold stream of air were blowing out through them - **THUJA**

Acute ophthalmia neonatorum > cold bathing - **SYPH**

Ophthalmia neonatorum - **ARG NIT**

Eyes- sensation as if room were filled with smoke; as if had been weeping: as if cold wind blowing across the eyes; closing lids tightly gives > - **CROC**

Eyes burn ache feels strained hot like balls of fire, spasms of lower lids - **RUTA**

Aching in and over eyes with blurred vision after using eyes at fine work watch making engraving – **RUTA**

Eyestrain from sewing < in warm room > in open air, disease due to defective accommodation - **ARG NIT**

Day blindness mist before eyes – **RAN BULB**

Stye, chalazae on eyelids or upper lids one after another, Leaving hard nodosity in their wake – **STAPH** (CON; THUJA)

Styes on upper lid from eating fat, greasy rich food or pork - **PULS**

Eyes wide open, prominent, brilliant pupils widely dilated - **STRAM**

Flickering before eyes, fiery sparks as of various colours glittering needles, dim vision of fog or smoke - **CYCL**

Yellow color of conjunctiva; clears up vision after keratitis - **CROT HOR**

Pupils dilates when child is reprimanded - **STRAM**

Amaurosis from atrophy of retina or optic nerve - **TAB**

Dryness of eyes; too dry to close the lids - **NUX MOS**

Nystagmus - **PHYSO**

Vision dim, from blur or film, object mixed - **PHYSO**

Eyelashes: loaded with dry, gummy exudation - **BOR**

Eczema of lids; eruption moist and fissured; lids red and margins covered with scales or crusts- **GRAPH**

Ptosis, paralysis of sup. oblique, sleepy look from drooping lids - **SYPH**

Drooping of upper eyelid can't keep them open (Caul.; Gels.; Graph.)- **CAUST**

Drooping of both eyelids- **SEP**

Great heaviness of eyelids; can't keep them open - **GELS**

Leucorrhoea with upper eyelids heavy has to raise them with fingers - **CAUL** (GELS)

Bag like puffy smelling under the eyes- **APIS**

Bag like swelling between the upper eyelid and eyebrow- **KALI CARB**

Lids swollen puffy edematous (whole eye swollen) – **PHOS.**

EARS

Chronic otitis, discharge purulent like putrid meat; granulation condylomata; polypi, pale red, cellular, bleeding easily - THUJA

Otorrhoea; thin, ichorous, horribly fetid discharge like decayed meat; chronic.; after measles or scarlatina - **PSOR**

Cracking: in ears, on masticating; of the joints, on motion - **NIT AC** (COCC; GRAPH)

Hardness of hearing > by riding in carriage or train - **GRAPH; NIT AC**

(*Sick-headache from carriage, boat or train riding – COCC*

Complaints > by riding in a carriage – NIT AC

Backache while riding in a carriage- NUX MOS.

Nausea or vomiting from riding in carriage boat or railroad car- COCC)

Polypi and fungous excrescences in ext. meatus - **MERC SOL** (MAR V; THUJA)

Painful swelling behind the ear (mastoid), extremely sore and sensitive to touch- **CAPS**

Hearing confused; cannot tell from what direction a sound comes- **CARB AN**

Catarrhal inflammation of middle ear - **MERC DULC**

Eustachian tube closed, catarrhal deafness and otorrhoea in psoric chidren; deafness of old age - **MERC DULC** (KALI MUR)

Sensation as if ears were plugged up with some foreign substance- **ASAR**

Pressive pain in root of nose- **KALI BI**

Pressive pain in forehead and root of nose- **STICTA**

Discharge of plugs, "CLINKERS"- **KALI BI**

Cracking in ears on masticating – **NIT AC**

Small boils in any part of body but specially in external auditory canal – **PIC AC**

Crops of small boils, intensely painful, successively appear in the nose; green, fetid pus - **TUB**

(Leucorrhoea acrid copious fetid green- CARB AC; SEC COR

Boils: small, painful with green contents – SEC COR)

Scanty green urine – RUTA)

Meniere's disease - **THER**

FACE

At puberty acne in anemic girls with vertex headache and flatulent dyspepsia >by eating – **CALC PHOS**

Acne all forms simplex rosacea < during menses - **PSOR**

Eruption on face of young women, especially during scanty menses - **SANG** (BELLIS; CALC; EUG J; PSOR)

Itching eruption on forehead during menses- **SARS** (EUG J; SANG; PSOR)

Red pimples or tubercles on forehead and cheeks as in brandy drinkers, stinging when touched- **LED PAL**

Acne: simplex, indurate, rosacea; bluish-red, pustular, on face, chest, shoulders; leaves unsightly scars- **KALI BROM** (CARBO AN)

Sensation of cobwebs on forehead tries hard to brush it if- **GRAPH** (BAR CARB; BOR; BROM; RAN S)

Sensation of cobweb on face- **BROM** ((BAR CARB; BOR; GRAPH)

Epistaxis hangs in a dark clotted string from the nose like an icicle- **MERC SOL**

Nosebleed black, tenacious, stringy every drop can be turned into a thread- **CROC**

Neuralgia of face amel. by kneeling down and pressing head firmly against the floor- **SANG**

Neuralgia of face, supra or infra orbital; right sided; intermittent, darting , cutting ; < touch, cold air, pressure ; > external heat-

MAG PHOS

Twitching of muscles of face- **MYGALE**

Leucorrhoea with "moth spots" on forehead - **CAUL** (SEP)

Yellow saddle across upper part of cheek and nose; a "telltale face" of uterine ailments- **SEP**

Dark brown "Liver spots" in climacteric years; jaundice the eyes skin and urine yellow— **PLUMB**

Middle of lower lip cracked- **HEP** (AM CARB; NAT MUR)

Cracks in commissures- **CUNDURANGO**

Skin of face greasy, shiny- **NAT MUR**

Necrosis of the (left) lower jaw- **PHOS**

Exostoses of bones of face- **FL AC** (HEKLA)

Caries of the nasal palatine and mastoid bones- **AUR MET**

(Caries and necrosis, especially of long bones, psoric or syphilitic, abuse of mercury or silica- FL AC (ANGUS).

Necrosis of the (left) lower jaw- PHOS

Bones, especially long bones, inflamed, swollen; nightly pains going from above downwards; after abuse of Merc., after veneral diseases; caries, exostosis, tumors soften from within out- MEZ

Interstitial inflammation of bones, scrofulous, sycotic, syphilitic, mercurial; periosteum inflamed, pains burning, tearing, as if scraped with a knife (Rhus); caries, rachitis, but not necrosis- PHOS AC

In rachitis, caries, necrosis, it apparently goes to the root of the evil and destroys the cause- THER

Rapid caries of teeth; fistula dentalis or lachrymalis - **FL AC**

Fistula lachrymalis- **SIL**

Prosopalgia: periodical, left-sided, orbit, eyes, malar bone, teeth; *from morning until sunset* – **SPIG**

MOUTH, SALIVA, TOOTHACHE, TONGUE

Saliva profuse, acrid corrodes the mucous membrane- **ARUM T**

Discharge from nose and all mucous membranes. are tough, stringy tenacious- **BOV**

Discharge of a tough stringy mucus which adheres to the parts and can be drawn into long strings – **KALI BI**

(*Leucorrhoea ropy, thick, viscid yellow hanging from as in long strings – HYDRASTIS*

Haemorrhages forming into long black strings hanging from the bleeding surface- CROCUS SAT

Dysmenorrhoea: flow black; stringy, clotted – CROCUS SAT. (Ust.)

Menses: flow in gushes bright red, viscid and stringy – LAC CAN

Epistaxis: hangs in a dark clotted string from the nose, like an icicle – MERC SOL

Saliva: tough ropy, viscid, frothy in mouth and throat, with constant spitting – LYS)

Ptyalism tenacious, soapy, stringy profuse, fetid coppery metallic tasting saliva - **MERC**

Strong, sweetish, metallic, copper taste in the mouth with flow of saliva – **CUP MET** (RHUS TOX)

Great dryness of the month, tongue so dry it adheres to root of month with no thirst – **NUX MOS**

At every menstrual nisus, throat, mouth and tongue intolerably dry, especially when sleeping - **TARENT** (NUX MOS)

Intense thirst although the tongue looks moist and saliva in profuse-**MERC**

Dry mouth but no thirst – **PULS**

Sensation of dryness without real thirst- **NUX MOS**

Thirstlessness with nearly all complaints – **AETH; APIS; PULS**

Secretion from all mucous membranes. are thick bland and yellowish green – **PULS** (KALI SULPH; NAT SULPH)

Prevents caries of teeth- **COCA**

Toothache if anything warm is taken in mouth - **CHAM** (BIS; BRY; COFF)

Toothache while nursing the child – **CINCH**

Toothache intermittent, jerking relieved by holding ice water in the mouth but returns when water becomes warm - **COFF** (BIS; BRY; PULS; CAUST; SEP; NAT S)

Toothache only when eating; throbbing; < when touched by anything warm or cold - **KALI CARB**

Toothache; unbearable when food touches the teeth - **MAG MUR**

Toothache, painful to touch of food or drink but not from biting or chewing – **STAPH**

Teeth begin to decay as soon as they appear- **KREOS**

Toothache during menses - **STAPH; AM CARB**

Toothache during pregnancy < night- **MAG CARB**

Terrible toothache during early months of pregnancy; tooth feels elongated; < lying compelling to rise and walk about- **RATAN**

Toothache during menses and pregnancy- **CHAM**

Toothache < from cold or warm thing, > by rubbing the cheek – **MERC**

Crowns of teeth decay roots remain – **MERC**

Crowns intact root decay – **MEZ** (THUJA)

Teeth decay at the roots, crowns remain sound - **THUJA** (MEZ)

Teeth decay on edges - **STAPH**

Blue line along the margin of gum - **PLUMB**

Teeth turn black, show dark streaks through them - **STAPH**

Toothache > with mouth open and drawing in air - **MEZ**

Toothache < drawing cold air into mouth - **STAPH**

Teeth decay at edge of gum and break of are cupped and serrated - **SYPH**

Toothache from tobacco smoking; > only on lying down and while eating (Plan); worse, from cold air and water; returns from thinking about it - **SPIG**

During dentition intense desire to press the gums together - **PODO**

Irresistible desire to bite the teeth or gums together during dentition – **PHYTO**

Saliva and all food tastes salty – **CYCL**

Expectoration: profuse like the white of an egg; sweetish, salty- **STAN** (KALI IOD, SEP)

Taste sweetish – **PYR**

Bad taste in the morning – **PULS**

Foul breath in girls at puberty - **AURUM MET**

Taste pus like as from an abscess - **PYR**

Constant protraction and retraction of the tongue, like a snake - **CUP MET** (LACH)

Weakness and trembling; of tongue, hands, legs; of entire body - **GELS**

Tongue dry, black, trembles, is protruded with difficulty or catches on the teeth when protruding - **LACH**

Tongue – smooth, glossy red as if deprived of papillae or as if glazed - **TEREB**

Tongue foul but becomes clean at each menstrual nisus, returns when flow ceases - **SEP**

Tongue mapped with red insular patches – **NAT MUR**

Tongue large flabby, shows imprint of teeth - **MERC** (CHEL; PODO; RHUS)

Tongue coated thickly yellow, with red edges, showing imprint of teeth (Pod. - large, flabby, with imprint of teeth, Mer.) - **CHEL**

Tongue: dry; sore, red, cracked; triangular red tip; takes imprint of teeth - **RHUS** (CHEL; PODO)

Tongue fiery red, smooth and polished– **CROT HOR** (PYR)

Tongue large, flabby clean, smooth as if varnished; fiery red- **PYR**

Tongue smooth glossy red as if deprived of papillae, or as if glazed - **TEREB**

A thick milky-white coating on the tongue – **ANT CRUD**

Coating peels off in patches leaving bright red spots, or entire coating cleans off suddenly – **TEREB**

Mapped tongue, covered with a white film with sensation of rawness. This film comes off in patches, leaving dark red tender very sensitive spots — **TARX**

Tongue: white or yellow with red streak down the middle- **VER VIR**

Mapped tongue - **TARAX** (LACH, MERC, NAT M)

In chromic cases when well select remedies fail to relieve or permanently improve- **PSOR**

Arrogant, proud, contemptuous, haughty, pitifully looking down upon people usually venerated – **PLAT**

Praying, beseeching entreating incessant and incoherent talking and laughing- **STRAM**

Tired heavy feeling all over the body specially limbs on exertion - **PIC AC**

Desires light and Company - **STRAM**

Burning in along the spine with softening of cord- **PIC AC**

Brain fag of literary or business people- **PIC AC**

Restorative of a wasted and worm out system, nervous prostration - **PIC AC**

Periosteum inflamed, pains as if scraped with a knife- **PHOS AC**

Interstitial inflammation of bones- **PHOS AC**

Indifferent even to one's fancily to one's occupation to those whom she loves best- **SEP**

Is listless apathetic; indifferent to the affairs of life to those things that used to be of great interest- **PHOS AC**

Cannot get asleep or remaining asleep unless legs are crossed - **RHODO**

Footstep on soles as if he had stepped in cold water - **SANIC**

Circumscribed red checks - **SANG.**

THROAT (E.N.T.) and DIPHTHERIA

Diphtheria- pseudo membrane deposit prone to extend downwards to larynx and trachea- **KALI BI**

Diphtheria where the membrane beginning in bronchi, trachea or larynx and extending upwards- **BROM**

Diphtheria and tonsillitis beginning on the left and extending to the right side - **LACH** (LAC CAN, SABAD)

Diphtheria spreads from right tonsils to left < cold drinks - **LYCO**

Diphtheria and tonsillitis < hot drinks and after sleep - **LACH**

Diphtheria tonsillitis can swallow warm food more easily – **SABAD**

In diphtheria can't drink, liquids more painful than solids when swallowing - **LACH**

(Can swallow liquid only –BAPT Inability to swallow anything but liquid – BAR CARB

Shining glazed appearance of diphtheritic deposits **LAC CAN**

Diphtheria pains shoot from throat into ears on swallowing – **PHYTO**

Diphtheria great pain at root of tongue when swallowing - **PHYTO**

In diphtheria burning as form coal of fire or red hot iron - **PHYTO**

Painless diphtheria - **DIPHTH**

(Painless hoarseness- CALC;

Painless cholera morbus - PODO

Painless sorethroat- BAPT

Painless quinsy – BAR CARB

Painless diphtheria- DIPHTH

Painless haemorrhage- MILL

Painless haematuria- TEREB

Painless gleet – Sepia

Painless gonorrhoea – NAT SULPH

Painless involuntary diarrhea – SEC COR

Painless diarrhea with good appetite – FERR MET

Painless stool, profuse, offensive – RUMEX

Painless diarrhea – SULPH; ACID PHOS

Painless, involuntary diarrhea – PYR)

Carotid and Submaxillary glands indurated after diphtheria, scarlet fever - **PHYTO**

Frequent inclination to swallow, with burning, pricking, stinging and dry constricted fauces- **AESC** (APIS; BELL)

Malignant diphtheria or scarlatina - **CROT HOR**

Malignant scarlatina and variola – CARB AC (AMM CARB)

Malignant jaundice; haematic rather than hepatic – CROT HOR

Malignant diseases of uterus, great tendency to haemorrhage, blood dark, fluid, offensive – CROT HOR

Malignant affections of stomach – KREOS

Metrorrhagia: at climacteric; profuse for weeks, flow dark clotted, offensive; in gushes, on moving; with malignant disease of uterus – MEDO

Malignant affections of mouth – MUR AC

Malignant ulcers; carbuncle, anthrax; gangrene – TARAX

Malignant scarlatina with deep sleep; stetorous breathing- AMM CARB

Gangrenous ulcers; felon, carbuncle, erysipelas of a malignant type- ANTHRAC

Corners of the mouth sore, cracked, bleeding with malignant tendency- CUNDORANGO

The sore mouth and nose are guiding in malignant scarlatina and diphtheria – ARUM TRI

Malignant diphtheria with intense redness of fauces and great difficulty of swallowing - **MERC CYAN**

Putrid sore throat; tendency to gangrenous ulceration of tonsils- **AM CARB**

< by empty swallowing – **LAC CAN (IGN)**

Throat sensitive to touch externally – **LAC CAN**

Burning spasmodic constriction worse between acts of deglutition- **CAPS**

Sensation of splinter in throat when swallowing- **ARG NIT** (DOLICHOS; SIL; HEP; NIT AC)

Sensation of splinter in affected parts, ulcers, piles, throat, in growing toe nail < on slightest contact - **NIT AC**

Sensation of splinter, fish bone or plug in the throat - **HEP** (ARG NIT; NIT AC)

(Sensation of feather in larynx, exciting cough – DROS

Sensation of lump in throat; descends on swallowing, but returns immediately - RUMEX

Sensation as if a thread were hanging down throat- VAL

Sensation as of a hair on the tongue- NAT. MUR. ; SILICEA)

Quinsy tonsils greatly swollen, difficult, painful swallowing; pain goes to ears when swallowing – **PSOR**

Mumps metastasis to mammae or testicle – **PULS**

Sensation of a skin hanging loosely in throat must swallow over it – **SABAD**

Illusions that she has some horrible throat dis. that will be fatal – **SABAD**

Sore throat < sweet things - **SPON**

Painless sore throat - **BAPT**

(Painless diphtheria - DIPHTH

Painless hoarseness- CALC;

Painless cholera morbus - PODO

Painless sorethroat- BAPT

Painless quinsy – BAR CARB

Painless diphtheria- DIPHTH

Painless haemorrhage- MILL

Painless haematuria- TEREB

Painless gleet – Sepia

Painless gonorrhoea – NAT SULPH

Painless involuntary diarrhea – SEC COR

Painless diarrhea with good appetite – FERR MET

Painless stool, profuse, offensive – RUMEX

Painless diarrhea – SULPH; ACID PHOS

Painless, involuntary diarrhea – PYR)

Throat affection after checked foot sweat - **BAR CARB** (GRAPH; PSOR; SANIC; SIL)

(Ailments caused by suppressed foot-sweat- SIL)

Tenderness of the feet, which are bathed in foul-smelling sweat- PET

Foot-seat between the toes, making them sore; offensive- SANIC (GRAPH; PSOR; SIL)]

Sore throat with constant desire to swallow - **LYS**

Sore throat < after eating sweet things - **SPON**

Clergy man's sore throat- **ARUM T; DROS**

Inability to swallow anything but liquid – **BAR CARB** (BAP; SIL)

< hot drinks, after sleep liquid more painful than solids when swallowing- **LACH**

Can swallow liquid only, little solid food gags- **BAPT** (BAR CARB)

Throat burning as from a coal of fire or a red hot iron- **PHYTO**

Sensation of lump in throat; descends on swallowing but returns immediately - **RUM**

Sensation as if a thread were hanging down throat - **VAL**

Globus hystericus – sensation of a large ball rising from stomach to throat, causing sensation of suffocation- **LAC DEF** (ASAF; KAL)

Chronic laryngitis of singers; the high notes cause cough - **ARG NIT (ALUM; ARG MET; ARUM T)**

Catarrhal laryngitis - **ALL CEPA**

Tubercular laryngitis- **SELEN**

Follicular pharyngitis- **AESC**

Tubercular pharyngitis - **MERC BIN IOD**

Nasal polypus - **ALL CEPA** (MAR V; SANG; PSOR)

Laryngeal or nasal polypi- **SANG** (PSOR; TEUC)

Fan- like motion of alae nasi - **BROM; LYCO** (ANT TART)

Nostrils crusty, inflamed ; tip of nose shining red ; red noses of young woman- **BOR**

Otorrhoea: bloody , offensive discharge, with stabbing tearing pain < rt. side , at night and lying on affected side - **MERC SOL**

VOICE

Hoarseness of professional singer, public speakers - **ARG MET** (ALUM; ARUM T)

Sudden hoarseness > when walking against wind – **NUX MOS** (EUPH; HEP)

Hoarseness with rawness andand aphonia in the morning- **CAUST**

Hoarseness evening, < warm wet weather– **CARB VEG** (PHOS)

Painless hoarseness-<in the morning – **CALC CARB**

(Painless cholera morbus - PODO

Painless sorethroat- BAPT

Painless quinsy – BAR CARB

Painless diphtheria- DIPHTH

Painless haemorrhage- MILL

Painless haematuria- TEREB

Painless gleet – Sepia

Painless gonorrhoea – NAT SULPH

Painless involuntary diarrhea – SEC COR

Painless diarrhea with good appetite – FERR MET

Painless stool, profuse, offensive – RUMEX

Painless diarrhea – SULPH; ACID PHOS

Painless, involuntary diarrhea – PYR)

Voice hoarse, uncertain, uncontrollable, changing continually; worse from talking, singing or speaking - **ARUM T**

Aphonia complete after exposure to north – west winds; from singing - **ARUM T**

Loss of voice from becoming overheated- **ANT CRUD**

Total loss of voice with professional singer- **ARG MET**

Hoarseness of professional singers and public speakers- **ARG MET**

GASTRO-INTESTINAL SYSTEM

DESIRES and AVERSIONS

Abnormal appetite for chalk and indigestible things - **CICUTA**

Great longing for eggs, craves indigestible things - **CALC CARB**

Abnormal appetite- craving for starch, chalk, charcoal, cloves, acids and indigestible things - **ALUM**

Longing for sour thing during hemorrhages - **CINCH**

Aversion to milk; diarrhea from it - **NAT CARB**

Longing for acid and pickles - **ANT CRUD**

Extraordinary craving for apple - **ANT TART**

Craves sugar - **ARG NIT**

Unconquerable longing for liquors - **ASAR**

Complaints of drunkards, after abstaining; craving for alcohol- **CALC ARS**

Longing for whiskey and tobacco- **CARB AC**

Craving for tobacco- **STAPH**

Cannot bear tobacco - **IGN**

Destroys craving for tobacco - **CALAD**

(Was first used as a tobacco antidote- COCA)

A/f. chewing tobacco – **ARS ALB**

Longing for spirituous liquors, an almost irresistible maniacal desire - **SELEN**

Inordinate craving for meat in children of tuberculous parentage - **MAG CARB**

(Cough after eating meat- STAPH

Styes from rich food and pork- PULS

Cannot bear the thought or sight of meat- **MUR ACID; NIT ACID; CALC**

Pork disagrees - **CYCL**

(Styes from rich food and pork- PULS

Cough worse after meat- STAPH)

Craving for ice – **MEDO**

Craving for salts – **NAT MUR (**CALC; CAUST; MED; CALC PHOS)

(Removes the bad effects of Iodine and excessive use of table salt – PHOS.

Abuse of salt, salt meats- CARB VEG

For the bad effects excessive use of salt- NAT MUR)

Craves salt or smoked meat - **CALC PHOS**

Insatiate craving:

For liquor, which before she hated (Asar.);

For salt (Cal., Nat.);

Sweets (Sulph.);

For ale, ice, acids, oranges, green fruit - **MEDO**

Desire for very hot drinks unless almost boiling stomach will not retain them - **CHEL**

Craving for acids and refreshing things - **VER ALB; PHOS**

Longs for: cold food and drink; juicy, refreshing things; ice cream > gastric pains - **PHOS**

Craves smoked meat - **CAL PHOS**

VOMITING

Child wants abdomen Uncovered, relieves nausea and vomiting; coldness in abdomen - **TAB**

Vomiting chronic with good appetite with nausea, profuse sweat and marked prostration - **LOB**

(Diarrhea with ravenous appetite – SEC COR; FER MET;

Constipation with good appetite – LAC DEF)

Vomiting with one effort vomits everything eaten and can sit down and eat again - **FER MET**

Vomiting incessant with no relation to eating – **LAC DEF**

Vomiting cannot lie on right side - **CROT HOR**

Vomiting in any position except when lying on right side - **ANT TART**

(Cough with utter inability to lie on right side –MERC;

Cough lying on left side –PHOS

Palpitation lying on left side- CACTUS (LACH)

Palpitation lying on left side, goes off when turning to right- LAC CAN; TAB

Pains < when lying on left side- PHOS)

Vomiting of water as soon as it reaches the stomach – **BISM**

Headache: ending in bilious vomiting - **ARG NIT**

As soon as water becomes warm in stomach it is thrown up - **PHOS**

Nausea or vomiting from riding in carriage boat or railroad car - **COCC**

(Sick-headache from carriage, boat or train riding – COCC

Complaints > by riding in a carriage – NIT AC

Hardness of hearing amelioration by carriage riding or train- GRAPH; NIT AC

Backache while riding in a carriage- NUX MOSCH)

Smell painfully acute, nausea and faintness from the odour of cooking food specially fish, eggs or fat meat - **COLCH**

Cannot bear the smell or sight of food - **ARS ALB** (COLCH, SEP)

Morning sickness of pregnancy: the sight or thought of food sickens (NUX); the smell of cooking food nauseates (ARS, COLCH) - **SEP**

Vomiting black or coffee grounds - **CROT HOR**

(Hematuria-blood thoroughly mixes with the urine, sediment like coffee ground- TEREB

Diarrhea stools black thin like coffee ground- CROT HOR

Urine: red, black, scanty, coffee-ground sediment- HELL

Vomiting: black or coffee- grounds - PYR)

Vomiting: persistent ; brownish coffee-ground; offensive, stercoraceous; with impacted or obstructed bowels - **PYR**

Vomiting as soon as he raises head from pillow - **STRAM**

Violent vomiting with cold sweat soon as he begins to move – **TAB**

Vomiting violent with cold sweat soon as he begins to move; during pregnancy when lactic acid fails - **TAB**

Vomiting: of pregnancy, sweetish water with ptyalism; of cholera during painful dentition; incessant with cadaverous stool; in malignant affections of stomach - **KREOS**

During pregnancy most obstinate vomiting, foetus moves too violently - **PSOR**

Regurgitation and eructation of food in mouthfuls; without nausea- **FER MET**

Vomiting: of drunkards, in pregnancy; seasickness; cancer; of dark, olive-green fluid - **CARB AC (PYR)**

(Diarrhea of Drunkard- APIS Drunkards, especially for their headaches; bad effects after a debauch- AGAR (LOB; NUX VOM; RAN)

Complaints of drunkards, after abstaining; craving for alcohol – CALC ARS (ASAR, SUL AC)

Vomiting: of drunkards, in pregnancy, sea-sickness, cancer; of dark, olive-green fluid – CARB AC (PYR)

Diseases peculiar to drunkards.- COCC

Follows well: after, Ars. in ascites of drunkards – FLUOR AC

Drunkards with congestive headaches and haemorrhoids; prone to erysipelas or apoplexy – LACH

Hypochondriac: literary, studious persons, who are too much at home, suffer from want of exercise, with gastric, abdominal complaints and costiveness; especially in drunkards – **NUX VOM**

Chronic alcoholism; dropsy and other ailments of drunkards – **SULPH**

Sensation as if trembling all over, without real trembling; internal trembling of drunkards – **SUL AC**

If the patient lies perfectly still, the disposition to vomit is less urgent. Every motion renews it - **COLCH**

Vomiting immediately after midnight - **FER MET**

Nausea especially on closing the eyes - **THER**

(*Vertigo on closing the eyes- THER; THUJA (LACH)*

Vertigo on opening the eyes - TAB

Vertigo on looking up- PULS, SIL

Vertigo on looking down – KAL; SPIG

Sweats as soon as he closes his eyes to sleep- CON MAC; THUJA; CINCH)

Profuse sweat over entire body during waking hours; on going to sleep dry heat returns – SAMB

DIARRHEA

Diarrhea in eruptive fever - **APIS**

Diarrhea: in summer, from *cold drinks*; epidemic in autumn, white stools - **NUX MOS** (COLCH)

Diarrhea especially if eruption be suppressed – **APIS; GRAPH** (PSOR)

(Asthma after suppressed eruption - HEP SULPH

Cough after suppressed itch , or eczema- PSOR

Epilepsy from suppressed eruptions- AGAR; (PSOR; SULPH)

Headache from suppressed eruption- ANT CRUD (PSOR)

Brain diseases from suppressed eruptions- CICUTA

Chorea from suppressed eruption; from fright- ZINC MET

The skin symptoms if suppressed, causes diarrhea - PET

Ailments: from suppressed itch or other skin diseases, when Sulphur fails to relieve – PSOR)

Diarrhea; the milk passes undigested in nursing children – **MAG CARB**

(Intolerance of milk: cannot bear milk in form; it is vomited in large curds as soon as taken- AETH

Children during difficult dentition are unable to digest milk; it causes pain and passes undigested- MAG CARB

Children during dentition are unable to digest milk - MAG MUR

Brain trouble during dentition- HELL; BELL; PODO)

Aversion to milk; Diarrhea from it - **NAT CARB**

(Constipation, with ineffectual urging >cold milk- IOD)

Diarrhea from boiled milk - **NUX MOS**

Diarrhea from drinking milk - **NAT CARB; CALC CARB; SULPH**

Unnatural, ravenous, appetite even with exhausting diarrhea- **SEC COR**

(Vomiting, chronic with good appetite- LOB

Constipation with good appetite - LAC DEF.)

Diarrhea – painless with a good appetite - **FER MET**

Hungry during Diarrhea - **ALOE**

Diarrhea: during acute hydrocephalus - **HELL**

Hungry during Diarrhea- **ALOE**

Diarrhea- during dentition – **CHAM**

(Constipation during dentition – MAG MUR

Brain trouble during dentition- HELL

Vomiting during dentition – KREOS

Skin prone to impetigo during dentition – CAUST; (LYCO)

Convulsion during teething with fever - BELL

Convulsion during teething without fever - MAG PHOS

Convulsion during dentition with pale face no heat – ZINC

Diarrhea in child-bed - **CHAM**

(Nymphomania: < in lying-in women – Plat

Should not be given in lying-in-women except in high potency- IOD

Paralysis of bladder, no desire to urinate in lying-in women- HYOS (ARN; OP)

Panaritia: with red streaks up the arm; pains drive to despair; in child-bed- ALL CEPA

Stool grassy green, of white mucous, bloody, fermented, foamy, slimy, like frothy molasses - **IPEC**

Stool green, watery, corroding like chopped eggs and spinach, hot very offensive like rotten eggs - **CHAM**

[Eructation tasting like rotten eggs like onions- MAG MUR

Belching, eructation; foul, putrid; like rotten eggs – arn

Eructations tasting of rotten eggs- PSOR (ARN; ANT TART; GRAPH)]

Diarrhea like scrambled egg - **SANIC**

Diarrhea: green mucous, like chopped spinach in flakes; turning green after remaining on diaper- **ARG NIT**

Diarrhea frothy grassy green, turns green on standing - **SANIC**

Diarrhea: white, jelly-like mucus; like frog spawn; involuntary - **HELL**

Diarrhea; stools green, frothy, like scum on a frog-pond; white tallow-like masses are found floating in stool- **MAG CARB**

Diarrhea as soon as anything enters the rectum- **PHOS**

Diarrhea with sago-like particles in the stool - **PHOS**

Stool with odour of limburger cheese - **SANIC**

Diarrhea profuse, pouring away as from a hydrant - **PHOS**

Diarrhea of children: white, very offensive, exhausting liquid stools running "Right through the diaper"- **BENZ AC (PODO)**

Diarrhea of children: of dirty water soaking napkin through- **PODO (BENZ AC)**

The bowels are moved as if by spasmodic jerks, "coming out like a shot"- **CROT TIG (GAMB)**

Diarrhea; *gurgling, as water from a bunghole* - **THUJA**

Diarrhea: watery, brown, gushing out in a violent jet - **AST RUB** (CROT T, GRAT, GUM, JATR, THUJA)

Diarrhea: preceded by cutting, doubling-up colic – **MAG CARB**

(Agonizing pain in abdomen causing patient to bend double – COLOCYNTH)

Sensation, as if anus remained open - **PHOS**

Diarrhea: as though anus was wide open- **APIS**

Diarrhea after 3 weeks- **MAG CARB**

When passing flatus, sensation as if stool would pass with it- **ALOE** (OLEAN; MUR AC; NAT MUR)

Diarrhea when she urinates – **ALUM** (MUR AC)

(Leucorrhoea after every urination- AM MUR

Leucorrhoea every time passes stool- MAG MUR

Haemorrhoids: prolapse while urinating- MUR AC

Haemorrhoids protrude every time he urinates- BAR CARB (MUR AC)

Diarrhea; stool involuntary while urinating; on passing wind; can't urinate without having the breath to move at the save time – **MUR AC**

Diarrhea from downward motion- **CHAM** (BOR; SANIC)

In diarrhea stool very changeable – **PULS; SANIC**

(No two stools alike very in color during constipation –AM MUR)

Diarrhea with great flatulence – **CALC PHOS**

Diarrhea after eating or drinking followed by great prostration- **ARS ALB**

Cholera morbus and summers complaints; when vomiting predominates- **BISM**

Asiatic cholera, first symptoms, where nausea and vomiting predominates- **IPEC (COLCH)**

Diarrhea: stool thin, involuntary black, of an intolerable odour - **CARB AC**

Diarrhea from anger or chagrin - **CHAM**

Diarrhea stools black thin like coffee ground - **CROT HOR**

(Urine: red, black, scanty, coffee-ground sediment- HELL; TEREB

Vomiting: black or coffee- grounds, of yellow fever - CROT HOR; PYR)

Diarrhea with great straining but little passes, as if faces retained and cannot be expelled - **NIT AC**

Inactivity of rectum, even soft stool requires great straining - **ALUM** (ANAC; PLAT; SIL; VER ALB)

(Fissures in rectum; lancinating even after stool- NIT AC (ALUMEN; NAT MUR; RAT)

Diarrhea after cabbage, sauerkraut- **PETR**

Diarrhea from cold drinks when overheated, from fruit or sauerkraut- **BRY**

Diarrhea from oysters - **BROM**

Diarrhea form eating pears –**VER ALB; CINCH**

Diarrhea from fruits cold food drinks or ice cream - **ARS ALB; PULS**

Diarrhea of drunkards- **APIS**

(Vomiting of Drunkards- CARB AC

Drunkards, especially for their headaches; bad effects after a debauch- AGAR (LOB; NUX VOM; RAN))

During pregnancy most obstinate vomiting – **PSOR**

Diarrhea of children while being bathed or washed- **PODO**

Painless cholera morbus - **PODO**

(Painless sorethroat- BAPT;

Painless hoarseness- CALC CARB;

Painless quinsy – BAR CARB

Painless diphtheria- DIPHTH

Painless haemorrhage- MILL

Painless haematuria- TEREB

Painless gonorrhoea- NAT SULPH

Painless gleet - SEPIA

Painlessness with all complaints – OP; STRAM)

Diarrhea **painless**, not debilitating, white or yellow watery- **PHOS AC**

(Painless Diarrhea in daytime only after eating – Cinchona)

Diarrhea: **painless** with good appetite; while eating or drinking - **FER MET**

Diarrhea: horribly, offensive; brown or black; **painless**, involuntary; uncertain, when passing flatus- **PYR**

Early morning Diarrhea from 5 to 10 am; **painless**, profuse, offensive; sudden urging, driving out of bed in morning – **RUM**

Diarrhea after midnight; **painless ; driving out of bed early in the morning**; as if bowelswere too weak to retain their contents- **SULPH** (ALOE; PSOR)

Diarrhea – early morning; expelled forcibly with much flatus gurgling as water from a bunghole; < after breakfast, coffee, fat food, vaccination, onions- **THUJA**

Bad effects: of onions- LYCO

Sweat in axilla smells like onion- BOV

Eructations like onions- MAG MUR

Breath smells like onion- SINNAPIS

Diarrhea involuntary at might from 1 to 4 am – **PSOR**

Diarrhea only in the daytime- **PETR** (ALOE)

Diarrhea only or usually at night – **PULS**

Diarrhea early in morning, continues through forenoon followed by natural stool in evening - **PODO**

Diarrhea urgent watery with nausea vomiting prostration and cold sweat - **TAB**

Diarrhea from fright - **PULS; OP; VER ALB**

Diarrhea as soon as he drinks – **ARG NIT** (ARS ALB; CROT TIG; TROM)

(Vomiting: of water as soon as it reaches the stomach, food retained longer – Bismuth)

Diarrhea in summer from cold drinks- **NUX MOS**

Diarrhea from cold -**CHAM**

(Headache from taking cold- ANT CRUD)

Diarrhea from taking cold in damp places, or damp foggy weather - **DULC**

Cholera morbus or asiatic cholera, with cramps in abdomen and calves of leg- **CUP MET**

Frequent, involuntary, cadaverous smelling stool, followed by burning soft stool voided with difficulty- **CARBO VEG** (ALUM; NIT AC)

Every stool is followed by thirst and every drink by shuddering- **CAPS**

Morning diarrhea- **ALOE; PODO; SULPH; NAT SULPH; PSOR; THUJA; PHOS; RUM; TUB**

Diarrhea: morning, of old people - **PHOS**

[Paralysis of bladder in old women – EQUIS

Dribbling urine of old men with enlarged prostate – BENZ AC

Shortness of breath, in old people – COCA

Vertigo: of old people – CON

Old people with great weakness and diarrhea – NIT AC

Dyspepsia of old people – NUX MOS

Tendency to gangrene following mechanical injuries, especially of old people – SUL PH AC.

Old people with weak, indolent circulation. Drunkards, especially for their headaches – AGAR

Constipation: of old people – ALUM (LYC, OP)

Old people with morning diarrhea, suddenly become constipated, or alternate diarrhea and constipation – ANT CRUD

Dysentry of old people – **BAPT**

Apoplectic tendency in old people; complaints of old drunkards – **BAR CARB**

Complaints of old age, or of premature old age – **FLUOR AC**

Slow pulse of old age – **GELS**

Aphthous sore mouth; of old people, often from plate of teeth – **BORAX (ALUMEN)**

Adapted to old maids with palpitation – **BOV**

Deafness of old age – **MERC DUL**

"Old sinners" with impotence and gleet – **AGNUS CAS**

Old men, with strong desire but imperfect erections – **LYCO)**

Diarrhea < in morning, on moving, even a foot or hand - **BRY**

Diarrhea during acute hydrocephalous - **HELL**

Alternate constipation and diarrhea, in persons who have taken purgatives all their lives - **NUX VOM**

Violent cramps in feet, calves, thighs; watery painless stool - **PODO**

CONSTIPATION

Constipation of bottle fed babies - **ALUM**

Constipation of infsnts - **LYCO**

Constipation- ribbon like stools- **ARN**

Alternate diarrhea and constipation - **ANT CRUD; ABROT; NUX VOM; CHEL; COLL**

Obstinate constipation accompanied by much flatus - **AM MUR**

No two stools alike very in color during constipation – **AM MUR**.

(In diarrhea stool very changeable –PULS)

Constipation of pregnancy after Nux fails - **PLAT**

From impaction of faeces when Platina fails- **PLUMB**

Constipation when Sulphur fails to relieve- **PSOR**

Constipation: painful, of infants and children, after lyco and Nux - **VERAT ALB**

Constipation since last confinement – **LYCO**

Constipation since puberty - **LYCO**

Feels better in every way when constipated - **CALC CARB**

Constipation with horribly offensive breath- **CARB AC**

Stool passes better when persons is standing – **CAUST**

Constipation in children with nocturnal enuresis –**CAUST**

Constipation: stool hard round balls like sheep'sdung – **CHEL**

Stool very offensive like rotten eggs - **CHAM**

(Belching foul, putrid, like rotten eggs - ARNICA

Eructation, tasting like rotten eggs, like onions – MAG MUR

Eructations tasting of rotten eggs PSOR (ARN, ANT T, GRAPH)

Stool green, watery, corroding, like chopped eggs and spinach; hot, very offensive, like rotten eggs - CHAM)

Constipation with stool large and painful child in afraid to have the stool on account of pain – **SULPH**

Dissatisfied especially when constipated - **ALOE**

Pain after stool as if splinters of glass were sticking in anus and rectum - **RATAN**

Constipation stool hand scanty, large, knotty, like sheep's dung - **CHEL; MAG MUR; PLB**

Constipation of infants during dentition – **MAG MUR**

Constipation painful extorting cries- **LAC DEF**

Constipation with frequent desire felt in rectum- **NUX VOM**

Constipation with frequent desire felt in epigastrium- **VER ALB**

Constipation with excessive urging, felt in upper abdomen- **IGN**

Constipation with frequent unsuccessful desire, passing small quantity of faeces, sensation as if not finished – **NUX VOM**

Constipation obstinate from impaction in fevers- **PYR**

Stool soft clayey adhering to parts – **ALUM**

Constipation stools adhere to rectum and anus like soft clay – **PLAT**

Constipation on going to sea- **BRY (PLAT)**

Constipation when away from home- **LYCO**

Constipation while traveling- **PLAT**

Constipation of emigrants - **PLAT**

Constipation after lead poisoning- **PLAT; OP**

The presence of others even the nurse in unbearable during stool - **AMBRA**

Stool hard impossible to evacuate, of grayish balls, like burnt lime - **SANIC**

Prolapse of rectum immediately on attempting a passage – **RUTA**

The odor of stool follows despite bathing- **SANIC**

Stool partly expelled partly recedes again - **SIL; SANIC; THUJA**

Can only pass stool by leaning very far back - **MEDO**

(Can only void urine while sitting bent backwards ZINC MET)

Constriction and inertia of bowels with ball-like stool - **MEDO (LACH)**

Constipation, difficult painful constriction in anus; throbbing fullness- **MELL**

Constipation with ineffectual urging > by drinking cold milk- **IOD**

Constipation sensation in abdomen as if something tight would break if much effort were used- **APIS**

Obstinate constipation accompanied by much flatus- **AM MUR**

Dissatisfied and angry about himself or his complaints, especially when constipated - **ALOE**

Constipation from inactivity or impaction following mechanical injuries - **RUTA (ARN)**

Constipation: inactivity, stool lies in rectum, without urging - **LACH**

Constipation after serious illness especially enteric fever- **SELEN**

Constipation: of corpulent, good –natured women - **OP (GRAPH)**

Constipation: sense of weight or ball in anus, not > by stool - **SEP**

(Sensation as of a ball rolling in the bladder – LACH

Sensation of a round ball in forehead sitting firmly there even when shaking the head –STAPH

Sensation of swelling in the perineum or near the anus, as if sitting on a ball – **CAN IND**

Sensation of a ball in inner parts – **SEPIA)**

HAEMORRHOIDS and ANUS

Hemorrhoids blue like bunch of grapes: relieved by cold water; intense itching - **ALOE** (MUR AC)

Chronic, painful bleeding piles; sensation as if sticks, sand or gravel had lodged in rectum – **COLL**

Rectum feels as if full of small sticks; burning, purplish rarely bleeding - **AESC**

Chest symptom alternates with fistula in ano - **SIL; CALC PHOS**

Chest complaints after operation of fistula – **BERB** (CAL PHOS; SIL)

Haemorrhoids after suppressed leucorrhoea - **AM MUR**

Mucous from anus; ichorous, oozing staining yellow- **ANT CRUD**

Mucous piles – **ANT CRUD**

Haemorrhoidal dysentery with tenesmus - **COLL**

Burning pains of hemorrhoids < by heat – **ARS ALB**

Congestion of pelvic viscera with haemorrhoids specially in later months of pregnancy- **COLL**

Haemorrhoids with stitching pains when walking or sitting, not at stool - **ARS ALB**

Piles swollen, pain most severe when sitting - **THUJA**

Haemoptysis in haemorrhoidal patient – **MILL**

After each period haemorrhoids- **COCC**

Rheumatism alternates with haemorrhoids, with dysentery - **ABROT**

(Rheumatism alternates with dysentery –KALI BI;

Alternating constipation and diarrhea – ABROT; ANT CRUD; BRY; NUX

Headache alternates with Diarrhea, headache in winter, Diarrhea in summer – PODO

Headache alternating with lumbago – ALOE

Croupy cough in winter alternating with Sciatica in summer- STAPH

Heart disease alternates with rheumatism – KAL

Headache alternates or attended with gastralgia- BISM

Mania following disappearance of neuralgia- ACTEA

Rheumatism alternates with gastric symptoms one appearing in fall and other in the spring - kali bi

Fistula-in-ano alternates with chest symptoms- CALC PHOS;SIL; BERB

Delirium alternates with colic- plumb

Headache alternates with diarrhea – ALOE

Mental symptoms alternate with physical symptoms – PLATINA; PLUMBUM; ACTEA R

Alternate diarrhea and constipation- ANT CRUD, COLLIN, NUX VOM (SULPH, VERT)

Cerebral congestion, or alternate congestion of the head and heart- GLON

Disposed to curse, strike, to think obscene things; alternates with uterine irritation-LIL TIG)

Piles with scanty menses - **LACH**

Fistula: painful offensive high spongy edges, Proud flesh in them - **SIL**

Haemorrhoids – bleeding profusely, as if back would break, bluish colour - **HAM; THUJA**

Itching and burning in anus preventing sleep- **ALOE**

Sharp needle-like pain in rectum - **MEDO**

(Pains sticking, pricking as from splinters- NIT AC)

Prolapse of ani from moderate straining at stool, stooping or lifting < when the stool is loose - **IGN**

Prolapse of rectum, immediately on attending a passage; from the slightest stooping, after confinement; frequent unsuccessful urging - **RUTA**

Haemorrhoids protrude every time he urinates - **BAR CARB** (MUR AC)

(Diarrhea involuntary while urinating- MUR AC

Diarrhea when she urinates- **ALUM**

Leucorrhoea after every urination – **AM MUR**

Leucorrhoea after every stool- **MAG MUR)**

Haemorrhoids: prolapse while urinating - **MUR AC**

Scirrhus of sigmoid or rectum, atrocious unbearable pain - **SPIG** (ALUM)

Anus fissured; painful to touch, surrounded with flat warts or moist condylomata - **THUJA**

URINE

Urine dark brown and the urinous odor highly intensified - **BENZ AC**

Urine scanty, dark brown, strong smelling "like horse urine" – **NIT AC**

Renal colic < left side- **BERB VUL**

Renal colic: violent spasmodic along ureter, left side with deathly nausea and cold perspiration - **TAB**

Renal colic < right side- **LYCO**

Neuralgic or renal colic, excruciating pains from Right kidney downwards- **SARS**

Renal colic, either side, with urging and strangury- **CANTH**

Bubbling sensation in kidneys – **BERB VUL (MEDO)**

Retention or incontinence of urine after labor- **ARN (OP)**

Urine retention post-partum or from excessive use of tobacco- **OP**

Paralysis of bladder: after labor, with retention or incontinence of urine, no desire to urinate in lying-in women- **HYOS (ARN; OP)**

Urine retained with bladder full in nursing children after passion of nurse- **OP**

Urine retained with bladder full in fever or acute illness- **OP**

Suppression of urine - **STRAM**

Severe, dull pain in the bladder as from distention not > after urinating – **EQUIS**

Pressure on the bladder as if constantly full continues after urinating - **RUTA**

Frequent voluptuous ticking in fossa navicularis – **PETROS**

Child, urine desire if cannot be gratified at once jumps up and down with pains- **PETROS**

Sudden urging to urinate - **PETROS** (CANTH)

Severe backache in renal region, amel by profuse urination - **MEDO** (LYC)

Pain in back relieved by urinating- **LYCO**

Constant desire to urinate on seeing running water - **LYS** (Canth; Sulph)

Urine; turbid when passed, turns milky and semi-solid after standing; white and turbid; involuntary- **CINA**

Catarrhal ischuria in grown-up children, with milky urine - **DULC**

Profuse urination at night of clear watery urine, which forms a white cloud at once- **PHOS AC**

Urine looks like milk mixed with jelly like bloody pieces – **PHOS AC**

Urine deposits white sand- **SARS**

Red sand in urine, on child's diaper- **LYCO** (PHOS)

Urine of deep range red color, copious red sediment – **LOB**

Urine deposits a reddish clay colored sediment which adheres to the vessels as if it had been burned on - **SEP**

Urine offensive and of a deep red color- **BENZ AC**

Urine coarse, red sandy, sediment involuntary dribbling while walking - **SELEN**

Urine involuntary when coughing, sneezing blowing the nose- **CAUST; NAT MUR; RUTA** (PULS; SQUILLA; VER ALB)

Constant desire to defecate and urinate with prolapsus – **LIL**

Frequent urging to urinate; if desire is not attended to, sensation of congestion in chest- **LIL**

Enuresis, bed is wet almost as soon as the child goes to sleep- **SEP** (KREOS)

Urination during first sleep from which child is aroused with difficulty – **KREOS**

Nocturnal enuresis –passes enormous quantity of ammoniacal urine in bed every night after over work or over play, extreme of heat or cold- **MEDO**

In children nocturnal enuresis with constipation - **CAUST**

Eneuresis during full moon, obstinate, with a family history of eczema- **PSOR**

Enuresis nocturna of delicate children- **BENZ AC**

Enuresis diurna et nocturna; profuse watery urine, where habit is the only ascertainable cause- **EQUIS**

Can only urinate when lying – **KREOS**

(Menses: flows only at night or when lying ceases when walking – MAG CARB; AMM CARB; KREOS

Menses flow only when moving about; cease to flow when she ceases to walk – LIL TIG; CAUST)

Can only void urine while sitting bent backwards - **ZINC MET**

(Can only pass stool by leaning very far back- MEDO.)

Urine bladder weak is unable to finish, seems as if some urine always remains- **HEP**

Urine voided slowly without force, drops vertically - **HEP**

Frequent and intolerable urging to urinate, with sensation pain at close of urination– **EQUIS** (BERB; SARS; THUJA)

Burning in urethra when not urinating - **STAPH**

Urging to urinate, has to sit at urinal for hours in- Young married lady; after coition; after difficult labor - **STAPH**

Urine dribbles while sitting standing passes freely - **SARS**

Urine scanty slimy, flaky, sandy, copious, passed without sensation - **SARS**

Severe, unbearable pair at the conclusion of urination — **SARS**

Haematuria cloudy, smoky, albuminous - **TEREB**

Hematuria-blood thoroughly mixes with the urine, sediment like coffee ground - **TEREB**

(Diarrhea stools black thin like coffee ground- CROT HOR

Urine: red, black, scanty, coffee-ground sediment- HELL

Vomiting: black or coffee- grounds, of yellow fever- CROT HOR; PYR)

Urine horribly offensive after standing — **INDIUM**

Urine Fetid so offensive must be removed from the room - **SEP**

Urine rich in albumin and blood but few if any casts < from living damp dwelling— **TEREB**

Urine passes unconsciously day and night - **ARG NIT** (CAUST)

Paralysis of bladder in old women- **EQUIS**

Urine cold when it passes - **NIT AC**.

GENITALIA

Impotence, after frequent attacks of gonnorrhoea - **AGNUS**

Seminal emissions almost every night, without erection - **ARG MET**

Coition followed by bleeding from vagina – **ARG NIT** (NIT AC)

(Discharge of blood from genitals during every stool – LYCO)

Discharge of mucus from vagina after an embrace causing sterility - **NAT CARB**

Sudden impotence – **CHLORINUM**

Impotence: erection fails when coition is attempted - **ARG NIT** (AGNUS; CALAD; SELEN)

Complete impotence with no sexual power or desire – **AGNUS** (CALAD; SEL)

Impotence with relaxed penis with sexual desire and excitement - **CALAD** (LYCO; SEL)

No erections even after caress; no emission no orgasm during an embrace- **CALAD**

Impotence: erection fails when coition is attempted - **ARG NIT** (AGNUS, CALAD, SELEN)

Decided aversion to coition (both sexes) - **GRAPH**

Sexual desire absent in fleshy people - **KALI BI**

Bad effects of suppressed sexual desire or non-gratification of sexual instinct – **CON MAC**

Complaints resulting from abnormal sexual desire- **LYS**

Sexual debility from sexual excess- **GRAPH**

Complaints from abstinence - **CON MAC**

Nightly emissions, with great weakness of genitals after coitus- **DIG**

Emissions during sleep with knee weak- **DIOSC**

Weak, ill-humoured after coitus, often involuntary dribbling of semen and prostatic fluid which oozes while sitting, at stool, during sleep - **SEL**

Nocturnal emissions stained with blood- **MERC** (LED; SARS)

Emissions during sleep; vivid dreams of women all night - **DIOS** (STAPH)

Must keep busy to repress sexual desire- **LIL TIG**

Crushed pain in testicles - **ARG MET** (RHODO)

Orchitis sensation in glad as if it were being crusted – **RHODO** (CHAM; AUR)

Spermatic cord swollen, painful; testicles swollen, bruised, squeezed; after suppressed gonorrhoea or maltreated orchitis- **SPON**

Excessive sexual development in virgins – **PLAT** (KALI P)

Nymphomania worse in lying-in women - **PLAT**

Should not be given in lying-in-women except in high potency – IOD

Paralysis of bladder, no desire to urinate in lying-in women – HYOS (ARN, OP)

Diarrhea in child-bed – CHAM

Panaritia: with red streaks up the arm; pains drive to despair; in child-bed- **ALL CEPA**

Sensitiveness of vagina, rendering coition painful - **LYS**

Sexual desire increased in women - **AST RUB** (LIL TIG)

Violent excitement in sexual organs, and excessive desire for an embrace - **MUR**

Seminal emission soon after an embrace with increased desire - **NAT MUR**

Emissions after coitus; desire inc. after emissions – **NAT MUR; PHOS AC**

Spermatic cord swollen painful - **SPON**

Indurations and swelling of testicle after gonorrhea or rheumatic exposure (Clem.) – **RHODO**

Spermatorrhoea with abashed look and followed by backache - **STAPH**

Persistently dwelling on sexual object - **STAPH**

Impotence with desire, lewd thoughts, but physically impotent -**SELEN**

Priapism glands drawn up – **SELEN** (BERB VUL)

Priapism glands drawn down- **CANTH**

Priapism, with spinal disease; erections; satyriasis - **PIC AC** (CANTH; PHOS)

Sexual desire: increased both sexes; preventing sleep; violent priapism, with excessive pain – **CANTH** (PIC AC)

(Decided aversion to coition (Both sexes) – GRAPH)

Week ill-humored after coitus often involuntary dribbling of semen and prostrate fluid which oozes while sitting at stool, during sleep - **SELEN**

Erections slow insufficient, too rapid emission with long continued thrill - **SELEN**

Catarrh of bladder after suppressed gonnorrrhea - **BENZ ACID**

Discharge of blood from genitals during every stool - **LYCO**

Sexual excitement extreme even to mania; spasms of uterus, pruritus vulva becomes intolerable -**TARENT**

Affects right side; enlargement or dropsy of right ovary or right testicle - **APIS MEL**

Weak eyes; after coition, pollution, abortion, measles - **KALI CARB**

FEMALE - GENITALIA

FEMALE CONDITIONS

Women who have not recovered from change of life have never felt well since that time - **LACH**

(Menorrhagia; has not been well since her last miscarriage- **SULPH**

They never have been well since that burn-**CAUST**

The 1st serious impairment of health is referred to puberic age, have "never been well since"- **PULS**

"Never well since" septic fever, following abortion or confinement – **PYR)**

Violent, corrosive itching of pudenda and vagina - **KREOS**

Climacteric ailments – **LACH**

Hot flushes and hot perspiration - **LACH**

Violent excitement in sexual organs and excessive desire for an embrace - **MUREX**

Sexual organs exceedingly sensitive cannot bear the napkin to touch her - **PLAT**

Least contact of parts causes violent sexual excitement - **MUREX**

(Haemorrhoids: swollen, blue, sensitive and painful to touch; appear suddenly in children; too sore to bear least touch, even the sheet is uncomfortable – MUR AC)

Coition painful in both sexes; followed by bleeding from vagina - **ARG NIT**

Sensitiveness of vagina, rendering coition painful - **LYSS**

Coition prevented by extreme sensitiveness of the vagina (Plat. - by dryness, Lyc., Lys., Natr.) - **THUJA**

Dryness of vagina; burning in, during and after coition - **LYCO (LYS)**

Discharge of mucus from vagina after an embrace causing sterility - **NAT CARB**

Violent stitches upwards in the vagina, lancinating pains from uterus to umbilicus - **SEP**

(Stitches from naval to uterus during haemorrhage – IPEC

Pain extending from sacrum to pubes- SAB

From back, going round the body to pubes- VIB OP)

The washer woman's remedy - **SEP**

Discharge of flatus from vagina- Physometra - **LAC CAN; BROM; LYCO; NUX M; SANG**

MENSTRUATION

Constipation before and during menses - **SIL**

Cholera like symptoms before and during menses - **AM. CARB. (BOV; VER ALB)**

Diarrhea and vomiting during menses – **AMM. MUR**

Vomiting: Every month after menstruation - **CROT. HOR.**

Diarrhea before and during menses - **BOV.**

Dysmenorrhoea: with vomiting and purging, or exhausting diarrhea with cold sweat - **VER ALB** (AM CARB; BOV)

After Am carb, Carbo veg and Bov in dysmenorrhoea with vomiting and purging - **VER ALB**

Bloody discharge from bowel during menses with neuralgic pains in the feet during menses - **AM MUR**

(Discharge of blood from genitals during stool – LYCO

Discharge of blood from vagina every time the child takes the breast - SIL)

Menses: Drinking a glass of milk will promptly suppress flow until next period - **LAC DEF**

(Constipation with ineffectual urging, > by drinking cold milk – IODUM)

Derangements at puberty; menses, suppressed from getting feet wet - **PULS**

Menses: delayed or suppressed by mental emotion, from cold, from fever - **ACTEA RAC**

Cold bathing causes suppressed menses - **ANT CRUD**

Menses: fatigue, especially of thighs - **AM CARB**

Backache before and during menses - **KALI CARB**

Epilepsy a day or two before menses - **KALI BROM**

Headache before and during menses – **KREOS**

Headache ceases during menses and return when flow disappear - **ALL CEPA**

Pain in malar bone during menses - **STAN**

Headache in place of menses - **GLON**

(Leucorrhoea in place of menses- COCC; NUX MOS)

Vicarious menstruation, nosebleed when menses should appear – **BRY; PHOS** (PULS)

Vicarious menstruation; in debilitated constitutions - **CROT. HOR** (DIG., PHOS.).

Nosebleed during menses -**NAT SULPH**

Mammae painful, as if they would ulcerate at every menstrual period; milk in breast instead of the menses - **MERC**

Congestion of brain from delayed or suppressed menses - **GLON**

Humming and roaring in ears with deafness before and during menses - **KREOS**

Sore throat and cough are apt to begin and end with menses – **LAC CAN**

Menses preceded by sore throat - **MAG CARB** (LAC CAN.)

Piles with scanty menses - **LACH**

(Heart disease complicated with haemorrhoids- COLL)

After menses exhausted physically and mentally scarcely able to speak - **ALUM**

After appearance of menses she can hardly speak – **CARB AN** (ALUM., COCC.)

During the effort of menstruation she is so weak she is scarcely able to stand from weakness of lower limbs - **COCC** (ALUM., CARBO AN.)

Is so weak can scarcely stand for 2 days at each menstrual nisus - **VER ALB** (ALUM., CARBO AN., COCC.)

Menses, irregular, exhaustive - **ACTEA**

Feels badly, week before menses – **KALI CARB**

Rashes before menses – **DULC** (CON)

Rashes before profuse menses - **BELL; GRAPH**

Menses with rash of small red principles over body which ceases with flow – **CON MAC**

Eruption on face of young girls specially during scanty menses -**SANG** (BELLIS, CALC., EUG. J., PSOR.)

Itching eruption on forehead during menses – **SARS** (EUG. J., SANG., PSOR.)

Acne all forms simplex rosacea < during menses - **PSOR**

All symptom better during flow - **LACH; ZINC MET; CYCL**

Worse during menses; All suffering < at menstrual period - **HAM** (PULS; ACTEA)

Menses, suppressed from getting feet wet - **PULS**

(*Colic: from cold by getting feet wet- ALL CEPA*

Rheumatic affections; from getting feet wet; from exposure to drafts to air while heated (Acon., Bry.);

< *in cold, wet weather, or cold wet clothes (Rhus tox)- NUX MOSCH)*

Menses delayed from getting feet wet - **GRAPH** (PULS)

Menses: stopped by taking cold; *by putting hands in cold water* - **CON MAC** (LAC DEF)

Menses: delayed; suppressed, by putting hands in cold water - **LAC DEF** (CON)

Difficult of wash off – **MED; MAG CARB**

Menses: flow in gushes bright red, viscid and stringy – **LAC CAN**

(Discharge of a tough stringy mucus which adheres to the parts and can be drawn into long strings – KALI BI

Leucorrhoea ropy, thick, viscid yellow hanging from as in long strings – HYDR

Haemorrhages forming into long black strings hanging from the bleeding surface - CROC

Dysmenorrhoea: flow black; stringy, clotted – CROC

Epistaxis: hangs in a dark clotted string from the nose, like an icicle – MERC SOL

Saliva: tough ropy, viscid, frothy in mouth and throat, with constant spitting – LYS)

Dysmenorrhoea: flow black; stringy, clotted – **CROC**

At every menstrual nisus, mouth, throat and tongue become intolerably dry specially when sleeping - **NUX MOS; TARENT**

Delayed 1st menstruation – **PULS**

In persons who menstruated very early in life - **SAB**

Menorrhagia; has not been well since her last miscarriage - **SULPH**

(Women who have not recovered from change of life have never felt well since than time – LACH

They never have been well since that burn – CAUST

The 1st serious impairment of health is referred to puberic age, have "never been well since"- PULS

"Never well since" septic fever, following abortion or confinement – PYR.)

Menstrual and uterine affection with great melancholy < at menstrual period - **AUR MET**

Discharge of blood between period at every little accident- a big walk, after every hard stool etc.- **AMBRA**

Menses: after over-exertion or too long a ride - **TRILLIUM**

Discharge of blood between periods with sexual excitement- **SAB** (AMBRA)

Least mental excitement causes profuse return of menstrual flow - **CALC** (SULPH; TUB)

Inflammation of ovaries or uterus after abortion or premature labor - **SAB**

Menses- flow dark with soreness in abdomen; after a blow on ovary or a fall; all suffering < at menstrual period - **HAM**

After: Arn in traumatic affections of ovaries - **PSOR**

Pain and numbness in right ovary, running down thigh of that side (Lil.) - **PODO**

Amennorrhoea with catarrhal symptoms of eyes and nose - **EUPH**

Menses too early, too profuse, sadness before pain in malar bone during - **STAN**

Menses- 1st day merely a show, 2nd day colic, vomiting, haemorrhage with large clots; each alternate period more profuse - **THLASPI**

Menses now lasting only one hour – **EUPH**

Intense menstrual colic, with drawing up of knees and terrible bearing down labor like pains; must press feet against support, as in labor - **MEDO**

Menses flow only when moving about cease to flow when she ceases to walk - **LIL TIG** (CAUST.)

Menstrual flow ceases when lying down - **CACTUS** (BOV., CAUST.)

Menses: flows only at night or when lying, ceases when walking - **MAG CARB** (AM MUR, KREOS)

Menses: only during the day; cease on lying down - **CAUST**

Metrorrhagia- flow in dark clots and fluid; thick, black tary or in a grumous mass - **PLAT** (CROC)

Suppressed Menses in young girls - **PODO** (PULS; TUB)

(Leucorrhoea in little girls- CAUL (CALC)

Leucorrhoea of children from atony- MILL (CALC)

Menses partly fluid partly clotted – **SAB** (FER MET)

Metrorrhagia in young widows or in sterility - **ARG NIT**

Amenorrhoea in plethoric young girls - **ACON**

Chorea, hysteria or epilepsy at puberty, during establishment of menstrual function - **CAUL** (ACTEA)

Menses with chorea, hysteria or mania; increase of mental symptoms during menses - **ACTEA**

(Leucorrhoea < mental depression, happier when leucorrhoea is worse- MUREX)

Menses with continuous discharge of watery blood until next period - **SEC COR**

Prolapsus; with pain in left ovary and back, extending forward and downward (right ovary, Pal.) - **ARG. MET.**

Weak and atonic condition of ovaries, uterus and pelvic tissues, resulting in anteversion, retroversion, sub-involution (Helon., Sep.) - **LIL. TIG.**

PROLAPSE

Pressing downwards as if the contents of abdomen. Would issue from the vulva, amel standing and sitting erect - **BELL**

Prolapsus uteri; many cases of years' standing cured - **LYSS**

Bearing down as if everything would come out < sitting, > moving - **NAT CARB**

Pressing, pushing towards genitals every morning; must sit down to prevent prolapsus - **NAT MUR**

Prolapsus of uterus and vagina, pressure and bearing down as if everything would protrude from pelvis must cross limbs tightly or set close to prevent it wish no sexual desire - **SEP**

Bearing down sensation as if abdominalorgans would be pushed out must sit down and crocs limbs to prevent; with excessive sexual desire – **MUREX**

Sore pain in uterus, a distinct sensation of womb - **MUREX**

A consciousness of womb, feels it move when she moves it is so sore and tender - **HELON**

(Distinct consciousness of a heart: it feels tired – PYR)

Prolapsus worse during stool - **STAN**

Prolapse, bearing-down pain almost intolerable - **AGAR**

Sleeplessness from prolapsus, uterine irritation, during climacteric - **SENECIO**

Prolapse of uterus and vagina; pressing and bearing down as if everything would protrude from pelvis; must cross limbs tightly or "sit close" to prevent it; with oppression of breathing - **SEP**

LEUCORRHOEA

Leucorrhoea after every urination - **AM MUR.**

(Diarrhea when she urinates- ALUM

Leucorrhoea every time passes stool -MAG MUR

Haemmorrhoids: prolapse while urinating - MUR AC

Haemorrhoids protrude every time he urinates - BAR CARB (MUR AC)

Leucorrhoea every time passes stool - **MAG MUR**

(Discharge of blood from genitals during every stool – LYCO

Discharge of blood from vagina every time the child takes the breast - SIL)

Leucorrhoea acrid copious foetid green - **CARB AC**

(Boils: small, painful with green contents – SEC COR

Crops of small boils, intensely painful, successively appear in nose; green, foetid pus – TUB)

Leucorrhoea- green brown offensive - **SEC COR**

Leucorrhoea with moth spots on forehead – **CAUL**

Leucorrhoea in little girls – **CAUL**

(Suppressed menses in young girls – PODO (PULS; TUB)

Leucorrhoea of children from atony - **MILL**

Leucorrhea. with strong odor of fish brine - **SANC**

(Oozing from rectum smelling like fish brine – MEDO

Discharge from ear smelling likes fish brine—TELL)

Leucorrhoea acrid corrosive, staining and corroding the linen - **IOD**

Leucorrhoea; transparent, but staining linen yellow; passes imperceptibly from the very relaxed parts - **AGN CAS**

Leucorrhoea stiffens like starch stains the linen yellow - **KREOS**

Leucorrhoea ropy, thick, viscid yellow hanging from as in long strings – **HYDR**

(Haemorrhages forming into long black strings hanging from the bleeding surface- CROC

Epistaxis: hangs in a dark clotted string from the nose, like an icicle – MERC SOL

Discharge of a tough, stringy mucus which adheres to the parts and can be drawn into long strings – KALI BI

Discharge from nose and all mucous membranes very tough, stringy, tenacious – BOV

Saliva: tough ropy, viscid, frothy in mouth and throat, with constant spitting – LYS)

Leucorrhoea <Mental depression, happier when leucorrhoea is worse - **MUREX**

Leucorrhoea: acrid and profuse, running down to the heels; < daytime; > cold bathing - **ALUM**

Leucorrhoea: profuse, soaking through the napkins and running down to the heels - **SYPH**

Leucorrhoea in place of menses – **COCC; NUX MOS**

(Headache in place of menses – GLON

Vicarious Menstruation – BRY, PHOS, CROT HOR, PULS

Nosebleeed with menses – NAT SULPH)

Leucorrhoea most abundant at time of menses - **IOD**

Leucorrhoea during pregnancy – **COCC**

Leucorrhoea 10 days after menses - **CON MAC**

Leucorrhoea worse between periods - **KREOS**

Leucorrhoea acrid corrosive, offensive – **KREOS**

AFTER-PAINS

After pains extending upto groins - **CAUL; ACTEA**

After pains extend upto shins - **CARB VEG; COCC**

After pains severe in calves and soles - **CUP MET**

After pains after long exhausting labor; spasmodic across lower abdomen - **ACTEA**

After pains too long, too painful hour glass contraction - **SEC COR**

BREAST

Fissures of nipples in nursing women - **RATAN (GRAPH; SEP)**

Nipples, sensitive, sore fissured; < intensely by nursing, pain radiates over the whole body - **PHYTO**

Loss of milk in nursing without any known cause - **LAC CAN (ASAF.)**

Serviceable in cases to bring back or increase milk - **LAC DEF**

Serviceable in almost all cases when it is required to dry up milk - **LAC CAN** (ASAF)

Deficient secretion or suppression of milk in nursing woman often with great sadness - **AGN CAS**

Suppression of milk in thin scrawny exhausted women - **SEC COR**

Milk runs out in nursing woman - **CHAM**

Milk runs out in weaning mother - **CON MAC**

Convulsions of children from nursing often a fit of anger in mother - **CHAM** (NUX VOM)

Convulsions in children from nursing after fright in mother - **OPIUM**

Child vomits as soon as it has nursed, after mother has been angry - **VAL**

Toothache while nursing the child - **CINCH**

(*Toothache during menses or pregnancy* – *CHAM*

Menses with toothache – *AMM.CARB*

Toothache during menses - *STAPH*)

Mammae heavy of a stony hardness pale but hard, hot and painful must support the breast - **BRY**

Breast inflamed, painful must hold them firmly when going up and down stones - **LAC CAN**

Breast cold as ice to touch, specially the nipples, rest of body warm (during menses) - **MEDO.**

Cancer of mammae; acute lancinating pain; drawing pain in breast; swollen, distended, as before the menses; breast feels drawn in - **AST RUB**

Mammae full of hard, painful nodosities. Breast, shows early tendency to cake; is full, stony, hard and painful, especially when suppuration is inevitable - **PHYTO**

Retraction of nipples; nipples are small, withered, unexcitable - **SARS** (SIL)

Nipple is drawn in like a funnel - **SIL** (SARS)

(Violent colic, sensation as if abdominal wall was drawn as if by a string to the spine – PLUMBUM)

Breast sore, hard and painful before and during menstruation - **CON MAC** (LAC CAN; Kali carb)

Mammae painful, as if they would ulcerate at every menstrual period; milk in breast instead of the menses - **MERC.**

Breasts swollen, nipples painful and tender - **HELON**

When child nurses pain goes from nipple to whole body - **PHYTO**

Discharge of blood from vagina every time child takes the breast - **SIL**

(Leucorrhoea every time passes stool- MAG MUR

Bloody discharge from bowel during menses with neuralgic pains in the feet during menses – AMM MUR

When child nurses pain goes from nipple to uterus - **PULS; SIL**

Drawing pain through the chest from breast to scapula, of the same side every time child nurses - **CROT TIG**

Breast is full stony hard and painful especially when suppuration is inevitable - **PHYTO**

Breast showing tendency to cake – **PHYTO**

A livid red spot appeared, broke and discharged; gradually invaded entire breast, very foetid odor; edges pale, elevated, mammillary, hard, everted; bottom covered with reddish granulations - **AST RUB**

ABORTION

Painless drainage after labor or abortion – **MILL**

(Painless cholera morbus PODO

Painless sorethroat- BAPT;

Painless hoarseness- CALC CARB;

Painless quinsy – BAR CARB

Painless diphtheria- DIPHTH

Painless haemorrhage- MILL

Painless haematuria- TEREB

Painless gonorrhoea- NAT SULPH

Painlessness with all complaints – OP; STRAM)

Abortion at 3rd month - **ACTEA; SAB; SEC COR**

Habitual abortion from uterine debility - **CAUL (ALET)**

Habitual abortion from anemia and profound melancholy - **HELON**

Threatened abortion; flow ceases and then returns with increased force; pains spasmodic, excite suffocation and fainting; must have fresh air - **PULS**

Feels a lack of room for foetus in uterus; inability of uterus to expand; threatening abortion - **PLUMB**

For the bad effects of abortions and miscarriages - **HELON**

Ailments: following abortion or premature labor - **SAB**

Never well since septic fever following abortion or confinement – **PYR**

(Menorrhagia; has not been well since her last miscarriage- SULPH

Women who have not recovered from change of life have never felt well since than time – LACH

They never have been well since that burn –CAUST

The 1st serious impairment of health is referred to puberic age, have "never been well since"- PULS)

Promotes expulsion of moles or foreign bodies form uterus - **SAB** (CANTH)

Foetus or secundines retained decomposed dead from days black - **PYR**

Inflammation of ovaries or uterus after abortion or premature labor - **SAB**

PREGNANCY and LABOR

In early months of pregnancy can lie comfortably only on stomach- **PODO** (ACET. AC.)

(Rest better lying on belly - ACET. ACID; AMM CARB

Amelioration lying on stomach – MEDO)

Sour belching and vomiting of pregnancy, burning water-brash and profuse salivation, day and night –**ACET. ACID**

(Salivation < at night – LAC ACID, MERC SOL

Vomiting of pregnancy with profuse salivation – LOB

Nausea with profuse salivation – IPEC)

During pregnancy – most obstinate vomiting, foetus moves too violently - **PSOR**

Nervous cough during pregnancy - **KALI BROM**

Cough during pregnancy - **APOC; CON**

Toothache during menses - **AMM CARB; STAPH**

Toothache during menses and pregnancy - **CHAM**

Toothache during pregnancy < night - **MAG CARB**

Terrible toothache during early months of pregnancy; tooth feels elongated; < lying compelling to rise and walk about - **RATAN**

Leucorrhoea during pregnancy - **COCC**

Constipation of pregnancy after Nux fails - **PLAT**

Constipation when Platina fails - **PLUMB**

Constipation: painful, of infants and children, after Lyc., and Nux. - **VER ALB**

Constipation when Sulphur fails to relieve - **PSOR**

Vomiting: of drunkards, in pregnancy; seasickness; cancer; of dark, olive-green fluid - **CARB. AC.**

Diarrhea of drunkards - APIS

Nux or Opium in haemoptysis of drunkards – HYOS

Drunkards, especially for their headaches; bad effects after a debauch- AGAR (LOB; NUXVOM; RAN))

Vomiting: of pregnancy, sweetish water with ptyalism; of cholera during painful dentition; incessant with cadaverous stool; in malignant affections of stomach - **KREOS.**

Vomiting violent with cold sweat soon as he begins to move; during pregnancy when lactic acid fails - **TAB**

After: Arn in traumatic affections of ovaries - **PSOR**

Congestion of pelvic viscera with haemorrhoids specially in later months of pregnancy –**COLLIN.**

Fear of death during pregnancy - **ACON**

Pain, nausea and vomiting, during pregnancy, from wearing pessaries - **NUX MOSCH.**

Tendency to faint after every labor pain - **NUX VOM**

Labor pains press up wards - **CHAM**

Labor pains causes urging to stool or to urinate – **NUX VOM**

During labor everything seems loose and open but no expulsive action – **SEC COR**

Convulsions during labor - **HYOS**

Spasm during parturition - **KALI BROM**

Phlebitis, puerperal; after forceps delivery - **ALL. CEPA.**

Prevents postpartum haemorrhage and puerperal complication - **ARN.; Mill**

Puerperal convulsions immediately after delivery - **AMYL NIT**

Puerperal convulsions: frequent suspension of breathing for a few moments, as if dead; upper part of the body most affected; continue after delivery - **CICUTA**

Lochia almost ceases, then freshens up again – **KREOS**

LYING IN PERIOD/CHILD-BED

Should not be given in lying-in-women except in high potency - **IOD**

Nymphomania worse in lying-in women - **PLAT**

Paralysis of bladder, no desire to urinate in lying-in women - **HYOS** (ARN, OP)

Diarrhea in child-bed - **CHAM**

Panaritia: with red streaks up the arm; pains drive to despair; in child-bed - **ALL CEPA**

Puerperal mania – **ACTEA**

RESPIRATORY SYSTEM

DYSPNOEA

Dyspnoea cannot inspire deep enough - **BROM**

In dyspnoea as if breathing through a sponge or the air passages were full of smoke or vapor of sulphur - **BROM**

Dyspnoea < with every labor pains seems to neutralize the pains - **LOB INF**

Dyspnoea must lie on right side or with head high - **SPIG..** (CACTUS, SPONG.)

As soon as he falls asleep breathing stops - **LACH**

Least thing coming near mouth or nose interferes with breathing- – **LACH**

Pleurisy or pneumonia from sudden exposure to cold when overheated or vice versa - **RAN BULB**

Chest pains running upwards - **BROM**

Dyspnoea agg. in open air, on sitting up and amel. by lying downand keeping arms stretched far apart - **PSOR**

Desire to be constantly fanned (rapidly) - **CARBO VEG**

Wants to be fanned, but slowly and at a distance - **LACH**

State of collapse, wants to be fanned all the time - **MEDO**

Dyspnoea; can inhale with ease, but no power to exhale - **MEDO; SAMB**

Cough with regular inhalations but sighing exhalations - **SAMB**

Unable to breathe well, or is chilly in warm room - **PULS**

Dyspnoea with palpitation worse in a warm room - **AM CARB**

Dyspnoea < by exposure to cold - **LOB**

Want of breath in those engaged in athletic sports - **COCA**

Dyspnoea < sitting, after sleep, in room, > dancing or walking rapidly - **SEP**

(Vertigo when moving slowly, but not when taking violent exercise – MILL

Sensation of congestion, pressure or weight in chest as if blood from extremities was filling it, > by rapid walking- LOB)

One of the best remedies in emphysema - **AMM CARB**

COUGH

Cough compels patient to grasp the larynx seems as if cough would tear it - **ALL CEPA**

Cough with utter inability to lie on right side - **MERC**

Cough lying on left side – **PHOS** (DROS; STAN)

(Vomiting in any position except lying on right side- ANT. TART

Vomiting cannot lie on right side- CROT. HOR

Palpitation worse when walking and lying on left side- CAC GRAND (LACH.)

Palpitation violent when lying on left side > turning on right- LAC. C, TAB

Pains < when lying on left side- PHOS)

Cough < entering a warm room - **BRY**

Cough going from warm to cold air - **PHOS**

Croupy cough in winter alternating with sciatica in summer - **STAPH**

(Headache alternates with Diarrhea; headache in winter, Diarrhea in summer- PODO)

Laughing excites cough - **ARG MET**

Cough worse after meat - **STAPH**

(Styes from rich food and pork- PULS

Aversion to meat- CALC CARB

Inordinate craving for meat in children of tuberculous parentage – MAG CARB

Cannot bear the thought or sight of meat – MUR AC (NIT AC)

Cough worse after eating meat- STAPH)

Cough excited by cleaning the teeth - **STAPH**

Cough < inspiration - **SPON**

Cough < reading, singing, talking, swallowing – **SPON**

Cough < sweat thing, cold drinks, lying with head low - **SPON**

Cough > by swallow of cold water - **CAUST.; CUP. MET.**

Cough > eating or drinking warm things - **SPON**

Expectoration, sweetish, salty - **STAN**

Expectoration Salty - **KALI IOD; SEP**

Great weakness in chest < from talking, laughing, reading aloud singing - **STAN**

Cough dry sibilant, like a saw driven through a pine board - **SPON**

Great dryness of mucous membrane of air passages "dry as thorn" - **SPON**

Cough not ceasing until he sits up in bed and passes flatus – **SANG**

Every mental excitement increases the cough - **SPON**

Short cough and chest complaints; esp. after operations for fistula in ano – **BERB VUL** (CALC. P., SIL.)

Fistula-in-ano alternates with chest symptoms - **SIL** (BERB.)

Cough dry spasmodic with gagging and vomiting - **BRY** (KALI CARB)

Cough – violent rattling with gagging from viscid mucus in throat < undressing - **KALI BI** (HEP)

(Itching when undressing- RUM; TUB)

Pain in distant parts on coughing - **CAPS**

Pain in hips with cough - **CAUST**

With every explosive cough there escapes a volume of pungent foetid air - **CAPS**

(Constipation; with horribly offensive breath- CARB AC)

Cough has gurgling sound, as if water was being poured from a bottle > by drinking cold water - **CUP MET**

Cough in paroxysm of 2 coughs – **MERC**

Cough in paroxysm of 3 coughs - **STAN**

(Whooping cough in paroxysm of 3 attacks- CUP MET)

Constant titillating cough in children begins as soon as head touches pillow at night - **DROS**

Cough; as soon as the head touched the pillow a spasmodic paroxysm of cough sets in - **CROT TIG**

(Vomiting as soon as he raises head from pillow- STRAM)

Cough: chronic, loose with chest sore; must support it with hands - **EUP PERF**

Great soreness of chest, during cough, has to set up in bed and hold the chest with both hands - **NAT SULPH** (NIC.)

Cough with stitches in side of chest with headache as if head would fly to pieces - **BRY**

Dry incessant fatiguing cough from slightest inhalation of cold air - **RUM**

Great sensitiveness to open air; putting the hand from under the bed-cover brings on cough - **RHUSTOX**

Cough when any part of the body is uncovered, croupy choking, strangling from exposure to dry west wind – **HEP SUL**

Cough with blood daily at 4 pm - **MILL**

Cough after a fall from a height – **MILL**

Tickling in throat pit causing dry teasing cough – **RUM**

Cough- dry from tickling in throat as from dust, every morning from 3 – 4 am - **AMM. CARB.** (KALI CARB.)

Sensation of lump in throat, descends on swallowing but returns immediately - **RUMEX**

Sensation of feather in larynx, exciting cough – **DROS.**

(Sensation of a splinter, fish bone or plug in the throat- HE. SULPH; ARG NIT; NIT AC (SIL; DOLICHOS)

Sensation as if a thread were hanging down throat- VAL

Sensation as of a hair on the tongue- NAT MUR; SIL)

Chronic laryngitis of singers, the high notes causes cough - **ARG. NIT.**

Cough on standing still during, > walk - **IGN**

Cough dry deep, precedes the fever paroxysm -**SAMB**

Cough returns every winter - **PSOR.**

Cough > relieved by lying down; > by eating (Spong) - **FER MET** (KALI BI)

Croup: *hoarse, metallic*, with expectoration of tough mucus or fibro-elastic casts in morning on awakening; with dyspnoea, > by lying down (*worse when lying down, Aral., Lach.*) - **KALI BI**

Cough < when lying down relieved by sitting up - **HYOS**

Cough < at night, from sweets, on lying down; > on lying on stomach - **MEDO.**

Cough, short and dry or deep and loose, during pregnancy - **APOC.** (CON.)

Nervous cough of pregnancy - **KALI BROM.**

Cough during pregnancy - **CON MAC**

Cough deep, hollow, even raising mucus in large quantity affords little relief - **LYCO.**

Cough loose after eating, dry after drinking - **NUX MOS**

Cough only after dinner - **STAPH**

Cough: only in the daytime, worse after eating meat - **STAPH**

Pertussis: *excessive lachrymation during cough; cough only in day time* - **EUPH.**

Cough only in the daytime - **STAPH; FER MET; EUPH**

Cough after suppressed itch, or eczema - **PSOR**

[Asthma after suppressed eruption -HEP SULPH

Epilepsy from suppressed eruptions- AGAR; (PSOR; SULPH)

Headache from suppressed eruption- ANT .CRUD

Diarrhea especially if eruption be suppressed- APIS

Brain diseases from suppressed eruptions- CICUTA

Chorea from suppressed eruption; from fright- ZINC MET]

ASTHMA

Asthma after the rose cold from odors - **SANG**

Breathing – must sit or bend forward unable to lie down for fear of suffocation < after 12.0 clock - **ARS ALB**

Asthma relieved when sitting up bending forward or rocking; worse from 2 to 4 a.m. – **KALI CARB**

Asthma < in open air; < sitting up, >lying down and keeping arms stretched far apart – **PSOR**

Asthma, must bend head back and sit up - **HEP SULPH**

Dyspnoea or Asthma, where the patient can only breathe by *standing up* - **CAN SAT**

Sailors suffer from asthma "on shore" - **BROM**

Humid asthma in children with every change to wet weather - **NAT SULPH**

Asthma only > by lying on face and protruding tongue - **MEDO**

Asthma after suppressed eruption - **HEP SULPH**

[Cough after suppressed itch, or eczema- PSORINUM

Epilepsy from suppressed eruptions- AGARICUS; (PSOR.; SULPH)

Headache from suppressed eruption- ANT. CRUD

Diarrhea especially if eruption be suppressed- APIS

Brain diseases from suppressed eruptions- CICUTA VIROSA

Chorea from suppressed eruption; from fright- ZINC MET]

WHOOPING-COUGH

Breathless, blue face rigid, stiff with whooping cough - **CUP MET**

Child loses breath, turns pale, stiff and blue in whooping cough - **IPEC**

Whooping cough in paroxysm of 3 attacks - **CUP MET**

In whooping cough wakes at 6-7 a.m. and does not cease coughing until a large quantity of tenacious mucous is raised - **COCC**

"Minute gun" during day whooping cough at night - **COR. RUB.**

Whooping cough < by being over-heated in the sun or in warm room - **ANT CRUD**

Whooping cough < from cold washing - **ANT CRUD**

Whooping cough with violent paroxysms which follow each other rapidly, is scarcely able to get breath - **DROS**

Whooping cough, but without crowing inspiration - **AMBRA**

Whooping cough; cataleptic spasm with each paroxysm - **CUP MET**

Cough in two paroxysms, worse at night - **MERC**

Cough: convulsive, in paroxysms of three coughs - **STANNUM**

CORYZA and SNEEZING

Profuse, watery and acrid nasal discharge with profuse bland lachrymation – **ALL CEPA**

Exhausting, fluent coryza with sneezing - **ARG MET**

Profuse fluent coryza in morning with violent cough and abundant expectoration, < from exposure to warm south wind - **EUPH**

Coryza; acrid, fluent; nostrils raw- **ARUM T**

Profuse, full of acrid tears, bland and fluent coryza - **EUPH**

Nose feels stopped up inspite of the watery discharge- **ARUM T**

Exhausting, fluent coryza with sneezing- **ARG MET**

Sneezing in spasmodic paroxysms; followed by lachrymation- **SABAD**

Sneezing < night – **ARUM T**

Coryza ending in Diarrhea- **SELEN**

Dyspnoea agg sitting; amel dancing or walking rapidly-**SEP**

Raw spot over bifurcation of trachea- **ARG MET**

Thick yellow green offensive musty hard discharge from; often ceasing after meal- **NAT CARB**

Cough- loose after eating, dry after drinking - **NUX MOS**

Acrid nasal secretion, having odor of old cheese; nostrils red, raw ulcerated- **MERC SOL**

Ozena: green casts from the nose every morning - **NIT AC**

Ozena, blowing bloody mucus from the nose frequently; blood rushes to tip of nose, when stooping - **AM CARB**

Takes cold easily without knowing how or where; sees to take cold every time he takes a breath of fresh air - **TUB**

Acrid, watery discharge dropping from tip of nose - **ALL CEPA** (ARS, ARS IOD)

HEART

Whole body feels as if caged, each wire being twisted tighter and tighter – **CACTUS**

(Sensation of a cord tightly tied around lower part of chest, marking attachment of diaphragm – CACTUS G)

Sensation as if the heart was squeezed together; as if grasped with an iron hand – **IOD** (SULPH)

(Violent twisting colic, occurring in regular paroxysms, as if intestines were grasped and twisted by a powerful hand – Dios)

Heart feels as if clasped and unclasped rapidly by an iron hand; as if bound "had no room to beat" - **CACTUS**

(Sciatica: crampy pain in hip, as though screwed in a vise – COLOC)

Sensation as if heart was grasped in a vise; as if blood had all gone to the heart feels full to bursting, inability to walk erect - **LIL**

Sensations of congestion, pressure or weight in chest as if blood from extremities was filling it > by rapid walking - **LOB**

(Dyspnoea: < sitting, after sleep, in room, > dancing or walking rapidly – SEP

Vertigo: when moving slowly, but not when taking violent exercise – MILL)

Sensation as if heart would stop beating if she moves – **DIG** (COCAINE)

Fears that unless on the move heart will cease beating – **GELS**

Palpitation from least motion - **ACTEA** (DIG)

Palpitation worse from least exertion- **IOD**

Palpitation worse from least mental exertion - **CALC ARS**

Palpitation worse from least exertion- IOD

Least mental excitement causes profuse return of menstrual flow- calc; (Sulph; tUb)

Discharge of blood between periods with sexual excitement -sab (ambra)

Discharge of blood between period at every little accident- a big walk, after every hard stool etc.- ambra

Heart troubles from reflex symptom of uterus and ovaries - **ACTEA**

Sensation as if the heart would stand still as though it ceased to beat and then suddenly gave one hard thumps – **AUR MET** (SEP)

Palpitation violent when lying of left side, goes off when turning to right - **TAB, LAC CAN**

(Cough lying on left side –PHOS (DROS, STAN)

Cough with utter inability to lie on right side- MERC

Vomiting in any position except lying on right side- ANT TART

Vomiting cannot lie on right side- CROT HOR

Palpitation worse when walking and lying on left side- CACTUS (LACH)

Palpitation violent when lying on left side > turning on right- LAC CAN, TAB

Pains < when lying on left side- PHOS)

Palpitation worse when walking and lying on left side - **CACTUS**

Palpitation in patients subject to piles and indigestion - **COLL**

Palpitation: day and night, worse when walking and lying on left side; at approach of menses - **CACTUS**

Palpitation before and during menses - **SPON**

Palpitation of heart is felt in the face- **MUR AC**

Heart's pulsations shake the body - **NAT MUR; SPIG**

Pulsation over whole body and full is distended feeling as if blood would burst through vessel - **AESC; LIL TIG**

Palpitation violent with pain and gasping respiration- **SPON**

Palpitation with valvular in sufficiency - **SPON**

Weak heart without valvular complication - **DIG**

For restoring a heart damaged by acute inflammation or from relief of suffering of chronic hypertrophy and valvular lesions - **NAJA**

Pulse full irregular, very slow and weak intermitting every 3rd, 5th and 7th beat- **DIG**

Slow pulse –35 – 40 beats/ min- **KAL**

Rapid heartbeat- 150 to 170/ min- **LIL**

Slow pulse of old age - **BAR CARB**

Pulse irregular in force, but regular in rhythm - **NAJA**

Pulse abnormally rapid out of all proportion to temperature - **PYR; LIL TIG**

Simple hypertrophy of heart - **NAJA**

Hypertrophy of heart from gymnastics in growing boys- **BROM**

Hypertrophy of heart from calisthenics in young girls - **CAUST**

After heart is relieved old piles reappear or suppressed menses return – **COLL**

Heart diseases complicated with hemorrhoids- **COLL**

Angina pectoris-tumultuous heart action; intense throbbing of heart and carotids- **AMYL NIT**

Chest complaints alternating with fistula in ano - **BERB VULG; SIL; CALC PHOS**

Anxiety about heart as if some evil was impending - **MENY**

Heart disease that have developed from rheumatism or alternate with it - **KAL**

Dropsy from cardiac disease - **COLL**

Threatened paralysis of heart: post diphtheritic - **NAJA**

(Post-diphtheritic paralysis, after Caust., Gels., fails - DIPHTHERINUM)

Sensation of coldness about the heart - **PET**

Heart –sensation as if suspended by a thread- **KALI CARB**

Heart –tendency to fatty degeneration – **KALI CARB; AUR MET; PHOS**

Deep seated pain at base of heart – **LOB**

Systolic blowing at apex - **SPIG**

Anxious pulsation about apex - **LIL**

Heart pain from base to clavicle- **SPIG**

Heart pain from apex to base - **MEDO**

Heart – lacerating pains from base to apex, at night-**SYPH**

Distinct consciousness of heart –**PYR**

(Consciousness of womb- HELONIAS; MUREX)

Severe stitching pain in region of heart - **NAJA**

Fatal syncope may occur when being raised to upright position - **DIG.**

BACK

Great sensitiveness between vertebrae sits sideways to avoid pressure against vertebrae - **THER**

Single vertebrae sensitive to touch - **AGAR**

Spine very sensitive to touch – **HYPER; AGAR**

Can't bear back touched- **ZINC MET**

Sacrum extreme sensitiveness can't bear the slightest touch even of a soft pillow, sits leaning forward as avoid contact with cloths – **LOB**

Pain in sacrum, coccyx, and back of hips running around and down limbs - **MEDO**

Lumbar vertebra sensitive to touch - **MEDO.**

Intolerable itching at tip of coccyx- **BOV.**

Spine aches from base of brain to coccyx, *very sensitive to touch or pressure* - **LAC CAN.** (CHIN. SULPH.; PHOS; ZINC MET)

Severe dull backache in lumbosacral articulation; more or less constant; affecting sacrum and hips- **AESC**

Chill especially along the spine running up and down the back in rapid wave like succession from sacrum to occiput – **GELS**

Burning along spine; softening of cord- **PIC AC**

Burning in spots along the spine bet. the scapulae or intense heat running up the back- **PHOS**

Sensation as of a piece of ice in between the scapulae- **LACHNANTHES**

(Sensation as if ice touched or ice-cold needles were piercing the skin; as from hot needles – AGAR)

Sensation of coldness in the back between scapulae - **AM MUR**

Pain between the shoulder when swallowing - **RHUS TOX**

Pain in back between scapulae; whole length of spine sore to touch - **MEDO.** (CHIN SULPH)

Backache < at night in bed and in the morning before rising - **STAPH.**

Backache: intense, unbearable, cross super-sacral region, extending to right natis and right sciatic nerve; < by rest and on first moving - **LAC CAN.** (RHUS)

Backache: must sit up to turn over in bed; lumbago – from sexual weakness, from masturbation- **NUX VOM.**

Backache while riding in a carriage - **NUX MOS.**

(Sick-headache from carriage, boat or train riding – COCC

Complaints > by riding in a carriage – NIT AC

Hardness of hearing amel by carriage riding or train- GRAPH; NIT AC.

Nausea or vomiting from riding in carriage boat or railroad car - COCC.)

Back gives out - **AESC.**

EXTREMITY

Itching chilblains- **ABROT** (AGAR)

Painful itching chilblains and chapped hands < cold weather- **PETR.**

Chilblains that itch and burn intolerably- **AGAR**

Chilblains painful< from rubbing- **ZINC MET**

Hamstrings feel painfully short when walking- **AMM MUR**

Painful contractions of the hamstring - **NAT MUR** (AM MUR; CAUST; GUAIC)

Rheumatic affections, with contraction of the flexors and stiffness of the joints; tension and shortening of muscles - **CAUST** (AM MUR; CIMEX; GUAIAC; NAT MUR)

When singing or using the voice, aching and weakness in deltoid and arms – **STAN**

Marasmus of lower extremity only- **ABROT**

Emaciation progresses every year, most marked in lower extremities, marasmus - **ARG NIT**

(Emaciation of affected part- LED PALARS, SEL; GRAPH)

Body large and fat, but legs too thin - **AM MUR**

Hydrocephalous; deathly coldness of forearm of children.- **ARN**

In gout and rheumatism, great fear of being touched or struck by persons coming near him – **ARN**

Rheumatism of cold weather, getting well in spring and returning in autumn - **CALC PHOS**

Rheumatism at top of shoulder and arm; pains extend to finger, >by motion- **MEDO**

Rheumatism of shoulder joint or at insertion of deltoid < from raising arising arm laterally – **SYPH**

Rheumatic in right arm and shoulder cannot raise the arm < right – **SANG**

Rheumatic affections left shoulder- **FER MET; NUX MOS**

Faint and weak, especially when going down stairs; can go up well enough - **STAN** (BOR)

(Reverse of CALC CARB)

Cracking if joint on motion (Coc.; Graph.) (compare Benz. ac)- **NIT AC**

Gouty concretions; arthritis vaga; affects all the joints, especially the knee, cracking on motion; nodosities -**BENZ AC** (BERB; LITH C; LYSS)

Ankles turn when walking – **CARB AN**

Ankles turn easily when walking – **MEDO** (CARB AN; LED)

Easy spraining of ankles and feet- **LED**

Chronic sprains - **BOV; STON CARB**

Easy dislocation and spraining of ankle - **NAT CARB** (LED)

Periosteal pains after wound have healed- **SYMPH**

Bruises and mechanical injuries of bones and periosteum; periostitis – **RUTA**

Pain in places where the bones are least covered, as tibia, back of hands etc (Rhus ven) - **SANG**

Pains: pressive, drawing or tearing of parts where bones lie near the surface- **CYCL**

Pain in periosteum of long bones < at night in bed, beast touch and damp weather – **MEZ**

Cramps of writers, piano or violin players - **MAG PHOS**

Rheumatic pains in muscles of neck and back; feel stiff, lame, contracted; spine sensitive, from using arms in sewing, type writing, piano playing –CIMIC (ACTEA) (AGAR; RAN BULB)

Rheumatism of women especially small joint - **CAUL** (ACT S)

Lassitude: faints on going into a room full of company - **PLUMB**

Gait unsteady; muscles refuse to obey the will - **AST RUB**; (GELS; ALUM)

Inco-ordination of muscles -**KALI BROM** (GELS)

For relaxation and prostration of the whole muscular system with entire motor paralysis - **GELS**

Great weakness of lower extremities, with trembling; cannot walk with the eyes closed - **ARG NIT**

Inability to walk, except with the eyes open, and in the daytime; tottering and falling when closing eyes - **ALUM** (ARG NIT; GELS)

The fingers go to sleep frequently and easily - **DIG**

When walking seems to be walking on air; when lying doesn't seem to touch the bed - **LAC CAN**

Great emaciation of face, hands, legs and feet or single parts - **SEL**

Muscular atrophy from sclerosis of spinal system - **PLUMB**

Nervousness, intensely felt about the ankles - **PULS**

(*Cannot bear to be touched; starts when touched ever so lightly; especially on the feet- KALI CARB*

Takes cold from exposure of feet- SIL)

Incessant and violent and fidgety feeling in feet or lower extremity; must move them constantly - **ZINC MET**

Fidgety hands- **KALI BROM**

Restless, fidgety moves continuously cannot sit stand still a moment- **PHOS**

Irritable; nervous; fidgety; hard to please - **APIS**

Fidgety while sitting at work – **GRAPH**

Restless, fidgety, starts at least noise- **SIL**

Intense restless and fidgety legs and feet- **MEDO** (ZINC MET)

Staggering uncertain gait- **KALI BROM**

Takes cold from exposure of feet (Con.; Cup.)- **SIL**

Sciatica: pain < when standing and letting foot rest on floor; when straightening out limb, during rest from previous exertion; > when walking- **VAL**

Intense pain along the sciatic nerve, from rt. hip joint down to foot < lying down, motion, stepping, >by sitting- **GNAPH**

Hands icy cold, body warm- **TAB**

Legs icy cold, from knees down; trembling of limbs- **TAB**

Upper part of body emaciated, lower part semi-dropsical - **LYC**

Deathly coldness in forearm of children in diarrhea - **BROM**

Gouty concretions; arthritis vaga; affects all the joints, especially the knee, cracking on motion; nodosities - **BEN AC** (BERB, LITH, LYS)

Easy dislocation and spraining of ankle - **NAT CARB** (LED)

Imagines he is hovering in the air like a spirit (Lac. c.); lightness of all the limbs. Cold "shivers" from any emotion - **ASAR EUR.**

PAINS

Stitching tearing pain < by motion > by absolute rest and lying on painful side – **BRY**

Amelioration lying on painful side - **BRY; CALC CARB; PULS; AMM CARB**

Amelioration holding painful side with hands-**BORAX**

Aggravation lying on right side - **NAT MUR**

Pains stitching darting worse during rest and lying on affected side- **KALI CARB**

Aggravation lying on painful side - **KALI CARB; PHOS; NUX MOSCH; BAR CARB; HEP SULPH** (IOD)

Aggravation lying on left or painful side - **PHOS**

Feels complaint more when thinking about them-**CALC PHOS** (HELON; OX AC)

Burning and smarting sensation as form cayenne pepper- **CAPS**

Pains with heat thirst and fainting with numbness of affected parts- **CHAM**

Inclination to faint ever from slight pain – **NUX MOS** (HEP)

(*Fainting feeling during hemorrhage-* TRILL

Skin affections extremely sensitive to touch, the pain often causing fainting- HEP)

Skin affections extremely sensitive to touch, the pain often causing fainting - **HEP**

Pain under the lower and inner angle of left scapula – **CHEN (SANG)**

Constant pain under the lower and inner angle of right scapula - **CHEL (KALI CARB; MERC)**

Sciatica left side crampy pain in hip as though screwed in a vise - **COLOCYNTH**

Intense pain along the sciatic nerve, from rt. hip joint down to foot < lying down, motion, stepping, >by sitting - **GNAPH**

Bone pains affecting back, head chest, limbs, especially wrists, as if dislocated- **EUP PERF**

Lameness after sprains, especially of wrists and ankles- **RUTA**

Gonorrhea intense biting, itching deep in urethra, must rub it with some rough article in urethra for > - **PETROS**

Pain at root penis or neck of bladder - **PETROS**

Pains sticking pricking as from splinters – **NIT AC**

Pains < 4 to 8 pm – **LYCO**

Changing from side to side every few hours or days, - **LAC CAN**

Daily colic in infants about 5 a. m. - **KALI BROM**

Daily colic in infants at 4 p. m. - **COLOCYNTH; LYCO**

Colic every day at the same hour- **CINCH**

Neuralgia every day at the same hour (Chin s.) - **KALI BI**

Pain in small spots can be covered by tip of fingers - **KALI BI (IGN)**

Pain in small spots, constantly shifting (Kali bi) - **LIL**

Lancinating pains from uterus to umbilicus – **SEP**

Drawing pains from sacrum to pubis in nearly all diseases- **SAB**

Pains from darkness to day light all symptom are < at night from sundown to sunrise - **SYPH** (MERC; PHYTO)

Pain flying like electric shocks; shooting, lancinating: rapidly shifting (Lac c., Puls.); worse from motion and at night - **PHYT**

Pain and numbness in rt. ovary running down thighs same side - **PODO** (LIL)

Intercostal rheumatism chest sore bruised from touch motion or turning the body - **RAN BULB** (BRY)

Pains: acute especially in the chest, < from pressure even slight, in intercostal spaces, and lying on left side - **PHOS**

(Vomiting in any position except when lying on right side- ANT TART (rev. CROT. HOR.)

Cough with utter inability to lie on right side –MERC

Cough lying on left side –PHOS; DROS.; STAN.;

Palpitation lying on left side- CACTUS (LACH)

Palpitation lying on left side, goes off when turning to right- LAC CAN; TAB

Pains < when lying on left side- PHOS)

Rheumatic drawing teasing in all limbs worse at rest and in wet cold windy weather - **RHODO**

Back pain bet shoulders on swallowing – **RHUS**

Pain and burning, particularly on sides of fingers and toes – **SARS**

Burning in all parts of the body as if sparks of fire were falling on the patient- **SEC COR** (ARS)

Pains are terrible; come suddenly last a short time disappear suddenly – **CARB AC** (BELL; MAG PHOS)

Headache or neuralgia – Pains begins lightly and inc. gradually to the highest point and then gradually decline - **PLAT; STAN; SYPH**

Pain of gradual and slow increasing intensity, which ceases suddenly when at its height - **SULPH AC**

Pains appear suddenly and leave gradually – **PULS**

Pains with numbness of parts – **KAL; PLAT; CHAM** (ACON)

Pains are accompanied with constant chilliness, more severe the pain, more the chilliness - **PULS**

Pains extend from other parts to back and are attended with shuddering – **SEP**

Pain from back going to pubes - **VIB. OP.**

Drawing pains in small of back, from sacrum to pubes, in nearly all diseases - **SAB**

Oversensitive to pains- **IGN** (COFF; CHAM)

Neuralgia with burning pain after zona- **MEZ**

Pain from darkness to daylight; begin with twilight and end with daylight - **SYPH** (MERC; PHYTO)

Pain as if pressure of blunt instrument – **SULPH ACID**

(After injuries with blunt instruments- ARN (SYMPH)

Lacerated wounds from blunt instruments- CARB ACID)

No pain with most complaints, painlessness is characteristic - **STRAM; OP**

Pain as if sprained; as if a muscle or tendon was torn from its attachment as if bones were scraped with a knife, worse after midnight and in wet rainy weather- **RHUSTOX**

Interstitial inflammation of bones; periosteum inflamed, pains burning tearing as if scraped with a knife - **PHOS AC**

Pain in periosteum of long bone, at night in bed, least touch in damp weather- **MEZ (MERC; PHYTO)**

Rheumatism, bone pains after mercury or checked gonorrhoea; pains < at night, in damp or after taking cold water - **SARS**

Syphilitic and mercurial affections of the bones - **AUR MET**

Painful sensitiveness of skin and whole body, all clothing is painful- **PET**

Pain on vertex as if the hair were pulled- **MAG CARB (KALI N; PHOS)**

Rheumatic pain are < by motion; < at night, by warmth of bed; > only when holding feet in ice- water- **LED**

Pain as if bones were all torn to pieces - **IPEC**

Bruised pain as if bones were broken - **EUP PERF (ARN; BELLIS; PYR)**

Pain in the bones all over, as if broken- **THER**

Pain pressive, drawing or tearing of parts where bones lie near the surface - **CYCL**

Pain in places where the bones are least covered; as tibia, back of hand - **SANG**

Pain are < by slightest touch, but > by hard pressure- **CINCH**

Stitching pain remains in chest after recovery from pleurisy - **CARB VEG; (RAN BULB)**

(Abrotanum after Acon. And Bry.)

In pleurisy, when pressing sensation remains in affected side impeding respiration. Has cured after Acon. And Bry. failed in pleurisy- **SABAD**

Pleurisy or pneumonia from sudden exposure to cold, while overheated, or vice versa – RAN BULB (ACON, ARN)

Mania following disappearance of neuralgia- **ACTEA**

Body painfully sensitive to touch; part touched feels chilly; touch sends shudder throughout the whole frame- **SPIG (KALI CARB)**

Cannot bear to be touched; starts when touched ever so lightly; especially on the feet - **KALI CARB**

Neuralgic pain like a thread; in face, head, neck, chest - **ALL CEPA**

Entire body painfully sensitive to slightest touch- **CAMPH**

Pain only ameliorated when feet hold in ice water - **LED.; SEC.**

Chronic sprains - **BOV.; STRON.**

NERVOUS SYSTEM

Epilepsy from valvular dis of the heart - **CALC ARS**

Epilepsy comes on during sleep - **LACH (BUFO)**

Epilepsy < at night during sleep – **CUP MET (BUFO)**

Epilepsy aura begins in knees and ascends - **CUP MET**

(Rheumatism ascends - LED.)

(Rheumatism descends – KALMIA)

Epilepsy a day or 2 before menses - **KALI BROM**

Epilepsy: twitching over the whole body four or five days before the attack - **AST RUB**

Epileptic spasms with clenched thumbs, red face, eyes turned downwards - **AETH**

Epilepsy from suppressed eruptions - **AGAR (PSOR; SULPH)**

[Asthma after suppressed eruption - HEP SULPH (Psor)

Cough after suppressed itch, or eczema- PSOR

Headache from suppressed eruption- ANT CRUD

Diarrhea especially if eruption be suppressed- APIS

Brain diseases from suppressed eruptions- CICUTA

Chorea from suppressed eruption; from fright- ZINC MET]

Brain diseases from suppressed eruptions - **CICUTA**

Bad effects of re-per cussed eruption resulting in brain affections, convulsions, vomiting - **CUP MET**

[*In the cerebral affections where the vis medicatrix naturae is too weak to develop exanthemata*- ZINC MET

(CUPMET; SULPH; TUB)

Bad effects of acute exanthema imperfectly developed or suppressed; measles, scarlatina; urticaria- APIS

Sudden retrocession of acute exanthema results in paralysis of brain or convulsions OP (ZINC MET)

Epilepsy about new moon at regular intervals (menses) - **CUP MET**

(Epilepsy at new moon- KALI BROM

Aggravation during full moon – CALC CARB

Aggravation at new and full moon – ALUM

Aggravation during new moon – SIL

Enuresis during full moon, obstinate cases, with a family history of eczema- PSOR)

Epilepsy: at new moon - **KALI BROM**

Sudden shrill piercing screams from children while waking or sleeping - **APIS**

Meningitis with the cri encephalique - **HELL**

Great greediness when eating – **ZINC MET**

Greedily swallows cold water – **HELL**

Automatic motion of one arm and leg - **HELL**

Automatic motion of hands and head or one hand and head - **ZINC MET**

Constant motion of left arm and leg - **BRY**

Constant and voluntary motion of one arm and one leg - **APOC**

Involuntary movement while awake cease during sleep - **AGAR**

Spasms reflex from uterus - **ACTEA**

Puerperal convulsions immediately after delivery - **AMYL NIT**

Convulsions during teething with fever - **BELL**

Convulsions: of teething children - **ACON**

Brain symptoms during dentition - **HELL** (BELL, POD)

Convulsions during teething without fever - **MAG PHOS**

(Meningitis during dentition – Glon.)

Convulsions of children from cerebral congestion - **GLON**

Convulsions during teething with pale face and no heat - **ZINC MET**

Convulsion with frightful distortions of limbs and whole body - **CICUTA**

Convulsions: from dazzling or reflected light from water or mirror - **LYSS** (STRAM)

Clonic spasms beginning in fingers and toes and spreading over entire body - **CUP MET**

A picture of acute idiocy – **HELL**

A picture of chronic idiocy - **BAR CARB**

(Children slow in learning to walk – CAUST (CALC PHOS)

(Scrofulous, rachitic children; slow in learning to walk – Sil.)

Hydrocephalous, post scarlatinal or tuberculosis, which develops rapidly - **HELL** (APIS; SULPH; TUB)

Acute hydrocephalous with open sutures, stupor with sight of one eye lost - **APOC**

Convulsions with extreme coldness of body except head or occiput, which may be hot; brain troubles during dentition - **HELL**

Constantly picking his lips, clothes, or boring into his nose with finger (while unconscious) - **HELL.**

(Constant picking of nose until it bleeds (while conscious) – ARUM T)

Urine red, black, scanty, coffee, ground sediment; suppressed in brain troubles – **HELL**

Convulsions of children from fright or the irritation of intestinal worms - **HYOS** (CINA)

(Worm affections of children- SABAD (CINA, SIL, SPIG)

Worms: with foul breath, choking- TEREB (CINA, SPIG)

Nervous diseases; twitching, convulsive tremblings, catalepsy; from worms - **SABAD** (CINA, PSOR)

Spasms of teething children, or from worms - **CICUTA**

Spasms every muscle in the body twitches, from the eyes to the toes – **HYOS**

Chorea, from simple motions and jerks of single muscles to dancing of whole body - **AGAR**

Twitching of muscles of face - **MYGALE**

Spasmodic contractions and twitchings of single set of muscle - **CROCUS** (AGAR; IGN; ZINC MET)

Twitching and jerking of single muscles - **ZINC MET** (AGAR; IGN)

Twitching, jerking, even spasms of single limbs or whole body, when falling asleep - **IGN**

Chorea from suppressed eruption; from fright - **ZINC MET**

Trembling extremity specially hands paralysis agitans – **MERC**

Convulsions from even thinking of fluids of any kind - **LYS**

Convulsions with consciousness, renewed by sight of bright light, of mirror or water - **STRAM**

Convulsion from dazzling or reflected light from water or mirror - **LYS**

Convulsions with consciousness - **NUX VOM; STRAM; (STRYCH)**

Spasms from nursing after fright of mothers – **OP**

Convulsions of children from nursing often a fit of anger in mother - **CHAM** (NUX VOM)

(Child vomits as soon as it has nursed, after mother has been angry- VAL)

Sudden retrocession of acute exanthema results in paralysis of brain or convulsions – **OP.**, (ZINC MET)

Bad effects of re-percussed eruptions (of non-developed, Zinc.), resulting in brain affections, spasms, convulsions, vomiting - **CUP MET.**

Hydrocephalous; deathly coldness in forearm of children - **ARN.**

Meningitis after mechanical or traumatic injury, from fall; concussion of brain etc. when suspecting exudation of blood, to facilitate absorption - **ARN.**

Injurious chronic effects from concussions of the brain and spine, especially spasms - **CICUTA**

Convulsions; after blows on head or concussion - **HYPER**

Apoplexy: apoplectic convulsions in inebriates, haemorrhage or broken down constitution - **CROT. TOG.**

Cataleptic condition, conscious, but without power to move or speak - **GRAPH**

Convulsion of children from fright or irritation of intestinal worms; during labor during puerperal state; after meals, child vomits, sudden shriek then insensible - **HYOSC.**

Convulsions: dim vision; basilar meningitis; head retracted; child on verge of spasms - **VER. VIR.**

Restless, fidgety; starts at least noise - **SIL.**

(Over sensitiveness of nerves, scratching of linen or silk, crackling of paper is unbearable- ASAR

Irritability: slight noises like crackling of paper drive him to despair – FER MET

Vertigo from any even least noise – THER

Headache, neuralgia, < by noise, touch, strong light and ameliorated by rubbing head against the pillow- TARENT)

Irritable; nervous; fidgety; hard to please – **APIS MEL**

(Fidgety hands- KALI BR

Fidgety feet – ZINC

Restless fidgety legs and feet with burning feet – MEDO

Restless, fidgety; moves continually, cannot sit or stand still a moment – PHOS

Fidgety while sitting at work (Zinc.)- GRAPH.)

Constant movement of the legs, arms, trunk, with inability to do anything; twitching and jerking of muscles - **TARENT**

INJURY

Glandular indurations after bruises and injuries of gland – **CON MAC**

Bruised soreness of affected parts - **HAM** (ARN)

(Sore, lame, bruised feeling all through the body, as if beaten- ARN)

Slightest injury causes suppuration - **HEP; GRAPH; PET; BOR; CALEND; MERC SOL**

Concussions and contusions, results of shock or injury; with laceration of soft parts; prevents suppuration and septic conditions and promotes absorption - **ARN**

Concussion of brain from fall or blow where skin is cold and body bathed in cold sweat - **SULPH AC**

Bad effects of spinal concussion - **HYPER**

Injurious chronic effects from concussions of the brain and spine especially spasms- **CICUTA**

Mental traumatism mental effects from injuries to head- **NAT SULPH**

Great prostration after injuries, after surgical shock, after anesthetic – **AC ACID** (SUL AC)

Resuscitates person sinking under anaesthesia - **AMYL NIT**

Bad effects of shock from injury - **CAMPH**

Nervous depression following wounds or surgical shock- **HYPER**

Removes bad effect of shock, fright and mesmerism- **HYPER**

Vomiting with congestive gagging and inexpressible pain after laprotomy – **BISM** (NUX VOM; STAPH)

Eneuresis after catheterization - **MAG PHOS**

Injuries to parts rich in sentient nerves- **HYPER**

Prevents look jaw – **HYPER**

The wounded parts especially are cold to touch - **LED**

Punctured wounds by sharp pointed instruments as awls nails - **LED** (HYPER)

Injuries from treading on nails, splinter - **HYPER** (LED)

Lameness after sprains specially of wrists and ankles - **RUTA**

Long remaining discoloration after injuries; black and blue, places become green- **LED**

For the bad effects resulting from mechanical injuries; even if received years ago - **ARN**

Bad effects of a long ago injury - **CARBO VEG**

Ecchymosis, Cicatrices turn blood red or blue, are painful - **SULPH AC**

Bluish discoloration of wounds- **LYS** (LACH)

Mechanical injuries from sharp cutting instrument - **STAPH**

Phthisis after mechanical injuries to chest (Mill.) – **RUTA**

Bad effects from mechanical injuries, with bruises, chafing and livid skin; prostration - **SULPH AC** (ACET AC)

Tetanus after traumatic injuries- **HYPER**

Idiopathic or traumatic tetanus; brought on or < by slightest breath of air from a person passing- **PHYSO** (HYPER; LYS; NUX VOM; STRYCH)

Antidotes stings of insects - **AMM CARB**

Suspicious insect stings, if the swelling changes color and red streaks from the wound map out the course of lymphatics- **ANTHRAC** (LACH; PYR)

Ailments from stings of venomous insects - **ARS ALB**

Rat bites, stings of insects, especially mosquito- **LED**

Mosquito and insect bites burn and itch intensely - **CALAD**

Ailments from sugar, insect stings, vapors of arsenicum or copper- **MERC**

Compound fractures and their profuse suppuration- **ARN** (CALEND)

Facilitates union of fractured bones; lessens peculiar pricking pain - **SYMPH** (CALC PHOS)

Non-Union of bones; promotes callous - **CALC PHOS** (SYMPH)

Similar to Symphytum and Calc phos in non-union of bones- **CALEND**

Irritability at point of fracture; periosteal pain after wounds have healed- **SYMPH**

After arnica, for pricking pain and soreness of periosteum remaining after an injury- **SYMPH**

Follows well after symphytum in bone diseases- **FL AC**

Decubitus in typhoid- **BAPT** (ARN; MUR AC; PYR)

Rapid decubitus - **PYR** (CARB AC)

After injuries with blunt instruments- **ARN** (SYMPH)

Lacerated wounds from blunt instruments- **CARB AC**

Pain in eye after a blow of an obtuse body; snow ball strikes the eye; infant thrusts its fist into its mother's eye - **SYMPH**

(To soft tissues around eye - ARN

Contusion of eye and lids, especially with much extravasations of blood- LED)

Lameness after sprains, especially of wrists and ankles - **RUTA**

Lameness after chronic sprains, especially of wrists and ankles - **BOV; STRON**

Easily strained from lifting even small weights – **CARB AN**

Neuralgia of stump after amputation – **ALL CEPA**

Necrosis in stump after amputation - **PHOS. AC.**

HAEMORRHAGES

Hemorrhage, forming into black strings hanging from the bleeding surface - CROC

Epistaxsis-hangs in a dark clotted string from the nose, like an icicle - **MERC SOL**

Nose blood black, tenacious, stringy every drop can be turned into a thread - **CROC**

Hemorrhage after hasty labor – **CAUL**

Hemorrhagic diathesis; blood bright red, coagulates easily- **FER MET; FER PHOS; IPECAC; PHOS**

Nosebleed flow passive long lasting blood non coagulable – **HAM; LACH; CROT HOR; SEC.**

(Small wound bleed profusely: PHOS; CROT H; LACH; KREOS; MILL; SEC C)

Nosebleed profuse > headache - **HAM** (MEL)

Violent congestive or nervous headaches; epistaxis affords relief - **MEL** (BUFO; FER PHOS; MAGN S)

Nosebleed preceded by intense redness, flushing of face and throbbing of carotids (Bell.); with general relief - **MEL**

Hemorrhagic diathesis small wounds bleed much - **KREOS; LACH; PHOS; SEC COR; MILL**

Hemorrhagic diathesis, with blood dark and non- coagulable - **LACH**

Oppressed breathing during hemorrhage – **IPEC**

Stitches from navel to uterus during hemorrhage – **IPEC**

Hemorrhage painless without fever – **MILL**

Very red face precedes hemorrhage from every organ - **MEL**

Nosebleed preceded by intense redness flushing of face and throbbing of carotids - **MEL**

Hemorrhage bright red, fluid blood – **MILL**

The more blood better indicated – **MERC**

Hemorrhage of black blood from all outlets of the body – **SUPH AC**

Discharge of sanious blood with strong tendency to putrescence- **SEC COR**

Slightest wound causes bleeding for week – **SEC COR; LACH; PHOS**

Passive hemorrhage, copious flow of thin, black watery blood, corpuscles are destroyed - **SEC COR**

Haemorrhagic diathesis, fluid blood and degeneration of red blood corpuscles - **AM CARB**

Sinking feeling during hemorrhage - **VER ALB**

Fainting feeling during hemorrhage - **TRILL**

(Pains with heat thirst and fainting with numbness of affected parts- CHAM)

Inclination to faint ever from slight pain –NUX MOS (HEP)

Fainting feeling during hemorrhage- TRILL

(Skin affections extremely sensitive to touch the pain often causing fainting- HEP)

Purpura hemorrhagica-fresh ecchymosjs in great no. from day to day - **TEREB**

Petechiae - purpura haemorrhagica blue spots, livid red itching blotches - **SULPH AC**

Traumatic epistaxis - **AC ACID**

Haemorrhage after extraction of tooth - **BOV**

Bleeding from cavity after extraction of a tooth - **TRILL** (HAM; KREOS)

Haemorrhage: long continued; longing for sour things - **CINCH**

Distended veins on lids, ears, lips and tongue - **DIG**

Ranula with foetid breath - **AMBRA**

Ranula: bluish or varicose veins in tongue or in mouth - **THUJA**; (AMBRA)

Pulsation over whole body and full, distended feeling as if blood would burst through vessels - **LIL TIG** (AESC)

Progressive pernicious, anemia, neurasthenia - **PIC AC.**

FEVER

Hay-fever; squirming sensation in the nostril as of a small worm - **NAT MUR**

Hay-fever; appearing regularly every year the same day of the month; with an asthmatic psoric or eczematous history - **PSOR**

Hay- fever, in August every year - **ALL CEPA**

Hay fever with violent sneezing on rising from bed- **ALL CEPA**

Fever paroxysm at 11a m. and 11 p.m. – **CACT**

Bilious vomiting at close of chill - - **EUP PERF**

(Headache ending in bilious vomiting- ARG NIT)

Insatiable thirst before and during, chill and fever; knows chill is coming because he can't drink enough - **EUP PERF**

Every stool is followed by thirst and every drink by shuddering - **CAPS**

Pulse abnormally rapid, out of all proportion to temperature - **PYR** (LIL TIG)

After sapraecaemia or septicemia when the best selected remedy fails to or permanently improve - **PYR**

Skin dry inactive rarely sweats – **PSOR**

Adapted to people with a dry skin, who rarely perspire- **NUX MOS**

Profuse perspiration after acute dis. with relief of all suffering – **NAT MUR; PSOR**

Profuse perspiration relieves - **NAT MUR; PSOR** (CALAD)

Profuse perspiration attends nearly every complaints but does not relieve- **MERC**

Sweats: profusely day and night without relief - **HEP**

No thirst in fever - **AC ACID**

In fever ravenous hunger for days before attack - **STAPH**

Feels unusually well day before attack - **PSOR**

Must be covered in every stage of fever – chill, heat or sweat – **NUX VOM**

(Chilly when uncovered, yet feels smothered if wrapped up – ARG NIT)

Extremely sensitive to cold air, cannot bear to be uncovered - **HEP SULPH**

Fever paroxysm at 7 am with great loquacity during heat and chill- **PODO**

Fever blisters like pearl around the lips - **NAT MUR**

(Corners of mouth ulcerated fever blisters around mouth and on chin- RHUS (NAT M)

Fever in which the cold stage predominates, coldness felt most acutely in abdomen and legs - **MENY**

When fever assumes a slow, " sneaking" , nervous form with vertigo ; with disposition to anger - **COCC**

Acute infl. stage of gonnorrhoea - **CAN SAT**

Second stages of gonorrhoea, burning after urination, discharge thick, yellow, pus-like- **CUBEBA**

Gonorrhoea: second stage, *greenish discharge*, < at night; great burning and tenesmus - **MERC COR**

All sequelae of measles - **CAMPH**

Typhoid scarlatina, with apathy, scanty or suppressed urine; threatened uraemia - **ARUM T**

Delirium during intermittents - **SABAD** (PODO)

Chill: begins in the back, between scapulae - **PYR**

Chill without thirst, especially along spine, running up and down the back in rapid, wave-like succession from sacrum to occiput - **GELS**

Burning along spine and great weakness of spine and back; softening of cord (Phos., Zinc.) - **PIC AC**

Chill beginning in the thigh - **THUJA.**

SKIN

Intolerable itching at tip of coccyx must scratch till parts become raw and sore - **BOV**

Sudden retrocession of acute exanthema results in paralysis of brain or convulsions - **OP** (ZINC)

Warts large jagged often pedunculated bleeding easily, exuding moisture, on face, eyelids and on the nose- **CAUST**

Warts large jagged pedunculated bleeding readily on washing; moist oozing; sticking pain- **NIT AC** (STAPH; THUJA)

Warts fleshy, large, smooth on face or back of hand and finger- **DULC** (THUJA)

Warts on palm of hand which is sore to touch- **NAT CARB**

Warts on palm of hands – **NAT MUR; ANAC**

Warts with sore pains; flat, smooth on palms of hands - **RUTA** (NAT MUR; NAT CARB)

Warts on eyelid, face on the nose – **CAUST**

Warts small, all over the body- **CAUST**

Figwarts with intolerable itching and burning; exuberant granulations-**SAB** (THUJA; NIT AC)

Figwarts: dry pedunculated cauliflower-like, after abuse of mercury - **STAPH** (SAB; THUJA; NIT AC)

Herpes about the anus and on borders of hair at nape of neck- **NAT MUR**

Herpes of anus- **TAB**

Herpes in bend of knees- **HEP; GRAPH**

Herpes about the genitals extending to perineum – **PETR**

(Excoriation of skin about anus (SULPH), covering perineum and extending to genitals – SANIC)

Herpetic eruptions on all parts of body - **SARS**

Herpes circinatus in isolated spots on upper parts of body - **SEP**

Herpes circinatus in intersecting rings over whole body - **TELL**

Herpetic eruption at end of nose- **AETH**

Shingles preceded or followed by intercostals neuralgia – **RAN BULB** (MEZ)

(Neuralgic burning pains after zona – Mez.)

Bunions and corns when pain is excruciating showing nerve involvement - **HYPER**

Corns sensitive to touch, smart, burn - **RAN BULB** (SALIC AC)

Large horny corns on soles of feet very sensitive when walking- **ANT CRUD** (RAN BULB)

Urticaria over whole body, no fever; itching burns after scratching; < in warmth, > in cold - **DULC**

Urticaria over whole body specially after violent exercise – **NAT MUR** (APIS; CALC; HEP; SANIC; URT)

When Rhus seems indicated though fails to cure in chronic urticaria- **BOV**

Eczema yellow, acrid moisture oozes from under crusts, new vesicles from contract of exudation, by scratching one place after itching ceases but appears in another place - **STAPH**

Thick brown yellow crusts on scalp, face, forehead, temples, chin, with reddish borders bleeding when scratched – **DULC**

Eczema no itching; exudation forms into a hard lemon colored crust- **CICUTA**

Head is covered with thick leather like crust under which thick and white pus collects here and there – **MEZ**

Scalp dry scaly or moist fetid suppurating eruptions oozing a sticky offensive fluid – **PSOR** (GRAPH; MEZ)

Eczema and itching eruptions after vaccination – **MEZ**

Ailments from bad effects of vaccination – **THUJA** (ANT TART; SIL)

Bad effects of vaccination especially abscesses and convulsions - **SIL** (THUJA)

From bad effects of vaccination when thuja fails and silicea is not indicated – **ANT TART**

Bad effects of vaccination - **CROT HOR**

Ulcers with lardaceous base surrounded by dark halo, apt to run together- **MERC**

Itching so violent toward evening as to make drive one wild – **KREOS**

Itching violent without eruptions - **DOLICH**

Driven to despair with excessive itching- **PSOR**

Corners of mouth ulcerated fever blisters around mouth and on chin - **RHUS TOX**

(*Fever blisters like pearl around the lips- NAT MUR*)

Skin of hands rough, cracked; tips of fingers rough cracked, fissured, every winter – **PET**

Cracks or fissure in ends of fingers, nipples, labial commissure; of anus; between the toe - **GRAPH**

The skin feels cold to touch yet patient cannot tolerate covering- **SEC COR**

Surface cold to touch, yet cannot bear to be covered; throws off all coverings- **CAMPH** (MEDO; SEC COR)

Skin cold yet throws off all coverings- **MEDO** (CAMPH; SEC COR)

Skin about neck wrinkled, hangs in folds - **SANIC** (ABROT; IOD; NAT MUR; SARS)

Throat and neck of children emaciate rapidly during summer complaints- **NAT MUR** (SANIC)

Child looks old dirty greasy and brownish - **SANIC**

Face oily, shiny, as if greased- **NAT MUR** (PLUM; THUJA)

Skin of face, greasy, shiny- **PLUM** (NAT MUR; SANIC)

Soreness behind ears with discharge of white, gray viscid fluid - **SANIC** (GRAPH; PSOR)

Profuse, scaly dandruffs on scalp eyebrows in the beard- **SANIC**

White scaly dandruff; hair dry and falling out- **THUJA**

Dandruff, falls out in clouds (LYC); hair fall out in bunches, baldness of single spots- **PHOS**

Falling of the hair especially in syphillis and mercurial affection- - **AUR MET**

Hair falls off, on head, eyebrows, whiskers and genitals- **SELEN**

Great falling of hairs; after chronic headache or at the climacteric- **SEP**

Hair falls out when touched, in nursing women - **NAT MUR** (SEP)

Hair, dry, lustureless tangles easily, gives toghether, plica polonica- **PSOR**

Plica polonica - **BOR; SARS; TUB; PSOR**

Hair becomes frowsy and tangled; splits, sticks together at each tips; if these bunches are cut off, they form again, cannot be combined- **BOR** (FL AC; LYCO; PSOR, TUB)

Skin itching when undressing uncovering or exposure to cold air - **RUM** (HEP; NAT SULPH; OLEAN)

(Cough < when undressing – KALI BI)

Eczema itching intense, < at night when undressing - **TUB**

Tumefied ulcers neither heal nor suppurates, is of a purple hue "hard as old cheese" – **PHYTO** (BRY; LAC CAN; PHEL)

A/f suppressed itch – **PSOR**

[Diarrhea especially if eruption be suppressed – APIS M; GRAPH (PSOR)

Asthma after suppressed eruption - HEP SULPH (Psor)

Cough after suppressed itch , or eczema- PSOR

Epilepsy from suppressed eruptions- AGAR; (PSOR.; SULPH)

Headache from suppressed eruption- ANT CRUD

Brain diseases from suppressed eruptions- CICUTA

Chorea from suppressed eruption; from fright- ZINC MET]

Sweat after 4 A.M. every morning - **STAN**

Sweat mouldy, Musky odor - **STAN**

(Complaints of imaginary odor before the nose, as of herring or musk- AGN CAS)

Cold perspiration on the forehead - **VER ALB**

Cold perspiration over entire body - **TAB**

Sweat smelling like garlic- **ART VUL**

Sweat in axilla, smells like onion -**BOV**

Bad effects: of onions- LYCO

Diarrhea from onion- THUJA

Eructations like onions- MAG MUR

Breath smells like onion- SINNAPIS

Perspiration, smelling like honey, on the genitals- **THUJA**

Perspiration has the odor of sulphur - **PHOS**

Sweet sweat attracts the files – **CALAD**

Sweat as soon as closing the eyes - **CON MAC; CINCH**

(Vertigo on closing the eyes – THER; LACH; THUJA)

Sweat only on uncovered parts; or all over except the head; when he sleeps, stops when he wakes - **THUJA**

Sweet on opening the eyes - **SAMB**

(Vertigo on opening the eyes – TABACUM)

Sweat on the face on a small spot only while eating - **IGN**

Sweat: of single parts, head, scalp, wet, cold; nape of neck; chest, axillae, sexual organs, hands, knees, feet- **CALC**

Profuse perspiration attends nearly every complaints but does not relieve- **MERC SOL**

Sweat profusely day and night without relief- **HEP**

< when perspiring- **VER ALB**

Profuse perspiration after acute diseases, with relief of all suffering- **PSOR** (CALAD; NAT MUR)

Sweat > pains - **NAT MUR**

Dry, inactive, rarely sweats- **PSOR**

People with a dry skin, who rarely perspires- **NUX MOS**

New vesicles form from contract of exudation by scratching one place after itching ceases, but appears in another- **STAPH**

Ulcers, herpes, surrounded by small pimples or pustules and spread by coalescing – **HEP**

Every spring skin affection reappears- **NAT SULPH** (PSOR)

Itch appears each year, as winter approaches- **ALOE** (PSOR)

Dry tettery, itching eruptions, worse in winter- **ALUM** (PET)

Persons who suffer from tettery eruption, dry or moist- **BOV**

Usually deep impressions on fingers from using blunt instruments like scissors, knife etc.- **BOV**

Desquamation in large flakes 2nd or 3rd time in scarlatina- **ARUM T**

Measles and scarlatina when eruption does not appear with pale or cold blue, hippocratic face; child will not be covered- **CAMPH** (SEC COR)

All sequelae of measles- **CAMPH**

Physical exertion, even much walking, brings on abscess in same part, but generally in the right ear- **CARB AC**

Small boils in any part of body but especially in ext. auditory canal- **PIC AC**

Furuncles and boils in ext. meatus- **MERC SOL;** (PIC AC)

Tendency to small, painful boils, one after another, extremely sore - **ARN**

(Small boils in crops – SULPH)

Boils: coming in crops in various parts of the body, or a single boil is succeeded by another as soon as first is healed- **SULPH** (TUB)

Boils-small painful with green contents - **SEC COR**

Crops of small boils, intensely painful successively appear in nose; green foetid pus- **TUB** (SEC COR)

Erythema from exposure to sun's ray (sunburn)- **CANTH**

Intense itching of skin, but so tender is unable to scratch; > by gentle rubbing; eczema over whole body- **CROT TIG**

Disposition to paronychia- **DIOSC** (HEP)

Naevus flat, of children, capillary aneurysm- **FL AC**

Eczema of lids; eruption moist and fissured; lids red and margins covered with scales or crusts - **GRAPH**

(Eyelashes: loaded with dry, gummy exudation; agglutinated in morning; turn inward and inflame the eye, especially at outer canthus; tendency to "wild hairs." – BORAX)

Violent corrosive, itching of pudenda and vagina- **KREOS**

Cold swelling; abscess, slow to suppurate- **MERC SOL**

Freckles: eczema solaris- **FL AC**

Parchment like dryness of skin- **SABAD**

Skin like parchments- **ARS ALB**

Excoriation of skin about anus, covering perineum and extending to genitals - **SANIC**

Herpes: of genital organs extending to perineum and thighs; itching, redness; skin cracked, rough, bleeding; dry or moist - **PET**

Gangrene; dry, senile< from external heat- **SEC COR**

Ulcerations tend to gangrene- **AMM CARB**

Gangrenous ulcers; felon, carbuncle, erysipelas of a malignant type- **ANTHRAC**

Eczema: itching intense< at night when undressing, from bathing; immense quantities of white bran- like scales- **TUB**

Eruptions only on covered parts, burns after scratching - **THUJA**

(Sweat only uncovered parts- THUJA)

Eruptions: dull, red, copper- coloured spots, becoming blue, when getting cold- **SYPH**

In the cerebral affections where the *vis medicatrix naturae* is too weak to develop exanthemata- **ZINC MET** (CUP MET; SULPH; TUB)

Bad effects of re-percussed eruptions, resulting in brain affections, spasms, convulsions and vomiting - **CUP MET**

Bad effects of acute exanthema imperfectely developed or suppressed; measles, scarlatina; urticaria- **APIS**

Sudden retrocession of acute exanthema results in paralysis of brain or convulsions - **OP** (ZINC MET).

SENSATIONS

Swashing sensation in intestines - **CROT TIG**

Sensation of swashing in brain – **RHUSTOX**

Sensation as if the brain was loose in forehead and falling from side to side - **SUL AC** (BELL, BRY, RHUS, SPIG)

Sensation of cobweb on face - **BROM;** (BARY CARB; BOR)

Sensation of cobweb on forehead, tries hard to brush it off - **GRAPH**

Cold sensation in larynx on inspiration > after shaving - **BROM**

Cold sensation in larynx-on inspiration < after shaving - **CARB AN**

Sensation of coldness in abdomen - **AMBRA** (CALC)

Sensation of coldness about the heart - **PETR** (CARB AN.; KALI M.; NAT M.)

Coldness in abdomen - **TAB**

Heat of the head, as if surrounded by hot air - **AST RUB**

Can't go to sleep because she can't get herself together; her head and body feels scattered about the bed – **BAPT**

In bed thought that she was three persons, could not keep them covered – **BAPT** (PET)

Delirium that another person were lying alongside him in same bed; that there were two babies in the bed ; that one leg double - **PET** (VAL)

Imagines all sorts of things; that she is double, lying crosswise - **STRAM** (PET)

Sensation as if something alive were moving in the stomach, abdomen, uterus, arms or other parts of the body - **CROC** (SAB, THUJA, SULPH)

Movement in abdomen as of a child - **SULPH** (CROC; THUJA)

Abdomen: as if an animal were crying; motion as if something alive; protrudes here and there like the arm of a foetus - **THUJA** (CROC, NUX M, SULPH)

Illusion that she is pregnant when merely distended from flatus - **SABAD**

Sensation of feather in larynx, exciting cough – **DROS**

Sensation of a splinter, fish bone or plug in the throat - **HEP; ARG NIT; NITAC** (SIL; DOLICHOS)

Sensation as if a thread were hanging down throat- **VAL**

Sensation as of a hair on the tongue - **NAT MUR; SIL**

Sense of relaxation of stomach with nausea - **TAB** (IPEC; STAPH)

Feels light as if floating in air- **VAL**

When walking seems to be walking on air, when lying, does not seem to touch the bed- **LAC CAN**

Feels light as if as if legs were floating in the air- **STICTA**

Imagine as if he is hovering in the air like spirit- **ASAR**

Oversensitiveness of nerves, scratching of linen or silk, crackling of paper is unbearable - **ASAR**

Irritability: slight noises like crackling of paper drive him to despair – **FER MET**

(*Vertigo from any, even least noise – THERIDION*

Headache, neuralgia, < by noise, touch, strong light and ameliorated by rubbing head against the pillow - TARENTULA

Restless, fidgety; starts at least noise- SILICEA)

Very sensitive to noise; slightest noise startles from sleep - **CALAD** (ASAR; NUX; TARENT)

Excessively nervous, easily frightened by the slightest noise or an unusual sharp sound, a cough, sneeze, a cry, lighting a match etc. - **BOR** (ASAR; CALAD)

Oversensitive to pains - **IGN** (COFF; CHAM)

Hyperaesthesia: least excitement irritates, followed by languid sadness; extreme on tips of fingers- **TARENT**

Oversensitive: to external impressions; to noise, odors, light or music - **NUX VOM**

Extreme sensitive to open air; hoarseness; worse evening; after exposure to cold; voice uncertain - **RUM**

Extremely sensitive to cold air, imagines can feel the air if a door is opened in the next room; must be wrapped up to the face even in hot weather - **HEP** (PSOR)

Great sensitiveness to cold air or change of weather; wears a fur cap, overcoat or shawl even in the hottest summer weather - **PSOR**

Takes cold easily without knowing how or where; seems to take cold "every time he takes a breath of fresh air" - **TUB**

Great sensitiveness to cold - **BAR CARB** (CALC; KALI CARB; PSOR)

Oversensitiveness of all the senses to external impressions, light, noise, odors, touch - **PHOS**

Sleepy, but cannot sleep (Bell., Cham.), sleeplessness with acuteness of hearing, clock striking and cocks crowing at great distance keep her awake - **OP**

Takes cold from exposure of feet- **SIL** (CON; CUP MET)

Oversensitive to open air; great aversion to wind, especially about ears- **CHAM**

Slight touch along the spine provokes spasmodic pain in chest and cardiac region- **TARENT**

Sensation of a ball rolling in the bladder – **LACH**

Sense of ball in anus, not > stool – SEP

Sensation of a round ball in forehead sitting firmly there even when shaking the head – **STAPH**

Sensation of swelling in the perineum or near the anus, as if sitting on a ball – CAN IND)

Globus hystericus; sensation of a large ball rising from stomach to throat, causing sense of suffocation - **LAC DEF** (ASAF, KAL)

Sensation as if a heavy, black cloud had settled all over her and enveloped her head so that all is darkness and confusion - **ACT RAC**

Illusion of a mouse running under her chair - **ACT RAC** (LAC C, AETH)

Sensation of heaviness and lameness in back - **AES HIP**

Sensation as if ice touched or ice-cold needles were piercing the skin; as from hot needle - **AGAR**

Feels pain as if beaten when standing - **AGAR**

Flesh feels as if beaten, from the bones - **THUJA** (PHYT)

Pain in back and limbs as if beaten - **ACID PHOS**

Pains burning, tearing, as if scraped with a knife (Rhus.tox) - **ACID PHOS**

Sensation of sinking in abdomen causing Dyspnoea - **ACET AC**

Absent minded, reduced power of insight; cannot recollect; has to read a sentence twice before he can comprehend - **AGNUS** (LYC; PHOS AC; SEP)

Dissatisfied and angry about himself or his complaints, especially when constipated –**ALOE.**

Feels better when constipated - **CALC**

Sensation as if the heart stood still; as though it ceased to beat and then suddenly gave on hard thump (Sep.) - **AURUM MET**

Thinks she is not at home (Bry.); this is continually in her mind - **OPIUM**

Great faintness and constant yawning - **ASAR EUR**

Profound and repeated yawning - **AMYL NIT** (KALI C)

Complete prostration – **VERAT ALB**

(Nervous prostration – PIC AC

Great prostration – ARS ALB)

Complete prostration of entire muscular system – **TAB**

TIME and TIME MODALITY

Aggravation after 3 p.m. – **BELL**

Fever chill at 9 am - **EUP PERF**

Intermittent fever paroxysm at 10 or 11 a.m. – **NAT MUR**

Intermittent fever chill 3 p.m.- **APIS**

Intermittent fever 3 a. m and at 3 p.m . – **THUJA**

Fever paroxysm at 11a m. and 11 p.m. – **CACT**

Fever paroxysm at 7 am with great loquacity during heat and chilly - **PODO**

Headache every afternoon- **SEL**

Headache < afternoon until midnight- **LOB**

Headache every six weak- **MAG MUR**

Headache every 8th day- **IRIS**

Headache every 7th day - **SANG** (SABAD; SIL; SULPH)

Headache ceases at 11 or 12 p.m. – **LYCO**

Headache worse from 10 to 11 and ceasing at daylight – **SYPH**

Headache commencing at 4 p.m.- **SYPH**

Weak empty, gone or faint feeling in the stomach about 11 a.m. – **SULPH**

Weak empty gone sensation at 10 or 11 a.m. > by eating- **NAT CARB**

Hunger ravenous about 11 or 12 a.m. – **ZINC MET** (SULPH)

Aggravation nearly all diseases from 4-8- p.m. - **LYCO** (HELL)

Aggravation from 4-9 p.m.- **COLOCYNTH; MAG PHOS**

Symptoms generally worse from 1-2-p.m. and 12-2- a.m. – **ARS ALB**

Worse from 2 –4 a. m – **KALI CARB**

Complaints return annually - **ARS ALB** ((CARB V; LACH; SULPH; THUJA)

Complaints return at precisely the same hour - **IGNATIA**

Neuralgia every day at same hour – **KALI BI** (CHIN S)

Fever annually returning; paroxysm every spring - **LACH** (CARB VEG; SULPH)

Hay fever; in August every year; violent sneezing on rising from bed; from handling peaches - **ALL CEPA**

This shrub flowers from September to November, when the leaves are falling - **HAMAMELIS**

Dysentery and summer complaints of intestinal canal, occurring from May to November - **MERC COR**

Rheumatism alternating with gastric symptoms, one appearing in the fall and the other in the spring; rheumatism and dysentery alternate - **KALI BI** (ABROT)

Every spring, skin affections reappear - **NAT SULPH** (PSOR)

Toothache, every spring and fall during sharp east winds; worse from *change of weather, thunderstorm*, **windy weather- RHODO**

Rheumatism of cold weather; getting well in spring and returning in autumn - **CALC PHOS**

Diarrhea: in summer, from *cold drinks*; epidemic in autumn - **NUX MOSCH**

Daily colic of infants about 5 A.M.- **KALI BROM**

Daily colic of infants at 4 p. m. - **COLOCYNTH; LYCO**

Sweat after 4 A.M. every morning - **STAN**

Early morning Diarrhea from 5 to 10 am – **RUM**

Diarrhea involuntary at might from 1 to 4 am – **PSOR** (ALOE; NAT S; PODO; SULPH)

Diarrhea after 3 weeks- **MAG CARB**

Complaints aggravated when waking at 4 am - **NUX VOM (SEP)**

Headache < 10 to 11 am or 4 to 5 pm – **MAG PHOS**

Headache in winter Diarrhea in summer - **PODO**

Headache returning every year in winter – **BISM**

Fever paroxysm returns at 11 a. m. and 11 p. m. - **CAC G**

Cough return every winter - **PSOR**

Intermittent dyspepsia, every other day at same hour - **IPEC**

Complaints return at precisely the same hour. - **IGN**

Intermittent fever: returns every seven or fourteen days - **CHINA**

Headache: for two, three or four days every two or three weeks - **FER MET**

MISCELLANEOUS

Very forgetful in business, but during sleep dreams of what he had forgotten - **SELEN**

Adopted to diseases with rapid sinking of the vital forces, complete, prostration collapse- **VER ALB**

Termini of nerves became so irritated and sensitive that some kind of friction was necessary to obtain relief- **TARENT**

Abscesses, boils felons, affected parts of a bluish color and atrocious burning pain compelling the patient to walk the floor for nights - **TARENT**

Hyper aesthesia – least excitement irritates followed by languid sadness - **TARENT**

RESTLESSNESS could not keep quiet in any position, must keep in motion, though walking < all symptoms- **TARENT**

Symptoms occur in paroxysms asthma, sick headache, vertigo sneezing- **TAB**

Cold perspiration on the forehead - **VER ALB**

Icy Coldness of surface, covered with cold sweat- **TAB**

Want of vital heat, always chilly even when taking active, exercise - **SIL**

Irresistible desire to lie down and sleep - **SELEN**

Wants to lie down and sleep - **SEL**

Great sleepiness or irresistible inclination to sleep, with nearly all complaints - **ANT TART** (NUX M; OP)

Itching of skin is not > by scratching and is apt to change to burning - **SEP**

Imagines he is hovering in the air like a sprint – **ASAR**

Thought she was 3 persons, could not keep them covered – **BAPT**

Red spots on left cheeks and drenching night sweat- **AC ACID**

One cheek red andother pale - **CINA**

One cheek red and hot, the other pale and cold- **CHAM**

One hand icy cold the other warm – **CINCH**

One foot hot and the other cold - **LYCO**

Hands icy cold, body warm- **TAB**

Legs icy cold, from knees down; trebling of limbs- **TAB**

Heat of upper part of body; coldness of lower- **ARN**

Music is unbearable makes her sad- **ACON**

Music makes her weep- **GRAPH**

Music in intolerable – **SAB**

Music causes weeping- **THUJA**

Attacks of anxiety and restlessness during on thunderstorms < from music- **NAT CARB**

Lively music makes her sad- **NAT SULPH**

Prevents excoriation from walking – **AGN CAS**

Sore and row spots on feet. Especially on heel from friction - **ALL CEPA**

Flushing of face abruptly limited, parts below one icy cold- **AMYL NIT**

Profound and repeated yawning- **AMYL NIT** (KALI CARB)

Irresistible desire to swear and curse- **ANAC** (LAC CAN; LIL; NIT AC)

Wants to pray continually - **STRAM**

Irresistible desire to talk in rhymes and repeated verse- **ANT CRUD**

Dropsy without thirst- **APIS**

Dropsy with thirst- **ACET ACID; APOC**

Everything on which he lies seems too hard- **ARN**

In whatever position the patient lies, the parts rested upon feel sore and bruised- **BAPT**

The bed feels hard; parts lain on feel sore and bruised- **PYR**

Burning pains as if hot coals were applied to parts > by heat – **ARS ALB**

Cannot bear the smell or sight of food - **ARS ALB**

The sight or thought of food sickens; the smell of cooking food nauseate- **SEP**

Smell painfully acute; nausea and faintness from the smell of cooking food – **COLCH**

Solitude is unbearable **BIS**

Dread of downward motion – **BOR; SANIC**

Unusually deep impression on finger, from using blunt instrument, scissors, knife etc.- **BOV**

Collar seems too tight must loosen it- **AMYL NIT**

Intolerance of tight clothing around the waist – **BOV**

Intolerance of tight bands about the neck or waist- **LACH**

Wants clothing loose around abdomen- **CARB VEG**

Complaints of drunkards from abstaining – **CALC ARS**

Pot belliedness of mothers- **SEP**

Persons who have never fully recovered from the exhausting effects of some previous illness- **CARB VEG**

Constantly desire to be fanned- **CARB VEG**

Wants to be fanned but slowly and at a distance- **CARB VEG**

Satiety after a few mouthfuls, food then becomes repugnant causes nausea- **CYCL**

Constant sensation of satiety; good appetite with a few mouthfuls fills up to the throat and he fells bloated – **LYCO**

Irritability: slight noises like crackling of paper drive him to despair – **FER MET**

(Oversensitiveness of nerves, scratching of linen or silk, crackling of paper is unbearable- ASAR

Vertigo from any even least noise – THER

Headache, neuralgia, < by noise, touch, strong light and ameliorated by rubbing head against the pillow- TARENT

Restless, fidgety; starts at least noise- SIL)

Always better by walking slowly about- **FER MET**

Acute diseases often result in dropsy- **CINCH**

A/f misdeed of others – **COCC**

Feels bad if they lose but one Hour sleep – **COCC**

Time passes two quickly – **COCC THER**

A\f bad effects of sudden emotion or pleasurable surprises – **COFF**

Bad effects of fright fear, exciting news and sudden emotions- **GELS**

Ailments that originate from fright, bad effects of fear still remaining – **OPIUM**

While drinking the fluid, it descends with a gurgling sound – **CUP MET**

Anticipation of any ordeal, preparing for church, theatre, or to meet an engagement, brings on Diarrhea- **GELS**

Apprehension when ready for church or opera Diarrhea sets in – **ARG NIT**

Is the aconite of the venous capillary system – **HAM**

What Pulsatilla is to puberty, graphite is to climacteric.

Trembling extremity, especially hands, paralysis agitans- **MERC SOL**

Sensation as if trembling all over in without real trembling – **SULPH AC**

Weakness and trembling of entire body- **GELS**

Extremely sensitive to cold air, imagines he can feel the air if a door is open in the next room- **HEP**

Remedy of great contradictions- **IGN**

Strange temper, laughs at serious matters and is serious over laughable things- **ANAC**

Changeable humor; are moment laughing the next crying; "sudden change from grave to gay, from lively to serene – **NUX MOS**

Frequent and extreme changes in sensations; sudden from greater hilarity to the deepest despondency – **CROC**

Mental conditions rapidly, in an almost incredibly short time, change from joy to sorrow, from laughing to weeping - **IGN**

Intense sleeplessness of irritable excitable persons from business embarrassments, often imaginary - **HYOS**

Restlessness and sleeplessness due to worry and grief, loss of property or reputation, from business embarrassments- **KALI BROM**

After business embarrassments, unable to sleep, must get up - **AMBRA** (ACTEA; SEP)

Loss of memory, forgets how to talk - **KALI BROM**

Very forgetful in business, but during sleep dreams what he had forgotten - **SELEN**

Weakness of memory; cannot remember names, words or initial letters; has to ask name of most intimate fried; even forgets his own name - **MEDO**

Cannot bear to be touched; starts when touched ever so lightly, especially on feet- **KALI CARB**

Cannot bear to be touched or looked at; does not want to speak or be spoken to - **ANT CRUD**

Left sided principally affected; disease begin on the left and go to the right Side- **LACH**

Affects right, side or pain goes from right to left – **LYCO**

Affections of right side of body; head, ear, face; chest, ovary, sciatic nerve - **MAG PHOS** (BELL; BRY; CHEL; KALI CARB; LYCO; PODO)

Affects principally left side- **LIL.TIG**

Great sensitiveness to touch- **LACH**

Dreads to go to sleep becauseshe wakes up with such a headache- **LACH**

All symptoms specially the mental worse after sleep, or the agg., wakes him from sleep – **LACH**

Worse after sleep or sleeps into aggravations- **SPON** (LACH)

Aggravation during and after sleep- **OPIUM** (APIS; LACH)

Aggravation after sleep- **APIS** (LACH)

Sleeps into the attack in dyspnoea- **SAMB**

Great loquacity; one words after leads into another story- **LACH**

Aggravation in clear fine weather and amel. in wet damp weather – **HEP; MEDO; CAUST; ASAR; ALUM**

All the ailments are accompanied by drowsiness and sleepiness – **NUX MOS**

Affects especially mucous outlets of the body where skin and mucous members join- **NIT AC**

Going without regular meals amel - **NAT MUR**

Sad weeping mood, without cause but consolation from other < her trouble - **NAT MUR**

Consolation < - **NAT MUR, HELL, LIL TIG**

Attacks of anxiety and restlessness during on thunderstorms < from music- **NAT CARB**

Cannot bear the heat of sun, exhausted in warm weather; < from overheating near the fire - **ANT CRUD**

Great debility as soon as he sits down his eyes close – **MUR AC**

Great debility caused by heat of sun - **NAT CARB**

Body large and fat, legs one thin - **AM MUR**

Upper, part of body emaciated, lower part semi dropsical – **LYCO**

Sour smell of whole body- **CALC; HEP; RHEUM;MAG CARB**

Cannot bear heat of sun- **LYS**

The sight or sound of running water or pouring water aggravates all complaints – **LYS**

Aimless hurried notion- **LIL**

Very forgetful, absent minded, makes purchases and walks away without then – **LAC CAN**

Sensation as if cold air was blowing over, even while covered up - **LAC DEF**

Somnambulism – **KALI BROM**

Great sensitiveness to cold air or charge of weather; wears a fur cap, overcoat or shawl, even in hottest summer weather- **PSOR**

Must be wrapped up to the face even in hot weaker- **HEP**

Aversion to open in- **CYCL**

Potencies of only this acid med. is prepared from alcohol- **CARB AC**

Constantly loses the thread of conversation - **MEDO**

Great difficulty in stating her symptoms, question has to be repeated as she loses herself. Cannot speak without weeping - **MEDO**

Anticipates death; always anticipating, feels matters most sensitively before they occur and generally correctly - **MEDO**

Hydrogenoid constitution of Grauvogl- **ANT TART**

Epidemic spleen disease of cattle, horses and sheep - **ANTHRAC**

Suited to persons of originally strong constitution who have become debilitated by loss of vital fluids- **CINCH; PHOS AC**

No pain with rest complaints; painlessness is characteristic – **STRAM**

Complains of nothing; wants nothing— **OP**

Ailments that originate from fright, bad effects the fear still remaining – **OP**

Was insulted, being too dignified to fight, subdued his wrath and went home sick, trembling and exhausted - **STAPH**

Adapted to thin, scrawny, feeble cachectic appearance- **SEC COR**

Disposed to talks continually - **STRAM**

Great falling of hair after chronic headache or at the climacteric - **SEP**

Ailments worse before and during a thunderstorm – **PET**

Hair falls out when touched in nursing woman – **NAT MUR**

A/F from chewing tobacco, Alcoholism- **ARS ALB**

Dreams of exertion, roaring swimming working hard at his daily occupation – **RHUSTOX**

Great restlessness cannot remain is bed must change position after to obtain relief from pain - **RHUSTOX**

Lameness stiffness and pain on 1st moving after rest or on getting up in the morning by walking – **RHUSTOX**

Too much summer bathing in lake or river – **RHUSTOX**

A/f over lifting particularly from stretching high up to reach thing s- **RHUSTOX**

A/f spraining or straining a single part muscle or tendon - **RHUS TOX**

Bad effects of getting wet specially after being overheated – **RHUSTOX**

Stormy weather he feels acutely feels restless for days before or during a thunderstorm- **PSOR**

Attacks of anxiety and restlessness during a thunder agg. from music - **NAT CARB**

Ailments which are worse before and during thunderstorm - **PET**

Nervous persons who dread a storm and are particularly afraid of thunder storm especially electrical storm – **RHODO**

Great restlessness must move constantly to amel. The soreness of parts - **PYR**

Symptoms ever changing; no two chills, no tow stools no two attacks alike – **PULS**

Hungry in the middle of night must have something to eat – **PSOR**

All excretions have a carrion like odor – **PSOR**

Feels restless for days before or during thunderstorm – **PSOR; PHOS**

Body has a filthy smell even after bathing- **PSOR**

Great weakness and debility remaining after acute dis. – **PSOR**

In acute dis. when well selected remedies fails to relieve or permanently improve – **SULPH**

RELATIONSHIP OF REMEDIES

ANTIDOTE

Coca was first used as a tobacco antidote

Lyco for bad effects of tobacco smoking and chewing.

Benzoic acid is incompatible with wine, which aggravates urinary, gouty and rheumatic affections

Vert alb often removes bad effects of excessive use of alcohol and tobacco.

Arsenicumum should be thought of in ailments from chewing tobacco

Ipec antidotes abuse of tobacco for excessive nausea and vomiting.

Nux antidotes abuse of tobacco for the gastric symptoms next morning after smoking.

Phos antidotes abuse of tobacco for palpitation, tobacco heart, sexual weakness.

Ign antidotes abuse of tobacco for annoying hiccough.

Clem or Plantago antidotes abuse of tobacco for tobacco toothache.

Sep antidotes abuse of tobacco for neuralgic affections of right side of face; dyspepsia; chronic nervousness, especially in sedentary occupation.

Lyco antidotes abuse of tobacco for impotence, spasms, cold sweat from excessive smoking.

Gels antidotes abuse of tobacco for occipital headache and vertigo from excessive use, especially smoking.

Tab potentized (200 or 1000) to relieve terrible craving when discontinuing use.

Camphor antidotes tobacco.

Dilute cider vinegar antidotes **Carbolic acid;** either externally or internally, when acid has been swallowed accidentally, or taken for suicidal purposes.

Amm carb antidotes, poisoning with Rhus and sting of insects.

Ars alb for ailments from dissecting woulds and anthrax poison; stings of venomous insects.

Mosquito and insect bites burn and itch intensively- CALADIUM

Dissecting wounds; insect stings; bad effects of vaccination- CROT HOR

Punctured wounds by sharp pointed instruments, as awls, nails (Hyper.); rat bites, stings of insects, especially mosquitoes –LED PAL

Ailments from sugar, insect stings, vapors of arsenicum or copper- MERC

Suspicious insect stings. If the swelling changes color and red streaks from the wound map out the course of lymphatics- ANTHR (Lach, Pyr)

Acet ac antidotes anaesthetic vapors (Amyl.); fumes of charcoal and gas; **Opium** and **Stramonium** *Resuscitates persons sinking under anaesthetics- AMYL NIT*

Bovista antidotes, effects of local applications of tar; suffocation from gas.

Camphor antidotes nearly every vegetable medicine; also tobacco, fruits containing prussic acid, poisonous mushrooms; should not be allowed in the sick room in its crude form.

Causticum antidotes paralysis from lead poisoning (bad effects of holding type in mouth of compositors). and abuse of **Merc.** or **Sulph.** in scabies.

Alumina is one of the chief antidotes for lead posioning; painter's colic; ailments from lead.

Petroleum is one of our best antidotes for lead poisoning.

Kali brom is one of the antidotes for lead poisoning.

Baptisia is indicated when **Ars.** has been improperly given or too often repeated in typhoid or typhus.

Benzoic acid is indicated after abuse of Copper in suppression of gonorrhoea.

Nux Mosch antidotes mercurial inhalation, lead colic, oil of turpentine, spiritous liquors and especially the effects of bad beers.

Chamomilla is indicated in cases spoiled by the use of opium or morphine in complaints of children.

Chel. antidotes the abuse of **Bry.**, especially in hepatic complaints.

Cinchona antidotes the direct action of **Digitalis** and increases the anxiety.

Hepar antidotes bad effects of mercury and other metals, iodine, iodide of potash, cod-liver oil.

The bad effects of **Ign.** are antidoted by **Puls.**

Lyco bad effects: of onions, bread; wine, spirituous liquors; tabacco smoking and chewing (Ars.).

The bad effects of **Merc.** are antidoted by **Aur., Hep., Lach., Mez., Nit. ac., Sulph.**, and by a strong (high) potency of **Merc.**, when the symptoms correspond.

Opium antidotes, for poisonous doses; strong coffee, **Nux, Kali per.** and constant motion.

When symptoms correspond, the potencies of **opium** may antidote bad effects of Opium drugging.

Podo antidotes the bad effects of mercury.

BAD EFFECTS OF/ AILMENTS FROM

Bad effects of checked perspiration: **ACON**

(Throat affection from checked foot sweat- BAR CARB)

Bad effects after a debauch - **AGAR** (LOB, NUX, RAN)

Bad effects of suppressed gonorrhoea - **AGNUS CAS** (MED)

Bad effects from getting wet - **ALL CEPA** (RHUS)

Bad effects of getting wet, especially after being overheated - **RHUSTOX**

Bad effects from inhaling foul odors of putrid fever or dissecting-room - **ANTHR**

Bad effects of disappointed affection - **ANT CRUD** (CALC PHOS)

Bad effects of unfortunate love - **HYOS**

Bad effects of anger, grief, or disappointed love - **IGN** (CALC PHOS, HYOS)

Ailments from grief, disappointed love - **CALC PHOS** (AUR; IGN; PHOS AC)

Ailments from long lasting grief; sorrow, fright, vexation, jealousy or disappointed love - **LACH** (AUR; IGN; PHOS AC)

Who have become debilitated by chagrin, or a long succession of moral emotions, as grief, care, disappointed affection - **PHOS AC**

Bad effects of violent mental emotions; anxiety, grief, or excessive sexual indulgence - **SAMB** (PHOS AC; KALI PHOS)

Bad effects: of **suppressed sexual desire**, or *suppressed menses*; non-gratification of sexual instinct, or from excessive indulgence; from abstinence - **CON MAC**

(Complaints resulting from abnormal sexual desire –LYSSIN)

For the bad effects of: onanism, sexual excesses, loss of vital fluids; chagrin, mortification, unmerited insults; indignation, with vexation or reserved displeasure - **STAPH** (AUR)

Bad effects from loss of vital fluids - **CARBO VEG** (CAUST.)

Bad effects from loss of blood - **HAM** (CHINA)

Ailments from loss of vital fluids, especially haemorrhages, excessive lactation, suppuration - **CINCHONA**

Aggravation from loss of vital fluids, especially seminal; self-abuse; sexual excesses - **PHOS AC**

Aggravation from sexual excesses - **SEP**

(Headache from sexual excess- THUJA

Spinal irritation due to sexual excesses- AGAR (KALI PHOS)

Nervous prostration after sexual debauch- AGAR

Premature old age arising in young persons from abuse of the sexual powers; from seminal losses- AGNUS CAS

Adapted to persons debilitated by sexual excesses- COCC

Sexual debility from sexual abuse- GRAPH

Impotence: of young men, from onanism or sexual excess- LYCO

Persons who have become debilitated by loss of vital fluids, sexual excesses- PHOS AC (CINCH)

For bad effects of vaccination when Thuja fails and Silicea is not indicated - **ANT TART**

Bad effects of vaccination - **CROT HOR**

Bad effects of vaccination, especially abscesses and convulsions - **SIL** (THUJA)

Ailments from bad effects of vaccination - **THUJA** (ANT TART; SIL)

Bad effects of acute exanthema imperfectly developed or suppressed - **APIS MEL** (ZINC.)

Bad effects of re-percussed eruptions (of non-developed, Zinc.) - **CUP MET**

Bad effects of poison wounds; post-mortem - **LACH** (PYR)

For the bad effects resulting from mechanical injuries; even if received years ago - **ARNICA**

Bad effects of a long ago injury- **CARBO VEG**

Bad effects of shock from injury- **CAMPHOR**

Bad effects of shock, of fright, of mesmerism - **HYPER**

Great prostration: after injuries; after surgical shock; after anaesthetics - **ACETIC AC**

Bad effects of spinal concussion - **HYPER**

Bad effects from falls, contusions or mechanical injuries of external parts - **EUPH** (ARN)

Bad effects of mechanical injuries, with bruises, chafing and livid skin; prostration - **SULPH AC** (ACET AC)

Bad effects of mental excitement, fright, fear, mechanical injuries and their later consequences; from having the hair cut - **GLON** (ACON, BELL)

Bad effects of sudden emotions or pleasurable surprises - **COFFEA** (CAUST)

Bad effects from fright, fear, exciting news and sudden motions - **GELS** (IGN)

Follows well: after, Opium, in bad effects of fright - **SAMB**

Bad effects of, the fear still remaining from charcoal vapors; from inhaling gas; of drunkards - **OPIUM** (ACON., HYOS)

Bad effects from decayed food or animal matter, whether by inoculation, olfaction or ingestion - **ARS ALB**

Often useful after bad effects from spoiled fish and decayed vegetables - **CARBO AN** (CARBO VEG, ALL CEPA)

For constitutions broken down by bad effects of mercury and syphilis - **AURUM MET**

For the bad effects or abuse of Mercury - **DULC**

It antidotes the bad effects of mercury - **PODO**

The bad effects of Mercury are antidotes by Aur., Hep., Lach., Mez., Nit. ac., Sulph., and by a strong (high) potency of Mer., when the symptoms correspond.

Bad effects of mercury and other metals, iodine, iodide of potash, cod-liver oil - **HEP SULPH**

Relieve ailments resulting from abuse of mercury, especially, if there be erythrism - **NITRIC ACID**

Bad effects of large doses or of too frequent repetition of mercury - **MEZ**

Bad effects of repeated doses of Digitalis- **NITRIC ACID**

For the bad effects of cauterizing with nitrate of silver - **NAT MUR**

Bad effects of Ign. are antidoted by - **PULS**

For the bad effects of exhausting diseases, whether in young or old - **CARBO VEG** (CINCH, PHOS, PSOR)

Antidotes paralysis from lead poisoning (bad effects of holding type in mouth of compositors) - **CAUST**

Useful in bad effects from excessive tea drinking abuse of chamomile tea, when haemorrhage results - **CINCHONA**

For abuse of chamomile tea - **VAL**

Ailments: from abuse of chamomile, quinine, mercury, tea-drinking, sulphur - *(Flatulence after meals or after eating, especially of tea-drinkers; are often subject to violent colic – DIOS*

Faintness, weakness and an indescribable feeling at epigastrium, from excessive use of tea or tobacco – LOB

"All-gone" sensation in stomach, in tea drinkers especially – PULS

Prosopalgia from tea – SPIGELIA

Headache overheating from tea – THUJA (SEL)

Toothache from tea drinking – THUJA

For the abuse of Chamomile tea – VAL)

Bad effects: from mountain climbing or ballooning (Ars.); of stimulants, alcohol, tobacco - **COCA**

Bad effects of beer - **KALI BI**

Headache from beer- RHUS TOX

Bad effects of drunkenness in people with light hair, blue or grey eyes, florid complexion, corpulent - **LOB INF**

One of our most effective remedies for *the bad effects of alcoholic beverages* - **RAN BULB**

Indicated in ailments from spirituous liquors or from charcoal vapors - **ARNICA** (AMM CARB; BOV)

Bad effects of opium eating, tobacco chewing - **VERT ALB**

Bad effects of: coffee, tobacco, alcoholic stimulants - **NUX VOM**

Bad effects: of onions, bread; wine, spirituous liquors; tobacco smoking and chewing- **LYCO** (ARS)

Diarrhea from onion- THUJA

Sweat in axilla smells like onion- BOVISTA

Eructations like onions- MAG MUR

Breath smells like onion- SINNAPIS

Great aversion to bread- NAT MUR

Bad effects: from **loss of sleep**, *mental excitement and nigh watching*; feel weak if they lose but one hour's sleep; *convulsions after loss of sleep*; of anger and grief - **COCC**

Bad effects from night watching - **COLCH** (COC.).

Compare with Staph. In ovarian or other diseases from bad effects of anger, reserved indignation or silent grief - **COLOCYNTH**

Bad effects: of anger (caused by offence); acid food, bread, quinine, *excessive use of salt*; of cauterization of all kinds with the silver nitrate; to grief, fright, vexation, mortification or reserved displeasure - **NAT MUR** (STAPH)

For the bad effects of abortions and miscarriages - **HELONIAS**

Ailments following abortion or premature labor - **SAB**

Bad effects of highly spiced or seasoned food - **NUX VOM**

Bad effects of: over-eating - **NUX VOM** (ANT C)

Bad effects of: long continued mental over-exertion; sedentary habits - **NUX VOM**

Bad effects of: loss of sleep - **NUX VOM** (COC, COLCH, NIT AC)

Bad effects of: aromatic or patent medicines - **NUX VOM**

Bad effects of: sitting on cold stones; specially in warm weather - **NUX VOM**

Removes the bad effects of Iodine and *excessive use of table salt* - **PHOS**

The bad effects of Plumbum are antidoted by - **ALUM; PET; PLAT; SULPH AC; ZINC MET**

Bad effects from suppression by sulphur and zinc ointments - **PSOR**

For the bad effects or abuse of Mercury - **DULCAMARA**

One of the antidotes for lead poisoning - **KALI BROM**

Cures the muscular weakness following excessive use of opium and tobacco - **MUR AC**

Relieve ailments resulting from abuse of mercury, especially, if there be erythism - **NIT AC**

Bad effects of repeated doses of Digitalis - **NIT AC**

Antidotes mercurial inhalation, lead colic, oil of turpentine, spiritous liquors and especially the effects of bad beers - **NUX MOS**

The bad effects of **Plumbum** are antidoted by - **ALUM., PET., PLAT., SULPH. AC., ZINC.**

Ailments: from abuse of chamomile, quinine, mercury, tea-drinking, sulphur - **PULS**

Relieves ailments from abuse of **Arsenicumum** - **SAMB**

After overaction, from repeated doses of Bell., in whooping cough - **STRAM**

Ailments from the abuse of metals generally - **SULPH**

Ailments from brandy-drinking - **SULPH AC**

For the abuse of Chamomile tea - **VAL**

When Fails

Collinsonia has cured colic after **Colocynth** and **Nux** failed.

Collinsonia is useful after **Nux** and **Sulph** have improved, but failed to cure piles.

(Aesculus is Useful after Nux and Sulph have improved, but failed to cure piles.)

Cocculus has cured umbilical hernia with obstinate constipation, after **Nux** failed.

Use **Platina** in obstinate constipation after **Nux** has failed and use **Plumbum** after **Platina** fails.

Use **Psor** in constipation when **Sulphur** fails to relieve.

Colchicum often cures dropsy after **Apis** and **Arsenicum** fails.

Blatta orientalis has cured bad cases of general dropsy, after **Apis, Apoc.** and **Dig.** Failed. - Haynes.

Apis has cured scarlatina albuminaria after **Canth, Dig** and **Hell** failed

Cina has cured aphonia from exposure when **Acon. , Phos. ,** and **Spongia** had failed.

Santonine sometimes cures in worm affections when **Cina** seems indicated, but failed (MAR. V; SPIG).

Sulph when patient have worms, but the best selected remedy fails.

In heart disease complicated with haemorrhoids consult **Collinsonia** when Cac., Dig., and other remedies fail.

Phos often cures lasciviousness when **Hyos** fails.

Benzoic acid is indicated after **Colch.** fails in gout;

Bromium has cured in croup after failure of **Iod; Phos; Hep** and **Spon.**, especially in relapses after **Iod.**

When **Rhus** seems indicated but fails to cure urticaria, **Bovista** is indicated.

Anth when **Arsenicumum** or the best selected remedy fails to relieve the burning pain of carbuncle or malignant.

Euphorbinum in the terrible pains of cancer, carbuncle or erysipelas when **Ars** or **Anth** fail to >.

Ant tart For bad effects of vaccination when **Thuja** fails and **Silicea** is not indicated.

The 200 or 1000th potency of **Arg nit** in watery solution as a topical application in ophthalmia neonatorum has relieved when the crude Silver nitrate failed.

In heart disease complicated with haemorrhoids consult **Collinsonia** when **Cac, Dig**, and other remedies fail.

Diphth post diphtheritic paralysis, after **Caust, Gels** fail.

Diphth laryngeal diphtheria, after **Chlor, Kali bi, or Lac c** fail

Kali carb will bring on the menses when **Nat mur** though apparently indicated, fails – (Hahnemann)

Mag phos relieves colic of horses and cows when **Colocynth** fails to >.

Phyto occupies a position between **Bryonia** and **Rhus**; cures when these fail, though apparently well indicated.

Psor when **Sulphur** seems indicated but fails to act.

Pyrogen during course of diphtheria, typhoid or tyhpus; *the best selected remedy fail to > or permanently improve.*

Sabadilla has cured pleurisy after **Acon** and **Bry**failed.

(Abrot after Acon. And Bry. in pleurisy, when pressing sensation remains in affected side impeding respiration.)

In metrorrhagia from retained placenta with characteristic delirium, **Sec cor** often acts promptly when **Stram** has failed (with fever and septic tendency, **Pyr**).

Sulph to facilitate absorption of serous or inflammatory exudates in brain, pleura, lungs, joints, when **Bryonia, Kali mur** or the best selected remedy fails.

Syph when the best selected remedy fails to relieve or permanently improve, in syphilitic affections.

Bromium cures hard goitre cured after **Iodine** failed.

Tuberculinum when **Psor., Sulph.**, or the best selected remedy fails to relieve or permanently improve.

ANALOGUE

Mezereum is the vegetable analogue of **Merc sol**

Valeriana is the vegetable analogue of **Platina**

Podophyllum is the vegetable analogue of **Plumbum**

All cepa is the vegetable analogue of **Phosphorus**

Ipecac is the vegetable analogue of **Cuprum met.**

Cham is the vegetable analogue of **Mag phos.**

Ign is the vegetable analogue of **Nat mur.**

Cinchona is the vegetable analogue of **Fer met.**

Bryonia is the nearest analogue of **Eup perf,** having free sweat, but pains keep patient quiet; while **Eup.** has scanty sweat and pains make patient restless.

Camphor antidotes nearly every vegetable medicines.

Kali mur is chemical analogue of **Puls.**

Kali iod is chemical analogue of **Phyto.**

Kali sulph is chemical analogue of **Dulc.**

CHRONIC OF

Alumina is chronic of **Bryonia**.

Nat mur is chronic of **Ign.**

Sil is chronic of **Puls.**

Calc carb is chronic of **Bell,** which is often required to complete a cure.

Sulphur is the chronic of **Aconite** and follows it well in pneumonia and other acute diseases.

COMPLEMENTARY TO

Aconite is complementary: To Coffea in fever, sleeplessness, intolerance of pain; To Arnica in traumatism; To Sulphur in all cases.

Alum and Rhus is complementary to **Bry**

Apis complementary **Nat. mur**.

Ant crud is complementary to **Squilla.**

Calcarea is complementary of **Bell.**

Ruta complementary to **Calc phos**

Hep., Sal. ac. Is complementary to **Calend**

Calc. phos. is complementary to **carbo ani.**

Kali carb. is complementary to **Carbo veg.**

Bell. is complementary to **Cham** in diseases of children; **Bell** – cranial nerves; **Cham**- abdominal nerves.

Colocynth is complementary to **Merc.** In dysentery, with great tenesmus.

China is complementary to **Ferrum**.

Cyclamen is complementary to **Calcarea carb.**

Drosera is complementary to **Nux vomica**.

Dulcamara is complementary to, Baryta carb., Kali s.

Fl acid is complementary to **Coca, Sil.**

Fer met is complementary: to, Alum., Cinch.

Graphites is complementary to **Caust., Hep., Lyc.**

Hammemelis is complementary to **Ferrum**, in haemorrhages and the haemorrhagic diathesis.

Hepar sulphis complementary to **Calendula** in injuries of soft parts.

Iodum is complementary to **Lycopodium**.

Ipecac is complementary to **Cuprum**.

Caust is complementary to **Carbo veg., Petros.**

Cuprum met is complementary to **Calcarea.**

Kali carb is complementary to **Carbo veg.**

Lachesis is complementary to **Hep., Lyc., Nit. ac.**

Lyco is complementary to **Iodine.**

Mag carb is complementary to **Chamomilla.**

Nat mur is complementary: to, **Apis,** acts well before and after it.

Nit ac is complementary to **Ars.**, and **Calad.**

Nux vom is complementary to **Sulphur** in nearly all diseases.

Phos is complementary to **Arsenicum**, with which it is isomorphic.

Psorinum is complementary to **Sulphur** and **Tuberculinum.**

Puls is complementary to **Kali m., Lyc., Sil., Sulph. ac.**

Rheum is complementary after Mag. carb., when milk disagrees and child has sour odor.

Rhustox is complementary to **Bryonia.**

Sabina is complementary to **Thuja**

Sepia is complementary to **Natrum mur.**

Silicea is complementary to **Thuja, Sanicula.**

Stannum is complementary to **Pulsatilla.**

Sulphur is complementary to **Aloe, Psor.**

Sulph acid is complementary to **Puls.**

Thuja is complementary to **Med., Sab., Sil.**

Trillium is complementary to **Calc. phos.**, in menstrual and haemorrhagic affections.

Tuberculinum is complementary to **Psor., Sulph.**

INIMICAL TO

Apis disagrees when used either before or after **Rhus.**

Acetic ac is inimical to **Arn, Bell** (in headache) **Lach, Borax, Dulc.**

Baryta carb is incompatible after **Calc.** in scrofulous affections.

Benzoic acid is incompatible with wine, which aggravates urinary gouty and rheumatic affections.

Borax is incompatible and should not be used before or after, acetic ac, vinegar, wine.

(Patients requiring Conium often improve from wine or stimulants, though persons susceptible to Conium cannot take alcoholic stimulants when in health.

Zinc met aggravates of many symptoms from drinking wine, even a small quantity (Alum., Con.)

Caust is incompatible with **Phos**, must not be used before or after Phos, always disagrees; the Acids; Coffea.

China is incompatible after, **Dig, Sel**

Coffea is incompatible with **Canth., Caust, Coc, Ign**

Dulcamara is incompatible with, **Acet ac, Bell., Lach.**, should not be used before or after.

Ignitia isincompatible to **Coff., Nux, Tab.**

Carbo veg. and **Kreosote** are inimical.

Lachesis is incompatible with **Acet ac, Carb ac, Amm carb, Dulc, Carb ac, Nit ac, Sepia.**

Mercurius should not be given before or after **Silicea**.

Nit ac is inimical to **Lach, Calc carb.**

Nux vom is inimical to **Zinc, Ignatia**

Phos is incompatible with **Caust**, must not be used before or after

Ran. Bulb is incompatible with **Sulph, Staph**

Sepia is inimical to, **Puls** (with which it should never be alternated) **Lach**

Calcarea must not be used before **Sulphur**

Cham. and **Nux** should not be used before or after **Zincum**.

Calc carb must not be used before **Nit ac** and **Sulph**

Sulph is inimical to **Calc carb** (must not be used before Nit ac and Sulph) **Ran bulb**

Tabacum is inimical to **Ignatia**

INSTRUCTIONS FOR PRESCRIPTION

Nat mur cannot often be repeated in chronic cases without an intercurrent, called for by the symptoms.

Lyco is a deep seated, long acting remedy, and should rarely be repeated after improvement begins.

Calc carb should not be repeated in aged people; especially if the first dose benefited, it will usually do harm.

Arum tri should not be given low or repeated often, as bad effects often follows. - Dr L. The higher potencies most prompt and effective.

Acon is rarely indicated in fever which usually brings out eruptions.

Nat mur should never be given during fever paroxysm.

Ferr met should never be given in syphilis; always aggravates the condition.

When lungs seem to fail, patient becomes sleepy cough declines or ceases, **Ant. Tart.** supplants **Ipecac**.

Acc to Hahnemann, **Calc carb** must not be used before **Nit ac** and **Sulph**; may produce unnecessary complications.

"One single dose of **Drosera** 30th potency is sufficient to cure entirely epidemic whooping cough. The cure takes place surely between seven and eight days. Never give a second dose immediately after the first; it would not only prevent the good effect of the former, but would be injurious." (Hahnemann)

Like **Sulphur** in many chronic diseases with abdominal plethora and congestion of portal circulation, **Aloe socortina** develops suppressed eruptions.

Children not easily impressed when **Ant. tart.** Seems indicated in coughs, require **Hepar.** In spring and autumn, when damp weather commences, coughs of children get worse.

Bapt is indicated, when **Ars.** has been properly given or too often repeated in typhoid or typhus.

"The chief distinction between **Brom.** and **Iod.** is the former cures the blue-eyed and the latter the black-eyed patients" - Hering.

In children **Calc.** may be often repeated. In aged people should not be repeated; especially if the first dose benefited, it will usually do harm.

According to Hahnemann, **Calc. carb** must not be used before **Nit. acid** and **Sulph.**

Calendula acts well in potency as in tincture, applied locally and may be administered internally at the same time.

In the skin be unbroken, apply an alcoholic solution of any potency and cover with cotton; **Canth.** will promptly relieve pain and often prevent vesication. If the skin be broken use in boiled or distilled water, and in each case give potency internally.

Want of susceptibility to well-selected remedies- **Carbo veg** (Opium, Val.).

Caust affects the right side most prominently.

Mental calmness contra-indicates **Chamomilla.**

Cina is frequently to be thought of, in children, as an epidemic remedy, when adults require other drugs.

"One single dose of **Drosera** in 30th potency is sufficient to cure entirely epidemic whooping cough. The cure takes place surely between seven and eight days. Never give a second dose immediately after the first; it would not only prevent the good effect of the former, but would be injurious."

Hepar sulph renders patient less susceptible to atmospheric changes and cold air.

The psoric skin affections of **Sulphur** are dry, itching, > by scratching, and not sensitive to touch; while in **Hepar** the skin is unhealthy, suppurating, moist, and extremely sensitive to touch.

In wounds where formerly **Acon.**, and **Arn.**, were given alternately, **Hypericum** cures.

Iodum acts best in goitre when give after full moon, or when moon is waning - Lippe.

Iodum should not be given during lying-in period, except in high potencies- Hering.

Drosera often relieves the constant, distressing night-cough in tuberculosis. Hahnemann says (Mat. Med. Pura.)

Kali carb will bring on the menses when **Nat. m.** though apparently indicated, fails - Hahnemann.

It is rarely advisable to begin the treatment of a chronic disease with **Lyco.** unless it is clearly indicated; it is better to give first another antipsoric. **Lyco.** is a deep-seated, long-acting remedy, and should rarely be repeated after improvement begins.

Mag phos sometimes acts best when given in hot water.

Mercurius if given in low (weak) potencies hastens rather than aborts suppuration.

Mercury is < by heat of, but > by rest in, bed. **Arsenicum** is > by heat of, but < by rest in, bed.

Nat mur should never be given during fever paroxysm.

Nit ac is often difficult to distinguish from **Merc.**; but is adapted to black-haired people, while Mer. is more useful in light-haired persons.

Nux vom should be given on retiring or, what is better, several hours before going to bed; it acts best during repose of mind and body.

In **Pet.**, skin symptoms are worse in winter, better in summer (Alum.); if suppressed, causes diarrhea.

Hahnemann says: "**Phos** acts most beneficially when patient suffers from chronic loose stool or Diarrhea.".

Puls is one of the best remedies with which to begin the treatment of a chronic case (**Calc., Sulph.**)

Rheum may be given after abuse of Magnesia with or without rhubarb, if stools are sour.

A single dose of **Sepia** often acts curatively for many weeks.

Sulph ac, one part, with three parts of alcohol, 10 to 15 drops, three times daily for three or four weeks, has been successfully used to subdue the craving for liquor - Hering.

Terebinth is recommended as a prophylactic in malarial and African fevers.

Cinnabaris is preferable for warts on the prepuce.

Hydrastis to fatten patients cured with **Tuberculinum**.

Belladonna, for acute attacks, congestive or inflammatory, occurring in tubercular diseases.

For pains in heels: **Agar., Caust., Cyc., Led., Mang., Phyt.**

In intermittent fever **Nat mur** follows **Lach** well when type changes.

Chin sulph is similar to **Cinchona** in intermittent fever, anticipating type.

Aloe like **Sulphur** in many chronic diseases with abdominal plethora and congestion of portal circulation; develops suppressed eruptions

Acet ac aggravates; the symptoms of **Arn., Bell., Lach., Mer.**, especially the headache from **Bell.**

Patients requiring **Conium** often improve from wine or stimulants, though persons susceptible to **Conium** cannot take alcoholic stimulants when in health.

Cinchona antidotes the direct action of **Digitalis** and increases the anxiety.

Mag phos acts well when given in hot water.

FOLLOWS WELL / AFTER

Tub follows **Psor** as constitutional remedy in hay fever, asthma.

Bell for acute attacks, congestive or inflammatory, occurring in tubercular diseases.

Medicines for pain in heels are **Agar, Caust, Cyc, Led, Mang, Phyt** and **Val.**

After **Baryta carb**, **Psor.** Will often eradicate the constitutional tendency to quinsy.

Vert alb after **Camph** in cholera and cholera morbus.

Vert alb after **Carbo veg, Amm carb** and **Bov** in dysmennorrhoea with vomiting and purging.

Graph follows well **Lyco, Puls** after **Calc** in obesity of young girl.

Hydrastis to fatten patients cured with **Tub.**

Blatta orient has cured bad cases of general dropsy after **Apis, Apoc** and **Dig** failed.

Colchicum often cures dropsy after **Apis** and **Ars** failed.

Euphor in the terrible pain of cancer, carbuncle or erysipelas when **Ars** or **Anthrac** fails to relieve.

The burning feet of **Sulph** and restless fidgety legs and feet of **Zinc met** are both found at the same time in **Med.**

Merc should not be given before or after **Sil.**

Merc given in low potency hastens rather than aborts suppuration.

Merc is indicated in diseases occurring in winter.

Epidemics occurring in January and February often call for **Mez.**

Mur ac cures muscular weakness following excessive use of opium and tobacco.

Apis acts well before and after **Nat mur.**

Con mac is followed well: by, **Psor** in tumors of mammae with threatening malignancy.

Ver alb follows **Cup met** well in whooping cough and cholera.

Ver alb follows **Apis** and **Zinc** well in convulsions from suppressed exanthemas.

Flou ac follows well after, **Ars** in ascites of drunkards

Flou ac follows well after, **Kali c** in hip disease

Flou ac follows well after, **Coff, Staph** in sensitive teeth

Flou ac follows well after, **Phos ac** in diabetes

Flou ac follows well after **Sil, Symph** in bone diseases

Calendula is similar to **Symp, Calc p**, for non-union of bones.

Flou ac follows well after, **Spong** in goiter

Graph follows well after **Calc** in obesity of young women with large amount of unhealthy adipose tissue

Graph follows well follows **Sulph** well in skin affections.

Graph follows well after **Sepia** in gushing leucorrhoea.

Hyos follows **Bell** well in deafness after apoplexy.

Aconite is the acute of **Sulphur**, and both precedes and follows it in acute inflammatory conditions.

Anacardium follows, and is followed by **Platina**

Calad. and **Selen.** follow well after **Agnus** in weakness of sexual organs or impotence.

Abrot after **Hepar** in furuncle

Abrot after **Acon.** And **Bry.** In pleurisy, when pressing sensation remains in affected side impeding respiration.

Sabadilla has cured pleurisy after **Acon** and **Bry** failed.

Acet ac follows well; after **Cinchona**, in haemorrhage.

Acet ac follows well after Digitalis, in dropsy.

Aesculus is useful after Nux and Sulph have improved, but failed to cure piles.

After **Collinsonia** has improved piles, **Aesc** often cures.

Calad. and **Selen.** follow well after **Agnus** in weakness of sexual organs or impotence

Anacardium follows well: after **Lyc.**, and **Puls.**

Ant crud follows well: after, **Puls., Mer., Sulph.**

Ars. and **Puls.** follow **Apis** well.

Lyc. follows well **Arg nit** in flatulent dyspepsia.

Arnica follows well: after, **Acon., Apis., Ham., Ipec., Ver.**

After **Baptisia; Crot., Ham., Nit. ac.** and **Tereb.** act well in haemorrhage of typhoid and typhus.

After **Bar. c.**, **Psor** will often eradicate the constitutional tendency to quinsy.

Borax follows: **Calc., Psor., Sanic., Sulph.**

Berb vul Acts well after, **Arn., Bry., Kali bi., Rhus, Sulph.**, in rheumatic affections.

After **Bryonia; Alum., Kali c., Nux, Phos., Rhus, Sulph.**

Calc ars follows well after **Conium**, in lymphatic, psoric or tubercular persons.

Calcarea follows **Nit. ac., Puls., Sulph.** (especially if pupils are dilated).

Calcarea phos acts best: before **Iod., Psor., Sanic., Sulph.**

Cina follows **Capsicum** well in intermittent fever.

Ars., Lyc., Sulph. follow well **Chel** and will often be required to complete the cure.

In pertussis, after **Drosera, Cina** has relieved the severe symptoms.

China follows well **Calc phos** in hydrocephaloid

Nux, Puls. or Sulph follow **Crocus** well in nearly all complaints.

Arum triphyllum after **Hepar sulph** and **Nit acid** in dry, hoarse, croupy cough.

Arum triphyllum after **Caust** and **Hepar sulph** in morning hoarseness and deafness, and in scarlatina.

Vert alb follows well **Cuprum met** in whooping cough and cholera. **Apis and Zinc.** in convulsions from suppressed exanthemas.

Drosera follows well after **Samb., Sulph., Vert. alb.**

Dulcamara follows well after, **Calc., Bry., Lyc., Rhus, Sep.**

Cinch. is the vegetable analogue of **Fer met**, follows well in nearly all diseases, acute orchronic.

Flouric acid follows well after, **Ars.** in ascites of drunkards.

Flouric acid follows well after, **Kali c.** in hip disease

Flouric acid follows well after, **Coff., Staph.** in sensitive teeth

Flouric acid follows well after, **Phos. ac.** in diabetes

Flouric acid follows well after **Sil., Symph.** In bone diseases

Flouric acid follows well after, **Spong.** in goitre.

Graphites follows well: after **Lyc., Puls,** follows;

Graphites follows well after **Calc.** in obesity of young women with large amount of unhealthy adipose tissue

Graphites follows well after **Sulph.** well in skin affections

Graphites follows well after **Sepia** in gushing leucorrhoea.

Ant. T. follows well **Kali bi** in catarrhal affections and skin diseases.

Kali brom often curative after **Eugenia jambos** in acne.

Kalmia follows **Spig.** well in heart disease.

In intermittent fever **Nat. mur.** follows **Lach.** well when type changes.

Lyco follows well after, **Calc., Carbo v., Lach., Sulph.**

Millefolium follows well after, **Acon.,** and **Arn.,** in haemorrhages.

Muriatic acid follows well after **Bry., Mer., Rhus.**

Nat carb follows well: after, **Sep.,** in bearing down.

Nit ac follows well **Calc., Hep., Mer., Nat. c., Puls.** or **Thuja**; but is most effective after **Kali c.**

Nux vom follows well after **Ars., Ipec., Phos., Sep., Sulph.**

Phos follows well after, **Calc.** or **Cinch.**

Podo after: **Ipec., Nux**, in gastric affections;

Podo after **Calc.** and **Sulph.** in liver diseases.

Psorinum is followed well by **Alum., Bor., Hep., Sulph., Tub.**

Psorinum after **Lactic ac.,** in vomiting of pregnancy.

Psorinum after **Arn** in traumatic affections of ovaries.

Sulphur follows **Psorinum** well in mammary cancer.

Sabina follows **Thuja** in condyloma and sycotic affections.

Spongia follows well after **Acon., Hep.,** in cough and croup when dryness prevails.

After **Spong.** in cough, **Hep.** follows when mucus commences to rattle.

Stannum follows well after **Caust.**

Caust., Col., Staph., follow well in order names.

Sulph., Calc., Lyc.; or **Sulph., Sars., Sep.** frequently follow in given order.

Sulph acid follows well after **Arn.** with bruised pain, livid skin and profuse sweat.

Sulph acid follows well after **Led.** in ecchymosis.

Symphytum follows well after **Arnica** for pricking pain, and soreness of periosteum remaining after an injury.

Theridion follows well after **Calc.** and **Lyc.**

Thuja follows well after **Med., Mer., Nit. ac.**

Tuberculinum follows **Psor.** as a constitutional remedy in hay fever, asthma.

Vert alb after **Ars., Arn., Cinch., Cup., Ipec.**

Vert alb after **Camph.** in cholera and cholera morbus.

Vert alb after **Amm. c., Carbo v.** and **Bov.**, in dysmenorrhoea with vomiting and purging.

FOLLOWED BY

Ant tart before **Silicea** in dyspnoea from foreign bodies in the larynx or trachea

Ant tart before **Puls.** in suppressed gonorrhoea

Ant tart before **Tereb.** from damp basements

Arnica is followed by **Sul. ac.**

Arum tri is useful: after Hep. And Nit. Ac. In dry, hoarse, croupy cough.

Arum tri is useful after Caust. And Hep. in morning hoarseness and deafness, and in scarlatina.

Asarum eur followed: by, **Bis., Caust., Puls., Sulph. ac.**

Borax is followed: by, **Ars., Bry., Lyc., Phos., Sil.**

Calcarea acts best: before **Lyc., Nux., Phos., Sil.**

Calcarea is followed by, **Kali bi.** In nasal catarrh.

Calcarea phos acts after **Ars., Iod., Tub.**

Conium is followed well by, **Psor.** in tumors of mammae with threatening malignancy.

Drosera is followed by **Calc., Puls., Sulph.**

Eupatorium is followed well by, **Nat. m. and Sep**.

Iodum is followed by Kali bi. in croup.

Ipecac is followed well by **Ars.** in influenza, chills, croup, debility, cholera infantum.

Ipecac by Ant. t., in foreign bodies in larynx.

Kali bi after **Canth. or Carb. ac.** has removed the scrapings, in dysentery.

Kali bi after **Iod.** in croup, when hoarse cough, with touch membrane, general weakness and coldness are present.

Kali bi after **Calc.** in acute or chronic nasal catarrh.

Kreosote is followed well by **Ars., Phos., Sulph.**, in cancer and disease of a malignant tendency.

Nat mur is followed by **Sepia** and **Thuja**.

If vertigo and headache be very persistent, or prostration be prolonged after **Nat mur, Nux** will relieve.

Nux vom is followed well by **Bry., Puls., Sulph**.

Phos ac after **Nux** in fainting after a meal.

Ruta after **Arnica**, it hastens the curative process in the joints; after **Symphytum**, in injuries to bones.

Sabadilla follows **Bry.** and **Ran. bulb.** Well in pleurisy, and has cured after **Acon.** and **Bry.** failed.

Sepia is frequently indicated after **Sil., Sulph**.

Silicea follows well after **Calc., Graph., Hep., Nit ac., Phos**.

Silicea is followed well by **Hep., Fluor. ac., Lyc., Sep**.

Stannum is followed by **Calc., Phos., Sil., Sulph., Tub**.

FOLLOWS AND IS FOLLOWED BY

Aconite is the acute of Sulphur, and both precedes and follows it in acute inflammatory conditions.

Anacardium follows, and is followed by **Platina**.

Aurum follows, and is followed well by **Syphillinum**.

Baryta carb is frequently useful before or after **Psor., Sulph.,** and **Tub**.

Iodum follows well after, **Hep., Mer**.

Mercurius follows well after, **Bell., Hep., Lach., Sulph.,** but should not be given before or after **Silicea**.

Phos ac. acts well before or after **Cinch.** in colliquative sweats, diarrhea, debility.

Puls follows and is followed by, Kali m.

MISCELLANEOUS

Unless indicated by exciting symptoms **Aconite** is nearly always injurious in first stage of typhoid fever.

Ant. Tart is similar to **Lyco;** but spasmodic motion of alae is replaced by dilated nostrils.

Ant. Tart is similar to **Ipecac** but more drowsiness from defective respiration and nausea > after vomiting.

Children not easily impressed when **Ant. tart.** Seems indicated in coughs, require **Hepar Sulph**.

Ant. Tart is indicated in spring andautumn , when damp weather commences, coughs of children get worse.

Bryonia is similar to **Ran. bul.** in pleuritic or rheumatic pains in chest.

Bryonia is similar to **Ptelea** in aching heaviness in hepatic region; > lying on right side, greatly < lying on left side; turning to the left causes a dragging sensation.

Sulph, Calc, Lyc; or **Sulph, Sars and Sep** frequently follow in given order.

Cina is indicated in Pertusis after **Drosera** has relieved the severe symptoms.

Stram. patients require light and company whereas **Coca** desires darkness and solitude.

Patients requiring conium often improve from wine or stimulants, though persons susceptible to **Conium** can't take alcoholic stimulants when in health.

Nitric acid resembles **Ars alb** morbid fear of cholera

When symptoms reappear they change locality or go from one side of the body to another side- **Ant crud.**